COLORS RARE

Poetry & Prose

Of

Mary Hill

Book Design by Deb Christiansen

ISBN 978-0-69226-289-4

Published by
Books For Dessert
P.O. Box 563
Schoolcraft, MI 49087
www.booksfordessert.com

Printed in the United States of America

CONTENTS

Chapter Seven | Color Heaven [sonnets]

Chapter Eight | Color Gate [farm]

Chapter Nine | Color Divine [praise]

Chapter Ten | Color Kin [family]

SOMETHING RARE

October 2011

There's something rare
That's in the air,
Like spending time with
God in prayer,
For autumn grows
As summer slows.

Sweet corn is past—
Peaches went fast—
The roadside stand just
Couldn't last;
Sun's heat is less,
Now clouds will bless.

Red leaves are few—
Few dropping too,
The soy beans sport
A golden hue,
For something rare
Is in the air.

To Mary Hill

We are like a couple of friends passing notes to each other in English class and hoping the teacher won't notice. Your poem was a pleasant surprise. Thank you. It is beautiful, complimenting our friendship and raising my self-esteem to its highest level. I shall cherish forever your message from the heart.

Thank you for your influence in my life, and I love you, too!

Betty C.

March, 2014

CHAPTER ONE

Colors Spun

[nature]

February Morning

February 2013

I was just racing off to the grocery
To finish my errands at dawn,
But the Lord had surprises and blessed me
As a sky of slate-blue met the sun.

They were soft, those pink clouds at the sunrise
[I thanked Him for clear roads to drive];
Then I passed Pleasant Lake and was happy
To watch the bright sunshine arrive.

SPRING FIRE

In spring blackbirds invade,
Can't even serenade,
And at my feeder lurk;
To steal the seeds they work,
Kirk, irk! Irk, irk! Kirk, irk!

They chase the little bird,
The suet fan deferred,
Each spring since time began.
But God keeps closed to man
Sometimes His perfect plan.

For when they all take flight
(A startled cloud of night!)
With or-ange wings so high,
There's fire as they fly!!
O! Fire in the sky!

WAKE UP!

March 1991

In March the spring aroused a sleeping world...
It stretched up to the sky...its limbs uncurled;
In flower beds, the crocus' sleep was done...
They rubbed their eyes and squinted: so much sun!

And down the road the brittle pond, knee-deep,
Threw off the icy blanket of its sleep;
To early birds, the mother robin said,
"It's only five o'clock...go back to bed!"

A momentary wall of snow returned...
Half-risen blades in swirling white were churned,
But underneath, the sleepers still arose,
And eager grass was wriggling its toes.

THE WIND

September 2012

Sunny or gray,
She loved the day
When fall was ornamental;
Down road of dirt
A lone convert
In search of El Viento.

Nor any car
Would silence mar
With passing detrimental;
With worldly heart
Such souls depart
From seeking El Viento.

From wafting breeze
And sight of trees,
Her view was incidental;
For pride and gain,
Man planted grain
Impeding El Viento.

But harvest soon
Will importune…
Man's touch inconsequential
And hearts will soar
To find once more
The joy of El Viento

SUMMER THUNDERSTORM

July 2010

The birds have all flown to a refuge,
The streets like a ghost town are bare,
The sun hides herself from the monster,
The odor of fish fouls the air.

The greenie-black heavens are rushing,
The trees bend away; the winds lash,
The rumble of thunder is distant
But heard as a warning, then CRASH!

The storm has begun with a fury,
The rain beats the glass whipping by,
The wind bangs the shutters in tempo,
The lightning is tearing the sky.

Then suddenly all has diminished,
Over now is the worst and the fears;
The sun will be queen of the weather
Until the next outburst appears.

THOSE IMPATIENT MAPLE TREES

The maples are impatient trees:
Come August they must flaunt and tease
With orange suggestion in the breeze…
Oh, yes. They are impatient!

They only want to do us good,
To show some lovely in the wood,
And, in September, well they should,
But, boy! Are they impatient!

Well, welcome fall, is what I say,
Chase ever-sultry heat away,
And raise in me this roundelay,
For I, too, am impatient!

SEPTEMBER DAY

September 13, 2013

We hiked the road, for the wind was cool,
You know how it is a September day
When all of the kiddies are back in school,
You're sure that summer's departed to stay.

Some leaves have "turned"...you pocket a few,
The sun comes out, the breezes die,
Surrounded by October's hue,
You start to sweat like it's still July.

THE FIRST SNOW

January 14, 1959

I woke up one morning
Aware of a warning
That winter was somehow quite near;
They way I was told
Was the unwelcome cold
That drove me as Regan did Lear.

The snow fell so deep
While in warm beds asleep
Others dozed, but I took in the sight!
Like cascades from the sky
Snow flakes beautify
The world had a fresh coat of white.

The land was a white
As pure witherite,
For snow drifts soon covered the ground;
The colors just there
(Though from autumn left bare)
Were in blankets of white warmly wound.

I looked on the scene
Like an ermine-robed queen
And saw fall going out on the wing;
Though winter seems long,
I can wait for the song
Of the first welcomed robin in spring.

YELLOW

Forsythia is yellower...
Like sparklers, how they sprout!
And daffodils appear in clouds...
Their trumpet-muzzles shout!
But dandelions on the lawn...
Now, that's what spring's about.

Where Autumn Leads

Green acorns dropped in a backyard glade,
And knowing it was an early sign
With more to follow, plans I made
To look and seek with a spaniel's aid
For autumn's early approach design.

I drove the highway far up and down
And saw or-ange tree boughs (just a few),
The sumacs red, corn tassels brown;
And walnut litter yellowed the ground;
I saw fall return as I traveled through.

The trees in wetlands are showing rust,
Their roots deep in water feeling glum,
Small saplings covered in summer's dust;
Up on crane legs the lily-pads come,
Old men, holding pantlegs up from scum.

In August berries in aftermath
Are luster-glossed for my survey;
Red, white, and orange, summer's wrath,
For summer follows along the path
Where autumn leads it to yesterday.

MICHIGAN, MY MICHIGAN!

I love to live in Michigan,
   And if I had the wish again,
   I'd wish to live right here.
In Michigan a di-a-mond
   Is made by snow beneath the sun,
   Not coal as may appear.

It's here the red bird stains the breeze
   Where other birds are gray like trees
   Upon a winter day,
And straw spikes up through fields of white;
   A lovely palomino sight,
   The bleakness to allay.

The remnant oak-leaves flutter bright
   In copper-bronze, a winter's sight
   To cheer the sullen breast,
And what is more, the seasons all
   With constant change, our spirits call…
   In Michigan I'm blessed

CHAPTER TWO

Colors True

[spectrum]

Blue and White

Summer's nearly over
  White and blue, white and blue
Chick'ry thick as clover
  Blue and white, blue and white
Queen Anne tats the roadway
Summer's nearly through

Summer's nearly gone
  Blue and white, blue and white
On blue lake a swan
  White and blue, white and blue
Lighthouse white...blue heavens
Summer's rain is dew

Summer rains are few
  White and blue, white and blue
White sails lavender
  Blue and white, blue and white
Whitecaps on the blue waves
Summer time, adieu

LORD, YOU MUST LOVE BLACK

Janury 2011

Lord, you must love black things:
Crows that soar on black wings,
Halloween cats arching,
And black stallions marching;
Lord, you made the night so
Black but with stars also,
Rings with stones of onyx,
Cockers black, our tonics
Just to stroke, and (yes) trees:
Sunset silhouette maps,
Rakish chickadee caps,
Bibles are bound in black
[From black sin they buy back],
My coat in black hue,
Lord, know what? I do too.

GREEN

Green smells like a Christmas tree
With sparkly lights aglow...
They warm and spread the balsam scent
Make Noel's essence grow.

Green tastes like lime gelatin
A-wiggle on a plate,
A kid a-chewin' spearmint gum
He swallows "by mistake."

Green looks like a shamrock worn
To tout our Irish starch!
Jake's shirt I bought he wears for me,
The chartreus lace of March.

Green feels like a perfect lawn
Beneath bare toes in May;
A costume Robin Hood would wear
On Sherwood's merry day.

Green sounds like meadow grasses
When summer winds blow through——
The waves of their creation roll...
The grasses murmur too.

Autumn Gold

October 2010

Just when the sun gets stingy with his hours,
    And even those are spent in southern sky,
God brightens up the fields with golden showers
    And yellow-dots the soy that we pass by.

Then goldenrod spills sunshine on our way,
    And black-eyed Susans flash a final glow;
We seek the mari-gold these autumn days
    As Spanish soldiers sought it long ago.

A gold unworthy of eternal streets,
    Yet here we welcome it as mother lode;
So that my one-with-nature is complete,
    I'll plant a gilded mum down by the road.

A Sapphire Sea

*Inspired by Exodus 24:10 and
the "colors" poetry of Elizabeth Ellen-Long*

God stands upon a sapphire sea,
And—'til I see it and we meet—
He gives to me like stars at night
On earth blue things for my delight.
The blue, fresh skies of early spring
To eye and soul refreshment bring,
And—when I turn my gaze around—
The blue extends from ground to ground.
Blue birds and jays of indigo
Dazzle my eyes in constant flow;
I feast on them; they dine off me:
The very best in life is free.
And bluejeans—more blue daily show—
(Though navy-hued, not indigo)
Are worn by all from sea to sea
Except for fat ones (One is me).
John's eyes of blue show tenderness,
And so for him the house I dress
In fashions of his favorite hue:
Blue drapes and linens, towels too.
And last, my ring of topaz blue
Returns my thoughts to rendezvous,
Where I shall walk the azure street
And praise God for His royal treat.

PUMPKIN ORANGE

October 2013

fall is orange
bonfires and trees
leaf jubilees
sweet candy corn and pies to please
very orange
O, so orange

fall is orange
bright pumpkins sown
so widely grown
'til everyone can claim his own
lantern orange
Jacks o' orange

fall is orange
the orbs grand
at roadside stand
in yards…to decorate the land
fall is orange
pumpkin orange

Red and Yellow Summer

2000

Summer is red and yellow:
The "purple" finches wear red bibs
Over brown when they have thistle lunch,
And the "gold" ones wear yellow to munch:
They are summer flowers,
But they never need water or care,
And the hoeing and weeding is rare.
And many summer holidays
Bring the red of the flags showing well;
Geraniums, of pungent smell,
And yellow flowers warble too;
Then as summer wanes we see the sun:
A red wafer above when it's done.

CHAPTER THREE

Color Me

[myself]

My Warm Sunshine

It was true love when first we met...
For nineteen years I'd waited;
Thru all those years I'd been in love...
Desire never abated.

I'd fall in love with men who taught,
With some friend of my father,
With singer, Zorro, high school stars...
All unrequited bother.

And then he kissed me, filled the void;
We climbed, in song, the love-vine...
He took my arm, he showed the way,
He was and is my sunshine!

Found Love

2013

Since we met and found love,
Close we had to be:
I just had to find you...
You, to follow me.

For a year of courting
When life gave respite,
With intensity we sought
Like a moth to light.

Phone calls, meeting, letters
Each the other bade...
Satisfying, marking
Way of man with maid.

O my love, soon fifty
Years we'll celebrate
Since we met and found love...
Found for life a mate.

THE IRISH WASHERWOMAN

I'm the Irish washer woman,
And I love to hang out clothes
On a chilly springtime morning,
For the wind fluffs as it blows.

And I get it from me Mither
(Though her Irish was but half)—
When I find it's time for laundry,
It's the old-time kind of bath.

I don't want to hear your blarney
That a dryer makes more sense;
It's just easier to pitch them
Than to hang them by the fence

Even in the dead o'winter,'
I can hang the sheets out fine;
And—though stiff as boards at even'—
They will freeze-dry on the line.

And when laundry day is over
And I carry armloads in,
They've a fragrance so from Heaven,
Sure it seems almost a sin.

When we're in our beds, I hollar,
"Smell the sheets!"—sweet as a rose—
Ah, the natural ways are best ways
Just as any Irish knows.

FLASH! FLUSH! FLASH! FLUSH!

March 1992

Covers fly across my hubby's form—
Get them off of me—I'm warm!
Can I help the midnight hormone flash?
I seek the faucet's cooling splash.

He has diarrhetic trouble though:
All the covers on me go
When he seeks the bathroom's sweet release;
Then the night returns to peace

Before April 4 (the "Hovel" bought)
Other things our nightimes sought;
Now it's flash & flush we 2 pursue
As our lives are ½ way through.

I will hear, above the house's hush
Once again, the toilet's flush,
And he pads across the kitchen cold…
Darling, we are growing old.

Just Sittin'

June 2009

When Pa wakes in the morning,
He doesn't leave the bed;
He sits awhile along the side
He says, "To clear my head."

When finally he rises,
He sits...well. you know where,
Performing his "ablutions"
Upon the bathroom "chair."

When Pa is dressed and sipping
De caffeinated brew,
He sits for hours in his chair
To read his Bible through.

This sittin' isn't wasted…
It's just his body's way
'Cause after lunch he's just about
On fire for the day!

HIS SILVER HAIR

April 2011

Old age is great...
I love my mate
Tho silver hair is glis'nin'...
With half his ears,
My words he hears...
With half his brain, he's lis'nin'

DRIVING MISS MARY

April 2012

In years gone by when we both worked,
Each went a separate way,
But now "retired," he has become
My driver for the day.

Of course, we merge our errands 'cause
The cost of gas is high,
But after all these many years,
Our bond we can't deny.

He gets the Buick with the quip,
"I'll see if it will start;"
He's always been the "motorman"
Whenever we depart.

We stop for Wendy's chili lunch,
We harmonize a song,
I shop for some "necessity"...
Good comrads all day long.

We ask the Lord what work He has
Each day for us to do,
And then we find fulfillment and
A day of blessing too!

My Hands

August 9, 2013

I miss my hands; they once could do
Each task I asked of them;
Pick up small things, or knit a scarf,
Or sometimes sew a hem.

And they were pretty, slender, quick
With long nails painted pink
And veinless skin so tan and smooth
With nary blotch or kink.

I miss my hands; oh, they're still here
Now clumsy, wrinkled, slow;
But they can clasp in frequent prayer.
That matters most, you know.

GERIATRIC FIX

Now, what did I come in here for?
(My heart begins to race.)
If I had come for glasses,
They were some other place.

Why am I here! I ask again...
I'm sure I've not a clue;
Perhaps if I return to START...
Oh, what am I to do?

What did I come up here for?
It was an uphill climb;
Perhaps I came to get my brain...
I'm sure I've lost my mind!

CHAPTER FOUR

Color Galore

[seasons]

EARLY SNOW

October 1987

When the first snow comes (the one that doesn't stay),
You must go to watch it fall without delay;
Though the snow-tires, true, are not yet on the car,
You must stop to watch the white from where you are.

Half of snow, half rain, in vain it tries to hide
Autumn's golden beauty, sprinkled far and wide;
It's a marvel in its whiteness that covers all you see
Even though bald spots remain under the tree.

It's the trees' fault, too, for they blow so very hard
As the storm continues all across the yard..
The stir grabs your attention...no matter how you try,
Your eyes just drift on upward to the sky.

Schoolwork, housework, or "workwork"—never mind...
Watch the snow...it's snowing!...and it's fine!

MORE THAN HALLOWEEN

October 2004

Halloween will be here soon,
Bringing with it the harvest moon,
Bringing legends, old and new,
Bringing trick-or-treaters too.

These things, of course, are known to all,
But what of shadows, short and tall?
What of unexplained events
Which few can see and few can sense?

They are more than legends told,
More than legends, new or old,
For it is truth and not a tale…
There's something to that midnight wail.

Ask yourself, though ill-at-ease,
Have you never felt the breeze
Of someone passing on the stair,
Yet, when you look, no one's there?

How many times walking down a dark street
Have you heard a second pair of feet,
Then found yourself in clammy sweat?
Once or twice, at least, I'll bet!

Don't say, "It doesn't matter,"
For someday it may, at that,
Especially now at Halloween—
Don't chance where spooks are at!

Scrooge-After-Christmas

January 2011

He calls me the Scrooge-after-Christmas...
I know in my heart that it's true
'Cause after sweet Christmas is over,
With Christmas, I really am through.

Now, don't get me wrong, I love Christmas:
October finds all my gifts done;
When Thanks are all Given, it's our house
That lights the dark...we're number one.

Perhaps all this scurrying weakens
(For Christmas I often am sick),
Perhaps 'cause I'm old, I desire
A return to normal...and quick.

I do leave the tree up (he wants that)
But down after New Years, and then
This Scrooge-after-Christmas by next year
Will dive into Christmas again.

Morning Walk

September 2011

I'll write no songs for fall this year,
Just soak it in instead...
Savor the sight of bluer skies
And flowers...leaves of red.

I'll watch and breathe the fragrance of
A bonfire's many charms
And feel the heavy challenge of
A pumpkin in my arms.

Can't wait to taste the acorn squash
And later pumpkin pie
And listen to the drying leave
That click a soft reply.

No poems for me...I've made my choice:
That musky autumn air
To just enjoy without the pen,
And that's for sure...so there!

SCAREY

October 2012

The witch at my doorstep is harmless and fun;
Complete with her broom, though, she's second to none!
I'd not be surprised if I saw her in flight
Afar o'er the houses on Halloween night.

And that ghost that comes out with the set of the sun
For treats at my house looks a genuine one,
But I know it is harmless and fun, just in play,
If only I treat him the Halloween way.

Such fun to watch youngsters on Halloween night!
But the ghoul in my mirror next morn gives a fright...
Not harmless the witchy hair, ghostly pale skin...
It's no fun; it scares me, this costume I'm in!

SNEAKY SNOW

February 2013

The sneaky snow of winter
Is easy to forget
From one year to another
In summer's warmth, and yet

It happens every winter:
When did the stuff begin?
That path or deck you shoveled
Is covered up again.

It's such an unseen nuisance
Except against a tree:
Just focus on an object dark
And soon fine flakes you'll see.

So, day and week the winter goes...
Accumulation rises;
It's hard to picture springtime
With sneaky snow surprises!

Christmas Takes Over the Stores

2013

It's not even Thanksgiving, and everything's changed.
The excitement came in with a roar!
It must be a birthday…for what lucky kid?
As Christmas takes over the stores.

Yes, there sure was a birthday so long, long ago,
And each day we watch for Him more,
And the anticipation is growing by bounds
While Christmas takes over the stores

Here's a present to open…you're special, you see,
Then a whole year to wait as before,
But we'll never have "let-down" when Jesus we see
Like when Christmas takes over the stores.

CHAPTER FIVE

Color Alive

[animals]

THE ALPHA GOOSE

May 2012

A sunny April lakeside morn
For time with God is blest...
A holy time, it seems to me,
A quiet scene of rest.

Until a goose off in the reeds
Begins to honk and shout;
He jabbers to himself, it seems,
'Til young goose rushes out.

The alpha goose pursues him then…
Across the lake they race.
He's jealous for his harem lest
A young goose take his place

Halfway across the lake they slow…
He turns from the attack;
And even though he flushed him,
He mumbles his way back.

Let's not be like the alpha goose
Whose anger builds a wall,
For sunny lakeside days of spring
Are plentiful for all.

THE CARDINAL'S COW-LICK

Behold the lovely redbird
As he frolics and he flits;
It's just too bad his top-knot shows
A cow has got her licks.

Beneath his scarlet flannels,
He's shaped like any bird,
But there! Observe his feathered pate…
It sticks up quite absurd.

So, lots of us have "cow-licks"
In hair or deep within;
Let's hope the world, in mercy,
Will look beneath the skin.

THE ROCKER RIVER STALLION

September 2011

The golden stallion leaped across the river on that day,
Pursued by rider spurring on a dirty, scarred bay;
Fiercely free, his snowy tail flew out as he raced by,
And one bright star hung like
                    a distant lamp in the morning sky.

Now, Wendy watched the chasing
                from the hilltop's lofty height
And knew Starfire could not be caught...
                the chase was useless flight;
Her horse's speed was rare, and Charlie might as well depart,
And she knew she alone
possessed the reins of
Starfire's heart.

Now much discouraged,
Charlie slowed and
pulled his horse away;
She thought about the
orphan colt she found
that springtime day
And too how easily her
friend had let her on his
back,
The Rocky river snaking
pink across the chilly
flat.

She gave a call, and Starfire reared to pivot in reply
'Til soon rode Wendy grasping silver mane...
                              how they did fly!
And then they saw that Charlie raced
                              again to claim the gold
And with his fever, anyone could see their doom unfold.
They leaped the reeds that grew
                              along the Rocky's varied shore
And pounded on through wetlands
                              where the Rocky's waters pour;
The clinging damsel leaning forward spoke to him her heart:
"Starfire, you know that even death can never make us part."

On wings of wind, their flight brought close
                              the edge of Skidmore Hill
Where Spirit Springs, the Indian camp,
                              the bottomlands distill,
And Wendy knew that Starfire's freedom merited the strife
And that he wouldn't hesitate to sacrifice his life.

The Indians say he sprouted wings like Pegasus of old...
One thing is sure: that nasty Charlie never got his gold,
For off the cliff they flew with heart
                              and met their ending thus,
And Charlie ground his teeth and muttered fiercely,
                              "Cuss, cuss, cuss!"

The Indians say that still today to those with spirits free
When evening sprays rise from the Rocky River eerily
And stars prick through a velvet dome of blue in afterglow,
A golden stallion and his rider race the Rocky's flow.

A slender, silver moon appears, they stop and stand alert,
And Starfire bugles in his pride their freedom to assert,
And then they vanish into mist along the river shore,
Unhampered by confines of time, together evermore.

COCKER SPANIEL

April 2014

How much is that doggie in the window?
    That's me: with ears so long
        And tail cut short, an arm's embrace
            So compact, sturdy, strong.

Look deep into my warm brown eyes
    To read my loyal plan:
        I'll love you right up to the death
            And after if I can.

I'll let you kiss my "hands" and ears,
    But let me kiss you too;
        I only want to lead your life
            And just to be with you.

PRETTY KITTY

February 2014

Lucy was a pretty cat,
All white against her gray,
And 'cause I like to keep a cat,
She came to us one day.

But in our house there was a dog
Who didn't want her there,
And so his area he marked!
And Lucy went elsewhere.

At first she wasn't welcomed
In the farm where she was at,
But soon this changed, for no one could
Resist this little cat.

Now Lucy's living in the house
(It's cold outside the door);
She shares their bed. Oh wait! I think
I heard a feline snore!

THE SENSE OF A GOOSE

Autumn snow geese migrate…
In a vee they go;
Lifting up each other,
On the thrust they flow.

When the lead goose tires,
Someone takes his place…
"Point" is sure demanding
In the southward race.

Listen to the honking
Of the ones behind
Cheering on the leaders:
Courage is refined.

When a goose is wounded,
Others follow down;
If a goose is weary,
Other geese surround.

We should live like geese do:
(Show we have some sense)
Stand by one another…
What a difference!

CHAPTER SIX

Color Mix

[haiku]

Summer

July 2013

summer
watermelon
biggest bite
melts like cotton-candy
water pouring
down your throat
freezing teeth
summer

GRAY TABBY

June 2014

when
a
small gray tabby
sleeping
in my bed
squiggles over
she shows
an apricot belly
and leopard spots
running up her chest
with four
black Siamese paws
airborne
where did you come from
kitty

StarLite

December 2014

Star
silver
blue: all-he-wanted
first snow
in the night/tinsel
morning-switch on lites/sapphire
Christmas tree
blue/trees reflecting
in other windows/green
get out the shovels
cold-indigo
tinsel
quiet peace
Saviour
blue/family

CAT IN MOTION

November 2012

cat
runs through
dry leaves of the forest
rustle, rustle, rustle
up onto a fallen log
tippity, tippity, tippity
rustle, rustle, rustle
flowing through the door ajar
like quick-silver
cold November morning

LOVING SPRING

2006

spikes
April likes
yellow forsythia
keeps again spring rendezvous
in generous abandon flings her hue
sun rays
freeforall

trees
(April breeze)
resemble women old
growing fluffy in disguise
or maidens growing hips and breasts and thighs
springtime
filling out

red
flying spread
and yellow on black wings
tells us when in sin we fall
the blood of Jesus heals if we will call
thank you
loving God

white
seen by height
for dogwood fills the air
seen by low there seem to grow
tril'um carpets in the wood like snow
high–low
lovely May

WAITING...

he's waiting…waiting…
for his morning cookies
a black widow waiting
at attention
his belly breathing
his tail most missing
his long ears dangling
watching the doorway

foal
medicine hat
sleeps in summer sun
her hide appears like flesh
pink although white
filly
peace

morning swans
still half frozen pond
red sun
rising yellow
earth nestling
in hoar frost's silver arms
dawn

sunrises
lilac
lavender
lilac
light
and neon pink all over

CHAPTER SEVEN

Color Heaven

[sonnets]

SUN SONNET

Shall I expound the lure of winter's sun?
It turns the biting cold to jubilee!
It makes each flake of snow a diamond
And comes with sky as blue as heaven must be.
The cat and dog move into shafts of light
That stretches cheer and warmth across the floor.
And I stand at the window, sun so bright,
To soak it up and then desire more.
But sun of summer chases me away--
It saps my strength; dry lips for moisture beg.
It blinds my eyes, so I just turn away;
The street's so hot that it would fry an egg!
Ah, yes. The winter sun's the wondrous thing:
It melts the snow and fills the heart with spring!

Sonnet to the Morning

The red sun rises like a Neptune ball,
And I sit down to spend a time with thee;
As bodies age some goods to us befall,
And time with you is best of all to me.
In spirit do we wander hand in hand,
And for this day Your grace and strength are free;
I read Your Word and find the daily plan,
And though corrupt, I see your purity.
I bring to You in Prayer no-longer-home-
Loved-ones whose absence silence this new start;
I write a journal entry or a poem,
Far from the world, so nearer to Your heart.
Thank you, great God, that when the hair is gray,
Still waters still each morning show the way.

To My Rose of Sharon

Farewell, you Rose of Sharon, small ladies in a row;
Last night was cold and windy, for summer's bent to go.
I pick up fallen branches and think of warming fires;
Your fuchsia, white, and purple had been my hearts's desires.
Farewell, my backyard maple: I love your yellow dress
With trim of red and often gold, each day as they progress.
Farewell, "November" maple: your colors rain on me;
With arms upraised I greet them to rake in jubilee.
This is my worship, Father: to glory in your earth,
Created for our pleasure, each year to know rebirth.
All this becomes my solace: whatever winter brings
Is worth it all because of days like these of autumn things?

Second Looks

October 2011

The poplars giggle up in golden glee
Now that the bright, cold days of fall are here;
We yield to second looks at all we see
As burnished orange and russet boughs appear;
We watch the fuchsia dawns rise up, then walk
Down quiet roads beside the fields of mist;
The beasts and birds, unstirred by human talk,
Add to our peace "til sun sets amethyst;
We drive through tunnels formed by golden trees,
A hint of glory in Shekhinah glow,
Beside the fields, scalped bare by reaper sprees,
Who wait for regal ermine cloaks of snow.
Men harvest now, for profit, beans and corn,
But we seek glory on an autumn morn.

Cloud Sonnet

Job 37 September 2014

The cloud spreads from the blue horizon's edge
To high above my head, a call complete...
A great, white, balanced stratum in the air
A child could dress up in, a spectral sheet.
And so I slowly raise my arms awide
In thanks and praise 'til high above my head;
I sense and clasp the great expanse of God
Who, as my savior, raised me from the dead.
He's bigger than the storm that dims my paths...
When both seem like the better path to choose...
He's all I need of beauty, shade, and rain,
A heavy, gentle gift: how can I lose?
Decide to take Him as your Lord and guide:
The great, high cloud...He'll be there at your side.

March Sonnet

March 2014

Between the winter white and pink of spring,
As snow recedes, new life delays for March,
The world becomes a bleak and dirty thing
Where all revealed the eager eyesights parch;
The whites most catch the eye, a bobbinet,
Discarded packages of man's debris:
Food cartons from McD's or cigarettes…
And steamers flap across the tops of trees;
Tan plastic Meijer grocery bags abound,
Metallic blue beer cartons, soiled and old,
And shining cans and bottles all around,
And broken icestorm twigs a thousand-fold;
But soon the earth in rain awash will gleam,
And then forsythia will reign supreme!

SONNET EQUUS

February 14

When I consider my God-given love
From birth (of all His creatures) for the horse
And how then just for me from up above
Was planned a Midas barb of grace and force,
Then mem'ries overwhelm of rides' ascent
Enthroned on gold to hilltops o'er the world...
I praise him for youth's golden virtue spent
(though short of snowy mane and tail empearled).
And so, though asking more is far from right,
I do, I ask this boon for end of time:
Although His soldiers' mounts will gleam in white,
I ask another palomino mine.
Then joy throughout the universe will ring:
A winged gallop serving such a King!

CANARY YELLOW

Come like sun, O wild canary,
Turn the winter doldrums merry;
Like the dandelions' mien,
Spring upon the virgin green;
Scatter back into the sky
If a leaf or blackbird shy…
Polka-dot the trees and wait
For your panic to abate…
Come back then to raid the feeder,
Be to me both bird and greeter,
Grip the cylinder asway,
Ride, your yellowness display;
Joy unfettered, finch so fine,
Dwell yet in my spirit-shrine…
Guard your freedom, yet be mine.

SONNET OF THE FIRMAMENT

Psalm 19:1

What is this "firmament," mysterious noun?
The great expanse of air wherein we live:
We look up to the blue, but God looks down [Ezek 1:25]
An atmosphere between, a transitive.
Where leaves may play, and winds through treetops roar,
Whence come the snow and rain, where night is made;
Where geese migrate and swans in splendor soar;
Where rosie dawns turn orange, and blue skies fade
To lilac and reflect on lake or pond
Or snow or, blazing blush, a wall once dim.
This vault, this arch, this canopy beyond!
Therein we see the handiwork of Him
Who set the lights to mark the year and hour. Gen 1:14
We praise Him in His firmament of power! Psa 150:1

CHAPTER EIGHT

Color Gate

[farm]

CANNING TOMATOES

August 2012

The jars and lids, collected up,
    Were washed in sudsy sink;
They'd bounce around with glassy sound
    And make their sudden clink.

The kettle rolled and bubbled:
    Tomatoes boiled there,
The cores and shreds of green and red
    In buckets everywhere.

Mom organized the workforce,
    Gram taking out the core,
While Jake, like boys, processed the noise
    And time-to-time yelled, "More!"

And when, at winter suppertime,
    They climb down wooden stair,
They'll find, all glassed, a summer past
    And bring it up to share!

TUBE LIFE

March 2013

Reaching for a tube I find
I have to read with care
Because the bathroom chest and drawers
A frightful burden bear.

Now, we have "boob tubes" (the TV)
And tubes for swimming's play,
But all the tubes of which I write
Create for me dismay.

We've tubes for pain in aching joints
And tubes to stop an itch;
We've tubes with stuff to brush your teeth,
Each in its bathroom niche.

We've tubes of stuff for places that
You wouldn't want to name,
And don't forget the de-germ tubes
And hair gels for your mane.

You squeeze the tube…outpops a glop!
To heal a wound's attack,
But watch it as you make your choice…
You might fluoride your back!

LIGHTNING STRIKES!

August 3, 1991

Lightning struck the iron bed
Where Grandma Millie slept, she said.
The fam-i-ly had all gone forth
To rent a cabin way up north.
Her sisters, too, could still recall
The entrance of the fireball—
Through open window, round the frame,
And out the other, still aflame.
Had it not happened, perhaps she
From every tempest would not flee;
But, I tell you, had I been hit,
It would have changed my life a bit!

LITTLE BOBBIE YONKER

Little Bobbie Yonker got a brand-new BB gun;
Dad warned, "Don't shoot birdies 'cause that really isn't fun."
  He was fine 'til he could see
  The old Dutch spinster on her knee:
Yielding to temptation, little Bobbie had to run.

Little Bobbie, innocently passing down the street,
Spotted old Miss VanderRoost down kneeling in the peat;
  Bent to flowers from the waist
  With her rear side to his face,
Man nor boy could such temptation with resistance meet!

Now they're marching to our house…she has him by the ear,
And the folks can tell she isn't overcome with cheer;
  Maybe his chagrin was rich,
  Maybe he escaped the switch,
But in just a day that gun was made to disappear.

MALARKAY

April 2014

Cell phones…direct TV…
They are not for me;
Cable TV and computers
Are unwelcome suitors.

They require a lot of "dough,"
And there's so much I don't know;
I could never "goo-goo" well…
At the Word I don't Excel.

All those "bytes" just make me twitch,
Vinegar can't stop the itch;
At my age it's all malarkey…
I'm for technical anarchy.

CHAPTER NINE

Color Divine

[praise]

Winter Sunrise

2007

"Did you see the sun this morning?"
We will ask throughout the day;
Who could see and not discuss it…
Such a radiant display!

Pink so bright (almost a scarlet)
Spread across the eastern sky;
Every cloud (and there were many)
Had a rosie underlie.

Good is God that, as we travel
Through this heartless world of strife,
He provides proof of his presence
Just to brighten every life.

True, the essence of the splendor
In mere minutes will be gone,
But the gloomy gray of one whole day
Will be brighter for the dawn.

DEAR LORD

Thank you, dear Lord, for all the stuff
(Contentment proves it is enough):
A home to keep, a good night's sleep,
Food, kids, a dog, sunshine skin-deep.

Thanks also, Lord, for acting fast
For special needs at times aghast:
A flattened tire, a woods afire,
That little doggie's funeral pyre

And last, but surely never least,
For Jesus' presence, holy peace,
Release of blame through His dear name
And Heaven 'cause He overcame

THE WHOA SPOT

We love our walks, the dog and I,
In snow we leave a toe blot,
Enjoying all God made for us
Until we reach the Whoa Spot

And there I say a hearty "Whoa,"
A vista claims my viewing
With silver, sand, and berry
As each new scene's debuting!

Perhaps you need to find a place
To stir your soul's renewing
With hues and shapes and movement…
A Whoa Spot for your viewing

You and Me

When you met me and I met you,
And everything for us was new,
You'd take my hand, a gesture warm,
And then you'd draw it through your arm.

I needed that: we could agree...
A man like you who wanted me!
Your doing was a gesture strong,
And I felt safe our whole life long.

So when we meet in Heaven's land,
Will you, my dear, come take my hand?
Help me to find the hearth my own...
Escort me to the Heav'nly throne?

EASTER

A lamb...a little lamb
For a burnt offering...how sad!
So little meat to eat on a lamb
For a Levite or priest...
Only good for loving
And the future (of the flock)
And for sacrifice

Thus was Jesus,
Our Lord, Our Savior, God:
He had no future here...
He died at 33...
Good for love,
Ah, yes!
And an offering!

CHAPTER TEN

Color Kin

[family]

SWEET VOICES

2011

Memories of a holiday
Fill my head with voices sweet:
Little children make requests…
They are angels at my feet.

"Grandma, can I have some juice?"
To their wishes I concede.
"Where's a blanket, Grandma" dear?
They think I have all they need.

"Grandma, do you have some gum?"
"Can we draw some pictures, please?"
We're so glad to have them come,
So I give them all of these.

Memories of a holiday
Linger in an afterglow…
Bless the long, dark winter days,
Melt away like springtime snow.

Simple...Or Is It?

Now comes the fall, and we all want
   To keep from getting sick
So wash your hands a lot, they say,
   And vaccinate real quick.
And daily drink eight waters too.
   Simple arithmetic.

But when we're with the grandkids, all
   Those rules go out the door:
The card Blake colored for me is
   With syrup smeared galore,
And Darren shares my soda, heck!
   We bother were sick before.

My napkin wipes, then, Julian's mouth
   (With virus we don't see?),
And last the hugs and kisses fly…
   a germy Jubilee!
But Grandpa says it's even worth
   A cold…don't you agree?

JULIAN

Julian saw me on the porch swing
(The porch swing on the hill),
So he left the trampoline
And the kids until
He could join me on the swing,
Tell me all that's new,
Talk about his birthday and
Things he likes to do.
When we left, he gave a card,
And so it seems to be:
The other kids seek the other kids,
But Julian seeks out me!

KETCHUP KING

There once was a kid we call Blake
Who to the restaurant we would take;
  We'd buy him some fries
  But what a surprise!
With ketchup a mess he would make.

He savored the flavor of spice
And thought tasting ketchup was nice;
  So he smeared his face
  Till hardly a trace
Of skin was not stained twice and thrice.

The ketchup would be up his nose
And cheeks—oh, yes—all over those…
  Down under his chin
  And—yes—with a grin
He would, if he could, smear his toes.

With fingers he'd slide it to feel
The satiny ooze—what a deal!
  We laugh till we ache
  But love this boy Blake,
Our Ketchup King, O, with a zeal!

THANKSGIVING AT OUR HOUSE

November 2005

They come amidst a snowstorm
("To grandmother's house we go")
And even ere they enter.
The fun begins to flow

Justin in the driveway falls,
And in the snow he lands,
So "gwamma" grabs a towel
And warms his snow-burned hands.

Then later in the bathroom,
"Gwam, get a wipe for me,"
And then he shows the candy
He's chewing up with glee.

Jake stands imperious to watch
The other children play,
And Blake must show on undies
Superman's array.

Julian drops Blake's silverware
And laughs when brother cries;
Then Julian falls down basement stairs
A bit more to the wise.

His hair's cut in a butch...
I stroke the others too,
And all come up to wrestle
And tickle 'til we're blue!

And Darren smiles and giggles
(He's only six months old);
A treasure-trove of grandsons...
Are Heaven-sent in gold.

FIVE LITTLE PRINCES

November 2005

Five little princes sittin' in a row…
When Justin gets droopy, he knows where to go:
His blanket and "pacy" in the kitchen drawer
Relieve his ill temper when he's feeling sore;
He raids grandma's toy chest for things to take home…
A bank like a duck or a purse or cell phone.

Four little princes, three live far away;
When we go to visit, we make it a day.
Then Engineer Julian when he sees we're here,
Says, "Stay with me, won't you?" and sits very near.
His hair is a "butch" and his face full of smiles…
A mem'ry that lingers through long homeward miles.

Three little princes, Jacob stands and stares…
Of all of his cousins he seems unawares;
Then suddenly he opens up on his own,
At which time he seems to ascend to his throne.
And when we must leave and would give him a peck,
He turns, so I kiss on the back of his neck.

Two little princes, now it's time for school…
The Potter will teach our Blake the golden rule
If he will behave with girls—not have to kiss,
(Grandpa's own "Hotlips" finds that to be bliss)
But he's a good student and likes to read books,
And at the TV with Daddy he looks.

One little prince…he was the last to come,
And we have discovered Darren isn't mum:
We hear thru the phone as he plays with his toys
That he is the loudest of all the boys.
Thank God for the princes on us to bestow…
Now we get the pleasure of watching them grow.

WAVING DOWN THE ROAD

November 2013

When family came to visit,
With hugs we all helloed,
But when they left we said goodby
Waving down the road.

It is an old tradition,
A loving family code,
To wave them down the drive, then stand
Waving down the road.

(Why, I can barely travel
For shopping episode,
But that a windowed hand is seen
Waving down the road.)

We watched for one another..
Our hearts with sadness flowed:
"Good-by! Good-by! We love you so!"
Waving down the road.

WHEN JUSTIN COMES

To the tune "Then Jesus Came"

We were so dull, so full of aches and sorrows,
Each task a chore, each movement not quite right,
We had our hope, but old age was a drawback,
Then Justin came to stay with us the night.

Chorus   When Justin's here, the day is filled with action,
        When Justin's here, a tractor he must ride.
        There's books to read and bb guns to practice,
        A bow with arrows he must shoot outside.

His hair is blond from swimming all the summer,
His skin is tan; he laughs like sleighbells do;
We hide the thimble shouting "hot!" or "freezing!"
When Justin comes, we act like children do.

Chorus When Justin's here, we scramble eggs for breakfast,
        He reads us books with kisses at day's end;
        Just like a young dog makes an old dog younger,
        When Justin's here, our oldness we transcend

LITTLE JAKE

Although this world has pleasures,
I have the joy that's best:
When Jake comes for a visit
And leans against my chest.

He's only just turned six…
He's still real close to mummy;
I wonder if he thinks of her
When he leans on my tummy.

His action says, "You know me"…
It says, "I know you care…
I know that I can trust you…
We are a special pair."

This world has much to offer—
So much to do and see,
But it espec'ly thrills my heart
When Jake leans into me!

My Dad's Hard-Workin' Hands

2012

Blessed are the families who can depend on their dads. If an award were given, my dad would have won. We could depend on him to provide for us.

His name was John Yonker, and for 43 years he worked seven days a week at one of the many paper mills that used to dominate the southwest Michigan area in the late 20th century. The literal sweat of his brow (the power plant could reach 105 degrees in the summer) provided a roof over our heads and food in our stomachs. Two tunes of the day rang out lyrics that fit him: "You load 16 tons, and what do you get?/Another day older and deeper in debt" as well as "Take a look at these hard-working' hands."

Dad played many woodwind instruments in the high school band with those hands, and enjoyed bowling and fishing with them as well (just another way of putting food on the table). Every summer he rented a cottage for his vacation weeks. We three kids spent every day in the lake. Meals consisted of bluegills, perch, or bullheads (all caught with a cane pole), sweet corn, and sliced tomatoes.

When my husband's job took us to Iowa and then Nebraska for nearly a decade, those same hard-working hands would drive him and Mom out, summer and winter, to spend a week. Our girls were little then and eagerly awaited the brown, paper grocery bags those big hands would cart in filled with treats, games, and surprises.

Life was simpler then...all it took was Dad to keep our world secure. And he did...with those hard-workin' hands. If that isn't love, I don't know what is!

God Was Good To Bless

God was so good to bless me with assurance that my parents went to Heaven when they died. One time when I was visiting, I asked Mom if she would like to go to church. She would, so we went to Berean Baptist…I don't know why I chose that one, but God knew Mom had an appointment with Him! When they gave the invitation, suddenly Mom had disappeared…I looked around, and there she was, scurrying down the aisle. When she returned, she said, "I just had to get that settled."

THE OL' KITCHEN TABLE

Our old table was purchased at the furniture shop in Sac City, IA, when we discovered the parsonage had a dining room, but we had no table. The price in 1975 was $666.00. It functioned for:

- writing letters "home" hundreds of miles away
- registering cocker Spaniel puppies
- studying the Bible and praying with the ladies
- enjoying sumptuous cooking (like Mom's) with Grandma & Grandpa, Aunt Donna (who fixed home-made noodles), Mr. Rehder (our resident Grandpa)
- celebrating graduations
- having the grandkids over for Christmas and barbecues
- setting out a "thing of beauty"

My Grandma Kate

March 14, 1993

Our old Dutch Grandma Kate Yonker was sober to me and probably one of the most beautiful Christians ever to grace this earth. I can remember, now that nearly 40 years have passed, all the fun and lovely things about the weekly visits to her house in Paw Paw, MI. Oh, yes, Grandpa was alive then too. Both were silhouettes in black and white…black clothes and shoes, silver-white hair, Grandma's done up in a bun. (I was told it was her glory and that when she let is down, it reached to her ankles.) They were reserved, undemonstrative people from a slower world than the one we were already entering.

Grandma would give us her thimble to play "Hide the Thimble" when she could see—or rather hear—that we were getting restless (evidenced by the thumps of the front porch swing against the back wall). Her house had lots of all-new places to hide the object. They had a wonderful garden—necessitated by a $100/month retirement allotment—full of good things to eat, smell and see, for there was one section devoted entirely to flowers, partly to grace the front of the First Baptist Church each Sunday.

The cookie jar held huge sugar cookies from the bakery where Grandpa once worked, and we could each have one while the grown-ups drank boiling hot coffee with theirs. When I made a note-holder in the shape of an owl in art class, my dad suggested I give it to them, and it hung forever after on the kitchen wall. The other wall-hanging I remember was at the front door: Jesus Never Fails.

Grandma would frequently ask if I had gone to Sunday School "last week", and I felt guilty if I had to say "no" and jubilant if I could say "yes" (some couple had offered me a ride). I believe the reason I saw them as threatening was because our parents strongly cautioned us three kids to be careful what we said so as not to betray our life of beer, bars and bashes. But we had also seen Grandpa's razor-strap hanging behind the bathroom door and heard his threats to use it on us…we were never sure if he was serious.

BEYOND THE CELLAR DOOR

A Michigan Cellar

Inspired by the Poetry Reading on February 12, 1990

I spent the major portion of my life,
If not in years then in intensity
Of experience, which I savor still,
In the neighborhood of Boerman Avenue.
Is middle-age the reason why all things
Back then smelled rich, looked bright compared to now?
In 1950 I could smell a storm
In November before it snowed.
I still remember soda-vinegar…
Its smell—the budding chemist's favorite mix
Because it foams and races up the glass
When basement scientists experiment.
Ah, yes! That basement. What we didn't do.
An outside cellar door gave access in
Or out to pirates who the coal bin used
As a secret cove to hide their treasures in.
But anyday that we could play outside
We did. We had an endless backyard field
Because it spilled over into the park.
And though each spring the city fixed the fence,
Each summer found a hole in it again.
And in that park the lilac bushes thrived
In spring, and in the fall we raked the leaves
In piles and jumped—always a spot was wet.
But getting back to that special cellar:
Besides the coal bin, it was one large room,
A portion of that room being the laundry
Where mom's old wringer washer cleaned our clothes;

A portion being the workroom with dad's workbench
Where we made "zip-guns" with clothes pin triggers
And rubber bands cut off tire inner tubes;
A portion for canned tomatoes and juice.
The stairs were open so the "boogie man"
Could grab our legs as we went spooky down;
And when we went back up, we looked away
Lest we might catch his leer between the steps.
The walls were rock; the light, one window dim,
But dimmer still the one adjoining room:
The coal bin, leading to the cellar door,
Had one window down which the "coal man" put
His chute to send a load of glist'ning black.
The other side was where dad and a daughter—
Seeking-praise would neatly stack wood scraps
Delivered gratis from dad's paper mill.
And on cold mornings, lying in upstairs cold,
We heard dad shake the furnace ashes down
Before he started that day's welcome fire…
Another blessing from the cellar's store.
And though mom let my dog go out to be
Run over on the road and killed, and though
Dad had to slap the neighbor boys fighting
To make them stop (one the other's finger biting),
My mind in generosity releases
All bitter and unpleasant memories
Of perverseness and abuse in favor of
The fun we found beyond the cellar door.

I Think of Mom

by Maria Johnson (Poet's Daughter)

Finding all the pretty rocks,
Raising puppies in a box,
Mending holes in pants and socks,
I think of Mom

When a kid comes in the dark,
Through a Cocker Spaniel's bark,
With a tent pitched in the park,
I think of Mom

Washing dishes in the sink,
Changing sheets with common stink,
Taking care of food and drink,
I think of Mom

As the foremost blooms unfold,
When heat has taken hold,
Watching trees turn red and gold,
I think of Mom

BROADHORN

M ARY C OLQUETT

ISBN 978-1-64114-691-3 (Paperback)
ISBN 978-1-64114-692-0 (Digital)

Christian Faith Publishing, Inc.
296 Chestnut Street
Meadville, PA 16335
www.christianfaithpublishingom

Printed in the United States of America

CHAPTER 1

An ironic smile touched the corner of Hart MacAlpin's mouth as he considered the years he'd spent avoiding this situation. Now here he was, trapped.

He was twenty-two when his father finally persuaded him to sail for Europe and an education at the University of Edinburgh, a rube from the wilds of the Mississippi Territory, and madly in love with the curvaceous Ada Albright of Brightway Plantation. His smile expanded to a chuckle. He had expected her to wait.

"Mr. Hart," a voice spoke from his bedroom door.

"What is it?"

"Your mother's asking for you downstairs," Ash replied, standing erectly just inside the door.

"I'm almost ready. Just putting on my boots," Hart replied, striding across the room toward them. "How have you been, Ash? Married yet?" he continued.

"Five years now," Ash replied.

"Children?" questioned Hart.

"Three boys."

"Still evading capture?" Hart continued, referring to Ash's free status. He'd been running from slavers when the MacAlpins had hired him.

"Yes, sir, and you?" Ash replied, grinning. "Are you still evading capture?"

"Permanently," Hart supplied. The ironic smile spread and was replaced by one of satisfaction. He had been away for eight years. It was late spring, 1811, but not much here had changed.

3

The year was proving ominous. He'd learned during his jour-
ney up from New Orleans that the Mississippi had frozen over twice
during the winter. The oldest inhabitants could never remember it
being so cold. Then the floods in early spring spread intermittent
fevers. Many people were ill. The oceans had suffered violent earth-
quakes, giving rise to new islands. Now there was a massive comet
hurling itself toward earth. The general outlook was apathetic at best.

"I'll tell Miz Flora you're about ready," Ash said.

Hart pulled on the freshly polished boots, then surveyed his
image in the long mirror before the window. His formal suit of nan-
kin breeches, white waistcoat, and black jacket still fit as though it
belonged to him, but more loosely. He much preferred his buckskins
and tam. He'd never felt comfortable in the confines of dress clothes.

Don't settle in too comfortably, he warned himself. As soon as he
could arrange a buying trip North, he was leaving again. Of course,
the comet could change his plans. He preferred to believe the reports
that it would reach its perihelion before it could slam into the earth;
otherwise, there'd be no need for plans of any kind.

He gave his appearance one last halfhearted appraisal then
walked downstairs to the sounds of merrymaking.

The drawing room was crowded. Rugs had been removed and
the furniture placed against the walls. Candelabra shone with a high
polish, casting jeweled prisms of light over dancing couples. The pas-
tel shades of the ladies' gowns created a blur as they moved ceremo-
niously around the floor.

As Hart savored this bit of nostalgia, he felt a pair of eyes boring
into his. Ada was watching him from across the room, oblivious to
Bruce's attempts to distract her. Although dressed in her usual flam-
boyant style, she was obviously expecting a child.

She signaled for him to join them. Deliberately letting his smile
fade, he turned his back, determined to find a partner for the next
dance, avoiding Ada and her woeful airs.

*****

Able Hand raised his bow and struck the chords of a currently
popular waltz, allowing the music to swell and ebb with the rhythm

4

of the dancers. Able wasn't one of the pillared folk, but he attended all the galas. His fiddle was his invitation, and he was paid handsomely. There were other benefits as well, and Able knew how to take personal advantage of them.

He was standing now with his back to a potted palm, behind which two feminine voices were heard.

"Hart's back," Viola Vespar spoke excitedly.

"Do you mean it? Here...at Crapewood?" Callie Warren returned.

"Of course, silly. Where else? He came in last night, or so Ma'ma said. She got it from the post courier who got it from the tavern keeper."

"My, my," Callie uttered softly. "I wonder what caused him to return. Never thought he would, did you?"

"Can't say I ever thought about it one way or the other," Viola proclaimed, a defiant tone to her voice. "But it beats me why Ada would choose Bruce over Hart. I mean, there's simply no comparison."

"Oh, I agree," Callie gushed, her voice surreptitious. "But don't think you can fool me. I know how you pined after him for years. You should have better sense. After all, look at us! We're not what you could call pretty, we're not rich, and our collective bloodlines can't produce even one aristocrat."

"Our bloodlines do sport a MacAlpin, even if she was the black sheep of the family." Viola's voice now held a note of spite. "Who is she? Just look at the way the men are swarming round her. You'd think she was pretty, or something."

"She is, in a way. Of course, she's awful thin and a bit too tall but has lovely skin, and with that pale hair properly dressed, she would be attractive, even pretty," Callie, who was the more observant of the two, contended.

"Lovely skin, my foot. She's much too pale, washed out. Sort of oversoaped, if you know what I mean."

At that, the cousins broke into unrestrained laughter, causing heads to turn and sending Able, his bow flying along the strings, across the room to get a better look at the object of their appraisal.

He wasn't alone. Hart MacAlpin was assessing the girl from the other side of the dance floor. Able chuckled to himself, knowing the envy this would create in Viola's vacant heart—and Ada's discontent one.

*****

Hart had walked away from Ada's pleading eyes purposely, casting a speculative glance around the dance floor. He noticed a straight back and proudly held head topped by light hair—the exact opposite of Ada, who was small and dark—standing in front of him. He approached it.

"May I have the pleasure of this dance?"

The back turned, and he was pleasantly surprised to discover a face of nice proportions and eyes that looked directly into his.

"Of course," the girl answered. "It will be my pleasure."

He took her arm and led her onto the dance floor, finding his attention totally absorbed. Which cousin was she, he wondered? He had been away a few years, but he ought to remember any female who looked like this. She was thin, but her small bones didn't protrude. And those eyes and that coloring wouldn't have gone unnoticed.

"I should introduce myself. I'm Hart MacAlpin, a member of the family. And you?"

"Lessie," she replied. "Lessie Lord."

As Able's nimble fingers quickened the tempo of the music, Hart swung his partner nearer the center of the drawing room. He was enjoying himself. The girl was a good dancer. She followed him easily. Able was playing a waltz. Tightening his hold on the slender waist, he spun her into ever faster circles. The sound of applause rang in his ears. Finally, exhausted, his feet slowed, ending their dance.

"You dance well, Ms. Lord. You've undoubtedly had a great deal of practice." He hardly realized he was baiting her. But since his betrayal by Ada, he had made it a point to place available young women at a disadvantage. The more obnoxious he behaved, the sooner they lifted their skirts and fled.

"Very little, in fact, Mr. MacAlpin," she answered blandly. "But thank you for the compliment."

"I say, Hart, elder brother, that was some dance. Home only a few hours and already the toast of the party." Adam's voice provoked from the other side of the table. "Surely, you don't intend harnessing this lovely lady all evening."

"Ms. Lord, may I introduce my brother Adam. Adam, Lessie Lord," Hart said.

"May I have a turn, Ms. Lord?" Adam came around the table and seized her arm as the music swelled again. "I'm much lighter on my feet than my elder brother." He thrust a sparring glance at Hart as he pulled Lessie toward the dance floor.

Hart watched as they began the measured steps and, then with their feet in perfect time, sailed around the room amidst a throng of dancers. The girl's skin was as pale as candlelight, her poise natural, as she paced herself with her new partner.

"Well, Hart, I see you have found a distraction. I wondered if you would. She seems a trifle pale to me, not your usual type," Ada thrust.

"On the contrary, I find her charming," he returned, not trusting himself to look directly into her eyes.

"You've changed," she responded, her eyes seeking his, her hand laid casually on his arm. "I wanted to speak with you last night when you arrived, but with the family around, there was no time."

"It's just as well. You're a married woman, the wife of my brother. Anything you have to say to me should be said in front of the family." He was rewarded by the quick inhalation of her breath.

She lowered her eyes. "You're not still holding a grudge, after all these years?"

"A grudge? No, Ada, I'm not still holding a grudge," Hart laughed. "I've grown up some."

"I'm so glad," she continued, behaving as though they were sharing a confidence. "There are things you don't know, couldn't know...about Bruce and—"

She was abruptly silenced as Hart spoke, his voice stern. "I don't care to know, Ada, now or ever. You married Bruce. Try and make him a good wife."

Without waiting to see what reaction his damning words had wrought, he turned and headed in the direction of the incandescent charmer with the hazel eyes.

*****

Lessie settled her white India muslin gown decorously around her feet as she seated herself on the settee near the potted palms. Her kid slippers were old, no longer white, and she disliked showing them. But she couldn't hide the stamped satin leaves that trimmed the neck of her gown and bordered its wide skirt. Like the slippers and satin cap that she wore atop her curls, they were yellowed with age.

"Not tired already, Ms. Lord?"

Lessie glanced up quickly, recognizing the voice. "Not tired, Mr. MacAlpin," she replied. "Just waiting for your brother to fetch me a glass of water."

"Then let's talk," he suggested, seating himself beside her. "I've been away for some time, and I'm having the devil of a time placing you."

"And what have you decided?"

"That you are totally unrelated to anyone I know."

"But you're wrong, Mr. MacAlpin," Lessie challenged, smiling at his perplexity. "Don't you see any local resemblance at all?"

"None whatever," Hart admitted, thinking that anyone with her coloring would certainly be known abroad the territory. Then he added carefully, watching her eyes, "I've never seen such coloring as you possess, Ms. Lord. And I'm certain *no* one else possesses your smile."

Lessie knew instinctively that he was testing her. She couldn't help smiling as she returned, "But as I said, Mr. MacAlpin, you are wrong."

"Then correct me," he demanded.

"I'm related to John Wellsley, of Wellsley Farm," she answered, laughing softly. She hadn't enjoyed herself like this for a long time.

"In what way?" Hart's brow rose quizzically.

"He's my father's nephew, and I believe his wife, Joan, is your mother's niece. Am I correct?"

She watched the long scar lift as Hart smiled in consternation. "So John is your first cousin. Then you are staying at Wellsley Farm?"

"Yes. For an indefinite period. I'm soon to travel to Nashville to stay with my widowed grandmother. The new mail carrier and his wife are to accompany me and my young brother, Nathaniel," she explained.

Hart regarded the young woman before him. She didn't seem the type to adapt to frontier travel. Her parents must be daft.

"I heard on the river boat up from New Orleans that they'd found someone for the job of mail carrier. But I had no idea they would send his wife along. The Trace is no place for women. Even in a large party, well armed, it's a gamble no sensible woman would undertake. How does your mother feel about you embarking on such a hazardous journey?"

"My mother has been dead for a number of years," Lessie replied, averting her eyes.

"Your father then?" Hart continued.

"My father was buried in Church Street Cemetery at Mobile only last month," she answered, lifting her face. Except for cousins and her grandmother Lord, whom she had never seen, she and Nate, her nine-year-old brother, were alone in the world.

"I am sorry," Hart responded immediately. "Please forgive my callousness."

"There is no need. I must become accustomed to being an orphan and not behave so childishly," she replied, still with a hint of defiance in her voice.

"Nonsense. You've behaved most naturally."

Their eyes met momentarily, each recognizing experienced sorrow.

"Come," Hart suggested after a moment. "Let's dance. We'll see if we can reignite your smile." He took her hand, insisting, just as Adam arrived with the glass of water.

"You drink it," Hart directed, laughing. "I'll get Ms. Lord a glass after this dance."

Once again, Lessie was enthralled. Just as he had done earlier, he maneuvered them around the perimeter of the floor, their feet keeping time with the music, his right hand pressing her close. She could see whispering behind carefully raised fans. It did not matter. She would be gone in a few months.

As the daughter of a distinguished, but impoverished, revolutionary war soldier who had taken to drink after the death of her mother, she had few chances for social occasions. She had beau until the state of their impoverishment had leaked out. Afterward, callers had ceased to come. If she issued invitations, they were gracefully refused. She had ceased to be angered by what she considered the avariciousness of men. They had their fortunes to make—or marry. And according to the scales of time, she had lost in the balance.

When the dance had ended, Hart turned her toward the wide double doors leading onto the front gallery.

"Let's get some air. I admit to being winded."

Lessie agreed, enjoying the rush of cool air as they stopped near the center columns. It was the middle of May; the evening sky was brighter than she could ever remember it being, almost as though the moon had somehow enlarged. The days, too, seemed wrong. Instead of becoming brighter, hotter, as spring progressed, they seemed colder, darker, as if the sun had gone to bed. Or at least that was Nate's definition for the lackadaisical sunlight.

There was talk of a pending disaster among the older folk. She prayed not. The last couple of years had been disaster enough for her and Nathaniel.

"Thank you," she said, after a moment or two, quite without thinking.

"For what?" Hart asked.

"For...the dances," she answered, then added, "I don't know when I shall have the pleasure of such an evening again."

Hart looked at her. What was it about her, he wondered, that had prompted him to dance twice with her, a feat which he guarded against. "Let's walk a while. The grass is dry this evening."

"I'd enjoy that," Lessie replied, relinquishing the thread of sorrow that had held her.

He offered her his arm, guiding her along paths he had walked as a boy. When they reached the edge of the lawn near the woods, they turned and looked back at the house. It was aglow with candlelight.

If it hadn't been for Ada's and Bruce's betrayal of him, he would make his home here. He had missed Crapewood and all it had meant in his young life.

After he had left Scotland, he had wandered around Europe for almost two years, Ada's numerous letters left unopened. Her rejection of him in favor of Bruce consumed his every thought; so much so that he often found he had crossed a border into another country without having been aware of it at the time. He had wanted to fight, to inflict pain, to wound—anything—to ease his own misery.

One day, he awoke to find snow covering him. He lay in an alley, his clothes a mess. He had closed his eyes against the knowledge that he had passed out in some barroom or bistro. Slowly, he checked his pockets, glancing around for the tam that had now become a part of his daily wardrobe. It lay near him, half-covered in snow. He had reached for it as he raised himself to his knees. His head hurt, he smelled to high heaven, and he was incredibly thirsty. But the tam was good news. He felt under the inside band for the gold coins that he kept hidden there, then sighed in relief when he discovered none were missing.

The first thing he had wanted was food, plenty of it and hot. Then he was going home. The thought had made him smile. He had at last purged his mind of Ada. He had laughed, his voice croaking hoarsely.

His decision to return home had kept him in great spirits until he attempted to book passage. No ships were sailing for North America. Madison was now president of the United States and had repealed the embargo, but the Napoleonic wars were still in progress, and Britain was still harassing American ships and confiscating American sailors. He had very little hope of leaving the Continent unless he could work his way across the Atlantic aboard a Spanish or Portuguese ship. This he managed to do—sailing from Portugal aboard a ship laden with goods for the Argentine. Once there, he had written his father from Buenos Aires, outlining his plan for purchasing horses to be shipped home and resold to the hungry territorial market. He had received a reply within a few months.

His father had agreed readily, stating that good horses were in short supply in the territory and that good breeding stock was in demand by squatters and landowners alike. Hart was soon in business, purchasing horses and other items that would be sought after in the territory and shipping them across the Gulf, then upriver from New Orleans.

He remained in Argentina until civil war broke out. The gauchos wanted their freedom from Spain. Because of his association with them, he was suspected of spying and expelled by the then ruling Spaniards.

It was April 20, 1811, when he finally sailed for home aboard a Danish ship heading for New Orleans.

He had spent much of his time in Argentina on the pampas where he had learned the ways of the gauchos. Spending each day guarding against death, struggling to find enough food and a safe place to spend the night, had instilled in him respect for the inevitable. Deprivation and battle served to correct many headstrong ideas, he mused, bringing his thoughts back to the present and Lessie.

"Would you care to sit down?" Hart asked, as they paused near a bench.

"Please," she replied. "You have a lovely home," she added, gazing toward the house in admiration.

"Thanks," Hart began, then stated, "After two dances and a walk on the lawn, we should be on a first name basis."

"I agree," Lessie replied, laughing lightly. "Friends should use first names."

"And cousins," Hart questioned, a wry twist to the corner of his mouth? "We're cousins several times removed. What should we call each other?"

"The same," Lessie replied, still laughing. "Although, I'm not certain we are cousins."

"We must be," Hart affirmed. "But Lessie and Hart will do."

Silence settled its cloak around them, staying further speech until Hart offered, "Would you enjoy seeing Crapewood?"

"Yes, I would indeed," Lessie returned.

"Come with me. Most of the guests are still in the parlor. We'll enter through the library. I'd like to see the place again myself."

Hart had taken Lessie's hand, assisting her to her feet, when a man spoke from directly behind him.

"It's a nice evening for a stroll, isn't it?"

"Yes, it is," he answered, turning to see who had spoken.

"I beg your pardon for intruding, but I've been admiring your companion from afar," the man said, his teeth gleaming in the moonlight. "I'm William Smythe, an officer on the governor's staff. And you?"

Hart turned his full attention to the interloper, his pampas sense stiffening his back. He stuck out his hand in introduction. "I'm Hart MacAlpin. This is Ms. Lord, a guest."

"Oh, I see. You're the parable son, the one just returned from where? The pampas?"

"There, among other places," Hart returned, taking Lessie's arm. "We were just about to return to the house."

"Please don't let me keep you, Mr. MacAlpin, Ms. Lord," Smythe said. "But allow me to request the next dance with Ms. Lord," he finished, bowing from the waist.

Hart ignored the man, moving briskly toward the house with Lessie almost skipping in order to keep up.

"Please, could we slow down?" she asked, tugging on his arm.

"Of course," Hart said, slowing his pace. "I didn't want the man ruining our tour of the house."

They walked back across the wide expanse of lawn toward the white-pillared veranda. Hart guided Lessie along the polished floor toward an entrance near the western end. Here a smaller replica of the Georgian doorway of the main entrance stood open. They entered, and Lessie found herself surrounded by walls of books.

"Wonderful," she exclaimed, not able to resist exultation at such a sight. Although ladies of the territory were not expected to exceed to acquired knowledge, she had spent many hours reading from her mother's special collection of volumes. They had long since disappeared due to her father's penchant for rum. Each volume had purchased one more night of oblivion.

Hart's attention was captured by the girl's ready admiration for his home. His parents had built Crapewood over a period of years as his father's wealth increased. The main section of the house had been sided by two identical wings, each continuing the architecture of the original structure, which had been a two-storied square with twenty-foot ceilings, an attic of approximately the same height, and front and rear verandas. A kitchen wing containing double fireplaces, a wine cellar, and a billiard room off to one side occupied the original one-story unit in which the young Angus MacAlpins had lived before the birth of Hart, their eldest child.

Lessie was smitten by the beauty of the library and its bounty of prose. The shelves were hewn from walnut, sanded smooth, and polished to a high luster. The floor and window casings were the same. Bright orange-and-green carpets from the Orient were strewn across the floor, imitating the pattern and color of the cretonne fabric on the numerous sofas and chairs.

"I'm surprised by your enthusiasm," Hart contended. "Most women have only a momentary interest in this room."

"Oh…but surely, everyone appreciates the abundance found here," Lessie responded. "I've never seen so many volumes. How many are there?"

"Something near two thousand, I believe," Hart answered. "My father sent away to England and Scotland for them. He wanted knowledge on hand, in case his sons exceeded to learning. I enjoyed certain aspects of it, I admit. But it was not my idea to go away to university. I did that to please him."

Lessie smiled at him, happiness glowing from her face as she pirouetted slowly around, marveling at such wealth.

"Let's continue through the house," Hart suggested. "I'd like to hear your opinion of it. Then we'll return here and stay as long as you wish."

Lessie accepted his arm, and they continued into the main hall along which were several rooms used for various family activities. The dining room was off to the rear of the east parlor and was entered from both the hallway and the parlor by double doors. The room reflected French and English tinctures. The buffet had been set for a late supper and displayed china, silver, and crystal. Through the open doorway, Lessie could see great gold-leaf pier mirrors, which were matched by an identical set in the parlor. The window hangings were of gold satin damask, as was the upholstery.

She had not visited in a home such as this since before her mother had died. Her mother's family had been for many years an accepted one in Mobile. But they had not accepted her marriage to Lessie's father, Nathaniel Lord.

His revolutionary heroics, handsome Irish features, and Gaelic charm had brought good business to his small gun shop until his wife's untimely death. Thereafter, his clients withdrew in proportion to his drinking. A few fast friends, those who had served with him in war, stayed close by until the end, attending his funeral with airs of acceptance and finality.

After viewing the first-floor rooms, Hart escorted Lessie upstairs and through the guest bedrooms, then along the hallway to his parents' room, which was furnished in English mahogany and was beautifully appointed with imported porcelain and silk fabrics.

"This is such a charming room. I know your mother enjoys spending time here," Lessie commented, noting the sewing basket and wool loom occupying one corner.

"She does," Hart stated. "I played here as a child while she wove fabric on that loom."

"Your home has an atmosphere of warmth and hospitality. You are much blessed," Lessie replied.

"I am that," Hart agreed. "Just at this moment, though, I feel a distinct need to eat. Let's return to the dining room and have supper."

When Hart had eaten his fill and Lessie had sampled various delicacies, they returned once again to the library, where the doors were still open to the evening breeze. Standing in one of them, looking right at home, was an Indian.

"Tchula," Hart exclaimed, hurrying forward and grasping the man's hand. "I am glad to see you. I'd no idea you would be here this evening."

"Not come to soiree. Come to see friend. You much skinny and much older. You not eat well long time," Tchula advised, picking up their way toward each other immediately as though eight years had been a day.

"Well, I can't say the same for you. You seem to be eating well," Hart laughed, pleased greatly by Tchula's presence. "Did you marry that sweet *ohoyo*?"

"We have two sons." Tchula beamed as he spoke, obviously proud of his family. "You bring wife home?"

"I've had other things to do," Hart answered. "Come inside and sit down. Bring me up to date on what's happening."

Lessie realized the two men wanted to reminisce after so many years. "I'll leave you to your reunion, Hart. No, please don't bother," she insisted, as he offered her his arm to escort her back to the other guests.

"Then let me say how much I've enjoyed our visit, Cousin," he returned, smiling at her. "And I hope we see more of you around Crapewood in the future."

"Thank you. I'd be happy to return for a visit, but I don't know if that will be possible. Perhaps we'll meet again," she added, turning quickly to leave the room. She felt they would not have such an opportunity and hastened quickly away.

Hart watched her departure momentarily before turning to Tchula.

"You have put on weight." Hart laughed again, as the two of them clasped each other's arms in a remembered salutation. "I'd not better you in a wrestle now. You're strong as a Calcutta boar."

"Achukma cook good. Much venison stew and bear steak," Tchula informed, seating himself in the chair he had favored since childhood.

Hart did the same, reclining himself across the sofa. "What news do you have?"

"Need to talk. Much worry here. Someone paying Creeks and Chickasaws to raid villages. Killing people, stealing horses, guns," Tchula explained, speaking quietly, exercising natural caution.

"I heard something about it on the boat up from New Orleans. Seems there's a British agent in our midst arming the renegade Indians," Hart submitted.

"Not renegades, Ishto Impa, warriors led by chiefs."

Hart smiled at the use of his Choctaw name, which meant Big Spoon, but was disturbed by Tchula's information about current problems in the territory. If the pillaging was being done by warriors led by chiefs, a full-scale war was in progress whether or not the local authorities cared to call it that.

"If you say it is so, it is so. What's being done about it?"

"Not much! I here to offer you commission. Governor sent for me. Pushmataha say we Choctaws not kill for money. Not all are against white men in territory. Some are. They take guns in payment for killing. Agent buys scalps," Tchula finished. "I tell him I will help if you will. He offers you, me, commission."

"Why me?" Hart asked, mystified. "I've never met the man."

"He knows from your father. Thinks you good man for job. I tell him you only man for job," Tchula explained, his red face alive with humor.

"Well, it will do you no good. I won't be around long enough," Hart said, chuckling. "After a short visit here, I intend traveling North and buying goods for Papa's commissary, bringing them down the Mississippi by broadhorn. I may settle in Nashville."

Tchula sat perfectly still, understanding Hart's reluctance to become involved so near home *and* Ada.

Hart considered the situation. He knew Tchula would take on the job alone if asked. He owed his friend a great deal, and he was in no particular hurry to leave for Nashville and Points North. He'd look into the problem and then make his decision.

"I make no promises, understand. We'll do some checking, then I'll decide if I want to be involved." He sat up on the sofa. "I'm tired. I want nothing so much as plenty of sleep."

Tchula nodded, agreeing. "We work together, like always?"

"Together, like always," Hart replied. "Just tell me all you know and where you think we should start. After that, I'll have to get back to the party, or Mam will have my scalp instead of the Creeks and Chickasaws."

They talked quietly for a few more minutes, then Hart returned to the parlor. He surveyed the room, recognizing most of the guests. Lessie Lord was dancing with someone he didn't know. When her partner turned, he recognized the man who had spoken to them on the lawn. As they moved nearer Hart's position, Smythe glanced his way and nodded in recognition. He was a powerfully built man of medium height, very polished and correct, military in his stance.

As the dance ended, Hart moved to break in when he was accosted by several old friends who were intent on welcoming him home. When he looked up, she had gone, leaving with her cousins, John and Joan Wellsley. It didn't matter, he told himself. She was just one more pretty ohoyo.

*****

Able placed his fiddle inside the suede sack in which he carried it. He had never understood why these social types kept such late hours. His fatigue and the ache in his arms were lightened, to some degree, by the weight of gold in his pocket. Old Angus paid well, he admitted to himself, as he tied the sack around the horn of his saddle. He'd soon be home, where Clemmie would have a hot bowl of soup and corn bread waiting. There might even be ham and greens. Things were looking up for the Hands.

"That was fine music, Able," Hart complimented, as he approached the man who was about to mount his horse.

"I'm much obliged, Mr. MacAlpin. That I am," Able returned, as he turned Joe's head toward Natchez.

"And that's a fine horse you're riding. Looks as though music pays well," Hart continued, appraising the lines of the big bay.

"From time to time," Able admitted, moving Joe into a trot. "And there's some who appreciate it mor'n others."

"I agree. Anyone with a talent like yours deserves good fortune," Hart shouted, as Able trotted Joe along the drive.

The horse was a good mover as well, Hart thought, watching their departure until darkness enclosed them. Then he walked slowly toward the barn. Neighing welcomed his arrival as he checked the stalls for Blister and was rewarded with a whinny as he neared the end one. There he was. Eight years showed very little. He seemed in fine shape. Hart put out his hand for the horse to get his scent. Blister's eyes widened perceptively as he snorted and stamped, seeking Hart's hand again and again, recognizing a familiar but long-absent friend.

"Good boy, good boy," Hart spoke softly, running his hand along Blister's neck, then patting him on the rump. "You remember me, don't you?"

When the snorting and stamping ceased, Hart lifted a bridle from the peg by the gate and placed it carefully over the horses head, securing it. Then as he led Blister from his stall, intending a short ride to reacquaint the two of them, Bruce spoke from behind him.

"Careful, Brother. No one has ridden him for a while. I'm the only one who works him out."

"I'll manage," Hart returned, proceeding out of the barn.

"Things have changed since you've been away, Hart. Don't get lost on some new byway," Bruce warned, walking along with him.

"As I said, I'll manage," Hart repeated, mounting Blister, who was prancing about, eager to be off.

The darkness was to Hart a known entity, a friend at times, an enemy at others. And just now it was due to low-level clouds. Earlier in the evening, the grounds were lit with light from the moon—and the brilliant comet.

"I'll just ride him around the farm. Be back in a while."

"See that you do. Papa wants to see all of us in the library for a smoke before bed. Sent me to tell you," Bruce added, as Blister's dappled gray shadow disappeared into the gloom.

Hart could feel the power of his horse beneath him. He nudged him into a trot, then a canter, and they shot down the drive and up the road. This he remembered. This he still enjoyed. It had been too long.

After a while, he reined Blister to a walk. They were both short of breath.

"Whoa, boy," he urged. "We'll walk awhile and get our wind back." He reached to pat Blister's neck when he saw light across the meadow to his left. He urged Blister forward at a walk until he spotted the gates to Wolloloy Farm. The light was from the house.

The young woman had been pleasant, he decided, considering what little he knew of her. He considered the possibility of calling on her later, after he'd settled in. *Hold up*, he told himself, *you've only just met her—and she's leaving soon*. Still.

The light was suddenly extinguished. "If that's not an omen, I don't know what is," he murmured, turning Blister's head in the direction of Crapewood.

CHAPTER 2

The clock struck three as an early morning breeze wafted through the open doors of the library, sending cigar smoke upward toward the high ceiling.

"War is certain to come," Adam asserted from his position by the door. "Clay and Calhoun are gaining support in Congress."

"Aye. They've a deal of support. But there are many Federalists who oppose it," Angus returned, "including some right here in Natchez."

"But don't you agree, Father, that England's high-handed practices of seizing and searching our ships and impressing American sailors has got to cease?"

"Cease? That's easier said than seen to, it seems to me. Will it cease ev'n we go to war again and win?" Angus had given the matter of British naval superiority some thought.

Hart, who had been content to listen, stretched his legs before the fire and drew on his cigar. He understood the point his father was making. "Not so fast, Adam," he inserted. "Father's right. Until we develop a sufficient force to repel her on the high seas, she isn't likely to stop harassing us even if we win in another land war."

"Aye," Angus concurred. "That's exactly what I meant. We won our independence from her in '76, and she's still dictating to us in every possible way."

"And she always will unless we learn to negotiate properly. Give her something she wants, and she'll come around," Hart affirmed, rising and standing before the fire. "If they've something to gain, something to claim as a prize, they'll change their tactics." He tossed his cigar butt into the fire. He'd learned that well enough, and a few other things as well... like how to survive on the marsh when campins and eat off the land, how to quickly and silently kill with his dirk before he could be strangled by a bola, and how to deal with loneliness and betrayal.

"That's just it, Hart," insisted Adam, earnest in his attempt to persuade them of the need for war. "You've lost track of things here. People are tired of being pushed around by other nations, especially England. I know the federalists are against war with England, especially now that Madison has lifted the embargo. We have a number of English sympathizers here in Natchez. They still maintain personal and social ties with her far beyond the rest of the country. And they're sympathetic in her struggle against Napoleon."

"I'm certain that's true enough." Hart marshalled his thoughts, not wanting an argument with his younger brother. "Father, you referred to sympathizers here. Anyone in particular?"

"Aye," Angus answered, pausing for a moment, before continuing candidly. "Bruce's father-in-law, Colonel Sheffield Albright, for one, feels we'd all be better off under the British flag."

Hart studied his father for a quick moment, noting the hard reflection in his eyes. "That's old news, at best. We've all known that since I was a boy," he said, glancing at Bruce who had turned his back, evidently seeking an ash tray.

"You're right. The colonel is harmless. But here's an even better argument for fighting," Adam continued. "It's a known fact that England is funding the Creeks and Chickasaws against the white settlers in the territory. They're wiping out entire settlements, women and children alike."

"How do you know?"

"They have new muskets, plenty of shells, and are spending money at the commissary in town," Adam stipulated.

Hart's attention was captured. "How about the Choctaws? Are they allying themselves with the others?"

"Nay. Their chiefs are against war. Lucky for us," Angus answered. "But who knows what may happen if Tecumseh has his way."

"And he most likely will," Bruce contended. "He's known as Tannap Abi, a killer of the enemy. And he considers all white men his enemies."

No one seemed to have a reply for that. Bruce took a glass of port and settled into a chair opposite Hart's. Smoke continued to swirl upward toward the high ceiling. Night sounds crept in through the open doorways.

"Well, Brother," Bruce said, breaking the contemplative thoughts of the others. "Tell us about you. Must have been different in Argentina?"

Hart settled into his chair. "Some."

"Oh come on, Hart," Adam interjected. "I'm dying to hear about your adventures."

At that, Hart laughed, long and hard. "Adventures? I wouldn't call the last few months an adventure. But since you ask, little brother, I'll fill you in."

He glanced at each of them. His father was listening carefully, his eyes picking up the subtle nuances of Hart's manner. Bruce seemed to be staring upward, unimpressed. Adam was sitting on the edge of the sofa, his elbows on his knees, waiting expectantly.

"As you know, when my term at university was finished, I decided to travel," Hart began, looking at Bruce. "I saw some of Europe before I decided to return home."

"We know all that. Get to the part about Argentina. What about the gauchos?" Adam interrupted.

"Yes, we were told you were much put upon before you got ship for home. Or was that just fabrication?" Bruce questioned, his voice sarcastic. He had never worshiped at Hart's feet, as did young Adam. It was Bruce's assumption that the stories arriving home in advance of his elder brother were obviously exaggerated out of all proportion, if not downright lies. "We didn't hear from you directly," he added.

"I had no way of posting mail from the pampas. And, of course, my main goal was to find a way home once I had purchased a few good horses. Occasionally, some settler or gaucho traveling back toward Buenos Aries passed my way. We'd share a meal or a night.

It was always wise to travel in a party—sleep, too, for that matter. It prolonged more than one life. There were thieves, murderers, roaming the wilds."

"Did you see any? Engage any in combat?" Adam asked from the edge of his seat.

"Some," Hart answered. He watched Bruce as he continued, noting the appraisal in his brother's eyes. "I did attempt to get messages out, though. I suppose some of them got through. Father received a number of reports, I believe."

"Aye, including one that you had died. Never believed that one," Angus stated positively.

"I can explain that," Hart grinned. "A number of men were tracking me after I had done some trading and was carrying a good bit of money. They almost got me one evening when I was alone. When the ruckus was over, two of them were dead and three more had fled. I placed my green tam o' shanter near the body of one fair-skinned hellion and spilled a few new coins near him on the ground. A few weeks later, in a small village, I heard talk of a fair-haired Scotsman who had gotten himself killed on the pampas. The only thing the authorities could identify was his hat. It seemed he had been carrying gold at the time."

"Thunderation! That's great, Hart," Adam praised. "I wish I had been there."

"Nay, Adam," Hart replied, using his father's word, "you wouldn't have enjoyed the reality of it. I couldn't sleep no matter where I was at night. Several attempts were made on my life. God only knows how I survived."

"By your wits, Hart. I always knew you were the type to come through unscathed," Adam continued, pleased with the prospect of adventure however past.

Hart smiled as he observed the excitement in his younger brother. "My wits may have saved my hide, but if I don't get some sleep soon, I may give up the ghost on my own."

"Aye, Son," old Angus replied, "you go on up to bed. We'll talk more tomorrow."

At the door, Hart said, "It's good to be back."

"Say, Hart. Why the green tam o' shanter…?" Adam asked, remembering the strange head gear his brother had been wearing when he arrived. "You mentioned it before."

"Most of us at school wore them. I got used to it," Hart replied.

He then proceeded across the hall and upstairs to his room, removing only his outer clothes before collapsing on the bed.

*****

"He looks fit enough," Angus said. "I had almost given up on his coming home at all."

Bruce gave his father a scornful look. "Petty behavior, in my opinion, his staying away all that time just because I won Ada from him."

The look in Angus' eyes silenced any further speculation about Hart's behavior—or absence.

Adam chuckled as Bruce stalked out of the room. "Come on, Papa, let's go to bed. Tomorrow shows great promise," he said as he proceeded his father from the room, a smile lurking in his eyes. *Hart hadn't been dubbed the big spoon for nothing*, he thought, the smile spreading to his lips.

*****

Flora MacAlpin bustled around the kitchen, busily preparing a large breakfast. Hart was home, and she intended to fatten him up. The joy of having him home at last had prompted her to rise earlier than she had in years, her bad heart notwithstanding.

"Cleo, hurry and set the table. Hart was always an early riser. He'll be down soon. I don't want him to wait on his breakfast," she instructed the cook as she slid a large pan of buttermilk biscuits into the oven. "And slice some ham to go with the bacon you're frying up."

"Don't fret so, Miz Flora. He'd not miss one of your breakfasts—not that man. I can remember having to run him out'r this kitchen most days. That boy could eat, he could," Cleo replied.

Flora smiled. "Yes, he could. But he burned it so fast it never seemed to take. He was always empty."

"Yes'um. He sho' could move." Cleo laughed, placing china on the table. "I could never catch that boy."

"That's a fact." Flora laughed happily. "You know, I don't think we ever did catch him."

"No'um. But he never dared run from the mister. Only time I ever saw that boy get his comeuppance was when he built that still down behind the barn. The mister caught him at it. Mr. Hart walked bent over for days."

"What's going on?" Hart stopped in the door of the kitchen, pleased to hear his mother's happy laughter. "I'm starved. What's for breakfast?"

At that, both women grabbed their apron tails, wiping their eyes, laughter and tears flowing together. "We were just discussing your appetite, and in you walk." Flora laughed. "Sit down, Son, and fill your plate. The biscuits will be out in a minute."

Hart sat, smiling. "My appetite hasn't changed much. So bring on the food."

For the next few minutes, Cleo employed herself in supplying all the ham, bacon, eggs, grits, and biscuits Hart could eat, along with assorted jams, butter, and a pitcher of fresh milk. When he had finished, he surveyed the room with a look of satisfaction. The women nodded to each other, pleased.

"Now I feel I'm really home," Hart offered. "I haven't had a breakfast like that since the morning I left for university."

"There's no reason you can't have them every morning now," Flora suggested, her intuition telling her that such would not be the case. Ada was here. Hart would not stay long. Her heart broke for her son. She knew him well. He had not put Ada's betrayal behind him yet—not entirely. And there was Bruce. Her love for him had somehow shriveled since his marriage to Ada, although she would never admit it. She hated this division in her family. She knew Hart would find it difficult to stay.

"Don't worry, Mam, I'll be around," Hart said, taking his mother's hand. "I'm fine now."

"Are you?" Flora asked, watching his eyes as she spoke. "You are young yet. You can build a good life for yourself here, with the family, if you can put the past behind you."

Hart rose, tossing his napkin on the table. "I intend to do just that. In fact, I already have a job to do," he finished, leaning down and placing a kiss on her temple. "You just keep the food coming."

"We'll do that, Mr. Hart," Cleo supplied. "I always do that, anyway." She giggled.

"Fine. I'll see you at lunch. Make sure it's a good one," he instructed, smiling at both of them, as he started for the stable and Blister.

*****

Blister was in fine fettle, whinnying in recognition as Hart approached him.

"Good morning, boy. Missed me, did you?" Hart said quietly, stroking the long soft muzzle.

"Morning, Mr. Hart," a voice spoke from the door of the barn. "I've a message for you."

"Thanks, Ash. Who sent it?" Hart asked, opening the note, as a sweet scent assailed his nostrils. For a brief moment he was lost in time. He had received many such notes, announced as he opened them by their particular fragrance.

"It was handed to me by Miz Ada, sir. She said to give it to you when you were alone," Ash explained.

Hart hesitated. He had no desire to read the contents of the note. He thrust his arm toward Ash, intending to hand it back to him when he thought better of it. Ada was not going to let up on him until he had a straight talk with her. He remembered well her tenacity for getting what she wanted.

"Never mind, Ash. I'll take care of this," he added, mounting Blister and moving out of the barn. "But hereafter, do not accept notes from Miz Ada to me. Tell her I instructed you not to."

"I'll do that, sir," Ash replied. "And gladly," he finished under his breath. He had never cared for Miz Ada. She was too uppity by half.

*****

Hart trotted Blister away from the farm and down the narrow road toward Natchez. Ada's note had asked him to visit her at Brightway Plantation. She would be visiting her parents for a few days and needed desperately to see him. Her choice of words had imparted urgency to her invitation. Hart was interested in spite of himself. What had she meant by "collusion"?

Blister's head was up. He wanted a run. Hart gave him his head, and off they went at a canter. It was only a few miles to Natchez from Crapewood, but Brightway was south of Natchez near the river. He had decided to stop at the tavern. At this time of morning, the only folk there would be the talkative kind, the kind that wouldn't work— and some who didn't need to.

It was still early when Hart reined Blister alongside the hitching rail, dismounted, and walked down the steps leading into the tavern. The tavern had been in existence since before the War of Independence. Hart could remember as a boy seeing its silhouette against the evening sky as he and his father had closed the commissary and headed home. It had changed little. He removed his tam as he entered.

"G'morning, Mr. MacAlpin," a robust voice greeted him as he entered.

"Morning, Ed," Hart returned. "Why the 'mister'?"

Ed Boles grinned, his teeth clasping his half-smoked cigar tightly. "Thought all that education might have raised the height of your nose," he emitted, dexterously balancing the cigar. "And that hat o' yours! Haven't seen one of them since those Canadians came through here before the war.

The thin scar widened as Hart smiled. "Not my nose, Ed, just my knowledge. And my tam serves its purpose well."

"Oh, aye, your intelligence, is it?" Ed laughed, his boisterous voice echoing off the low beamed ceiling. "I recollect you had plenty of savvy before you left—and a good hat."

"Savvy, maybe. Knowledge, no," Hart replied, seating himself along the bar.

"It's good to have you back, son. All jokes aside, I had little time to talk to you the other night when you first arrived." Ed stuck out his hand and grasped Hart's in a firm clasp.

"Thanks, Ed. I understand how busy you are in the evenings." Hart returned the handshake willingly.

Ed Boles considered himself as American as the flag that flew daily from the mast outside his tavern. He leveled his gaze at Hart, wondering what had brought him to the tavern so early in the morning. In fact, as he remembered, Hart had never been a regular in the evenings, either.

"What will you have, beer or rum?" Ed asked.

"A cup of good coffee, Ed," Hart replied, glancing casually around the room. Its interior seemed smaller than he remembered. There were only two customers, one he didn't know but guessed to be a planter. The other one he knew well.

"Sam Shute, how are you? It's been a long time," Hart said, smiling broadly as he moved toward the table where a small wizened man sat, nursing a glass of rye.

"Well, boy, I see you made it back in one piece," Sam fired, his voice echoing hollowly.

"More or less," Hart replied, straddling one of the stools at the table where Sam sat.

Sam leaned his scrawny elbows on the rough table, his manner that of a blue hound at point, his voice secretive. "You want something?"

Hart laughed. "Right to the point, as usual."

"I find it saves a lot of time," Sam returned.

"Right. I am glad to see you, Sam, for a number of reasons. The more important one just now is this. You always have your ear to the ground and your eyes open. You know more about what's going on at any given time than any man who travels the Trace," Hart said quietly.

A wet smile crept across Sam's face. He leaned his head toward Hart as he spoke, his hawk-like nose raised defiantly. "Could be, Mr. MacAlpin."

"You know me better than that, Sam. Call me Hart."

"True. I know you. Don't many men of your station get so friendly with a backwoodsman like me, though."

Hart did not reply to that. Instead, he fixed his gaze on Sam and said, "Sam, we've known each other a while. You don't mind answering a few questions, do you?"

"That I do. I knew when you walked in here, you were after something."

Hart roared with laughter as much at himself and his feeble attempt to secret information from an old coon like Sam as at Sam's perspicacity.

He decided to change tactics. Placing his hands flat on the table, he began. "These rumors of war, Sam, are raising tempers all over the territory. The Chickasaws and Creeks under the Shawnee medicine man, Tecumseh, are trying to align the Choctaws against us colonials. You know that. And you know what will happen if they're successful. Every white family from Nashville to New Orleans will be slaughtered wholesale."

"Agreed," Sam said, his manner less aloof.

"Then we've all got to stand together, Sam. We must forget our differences in order to survive."

"Are you telling me that you're an agent in the pay of the territorial government?" Sam was quick to surmise that Hart's curiosity was more than personal.

Hart surveyed the weathered little man across the table. In spite of the insignificant size of his body, his brain surpassed that of most men. He decided to offer a confidence in exchange for what he wanted. "Something like that, Sam. It's being said there's gold changing hands. Someone is selling us out."

Sam's eyes glittered as he replied. "What if I'm the man you want? Could be you won't reach your four score and ten admitting that to me."

"If I thought that, I would not be talking to you. You're known as a trustworthy man in a fight, if not always on the right side of the law. You've as much to lose as the rest of us if the British drive us out of the territory."

Sam's response was to lean back in his chair, his bulbous eyes obscured by lowered lids. After a moment, he replied. "I guess you're right. Don't think I'd be spared when the British discovered I'd spied against them in '75."

Hart remained still, waiting. Sam would make up his mind in his own time. He hoped he would decide to cooperate. He watched as Sam mulled over the situation, leafing absentmindedly through the pages of the worn Bible, which he always had with him.

"There was two hunters through here last fall, heading north toward Nashville," Sam finally offered. "After several days of drinking and sleeping it off, they let it slip they'd spent the summer south o' here, visiting with the Indians. I asked them if they'd run into Tchula, just to see what they would say. Said they hadn't spent their time with no-account Choctaws. Don't leave much of any other place for them to have been than with a band of renegade Creeks or Chickasaws. Some of them are hiding out south of here. When they're full of rum, they make strikes at the nearer farms."

"Did you learn their names?"

"Nope. Never mentioned them to anyone as far as I could dig up. Suspicious fellows they was too, carrying new muskets and plenty of shells, but no skins. Hadn't done no trapping or shooting of game that I could see."

"Did they mention other people, places?" Hart was suspicious as well. Men didn't spend their time in low country in the summer without something to gain.

"Just one. They was pretty far gone on rye one night and got to laughing and talking about this flatboat down in Natchez harbor operated by a big woman. Seems they had spent some time aboard," Sam answered.

Hart deliberated for a moment. There could be only one woman who fit that description. "Must be Flatboat Fanny," he replied, grinning.

"That's the one," Sam said. "I remember that's what they called her. Said she was big enough to handle any two men. That true?"

"That it is, Sam. Flatboat Fannie is at least six foot six inches tall and as big around as a wagon wheel," Hart explained, remembering the woman from trips to Natchez under the hill.

"Can't imagine how I missed her," Sam responded, amused.

"I don't suppose their being aboard her boat necessarily means much," Hart continued.

"Why not?" Sam asked, his mind still considering the woman's size and dimensions.

"She operates a bordello," Hart supplied. "She moves it often."

"Interesting," Sam retorted. "Must be a natural wonder, a woman like that," he chuckled, his usually somber countenance alive with curiosity. "How-some-ever, I'm a one woman man. I've got a family."

"I remember," Hart said.

Hart considered Sam's position while he finished his coffee. If he was going to get mixed up in this affair, he would need men like Sam Shute on his side. They would need to know what they were up against and who to seek out for shelter and arms when necessary. He had time yet, though. He could wait before enlisting Sam. He placed his empty mug on the table, rising as he did so.

"Sam, let me know if you hear anything else, will you? I'll pass it on to the proper authorities—with your permission, of course. I respect your privacy." He placed his tam on his head and moved toward the door.

"I'll think it over," Sam stated, a smile almost escaping his stoic countenance as he stared at Hart's green bonnet. "Where'd you get such a thing?"

"In Aberdeen, Sam. Like it?"

"Can't say as I do. What's it for, anyhow?"

"It's a hat, Sam, pure and simple, just a hat," Hart answered, as his dark silhouette moved through the open doorway into the morning sun.

As he mounted Blister and turned him in the direction of Brightway Plantation, he heard hearty laughter following him. Let them laugh. A man's hat was his own.

*****

Ada stood near the drive under the shelter of an ancient oak. She twisted her handkerchief in her hands as she strained to see who was coming. At last, it was him. She sighed in relief as she moved forward, standing in his way so that he must stop.

"I'm so glad you came, Hart. I'm so worried. I need you to advise me," she began in a rush before he could bring Blister to a halt and dismount. "Now don't look at me like that. I do need you. You'll see," she added, watching his face harden.

Hart led Blister under the spreading arches of the oak, tying him to a low limb, then turned, brushing Ada's hands from his arm as he selected a spot on the grass and sat down, leaning against the trunk. "Just what is on your mind, Ada?"

"I...I don't know exactly how to tell you," she began, hesitantly. "It's Bruce. Now don't go, Hart," she added, as he began to rise at the mention of Bruce's name. "Be patient with me. You never used to be so hard."

"You never used to be married to my brother. I don't care to hear about your domestic problems. They are better settled between the two of you."

"Oh, but it isn't domestic problems, Hart. Oh no! It's much more than that," she confided, scanning the lawn with her eyes. "We must be careful."

"Careful of what, Ada? You are beginning to annoy me with your hesitancy. Just why must we be careful?" Hart had loosened Blister's rein and was standing now beside the horse. "I've other things to do than play guessing games."

"We must be careful...of those who are in the pay of the spy," she whispered, her upturned face near him, her eyes wide. He paused, half in the saddle, then dropped his leg to the ground and stood silently before her. She was definitely agitated about something. "What do you know about a spy?" he demanded, removing her hand from his horse's reins.

"Oh, Ishto Impa," she began, tears glowing in her eyes, spilling over onto her cheeks, "someone here, and at Crapewood, is in this spy thing. You know, paying the Indians to pillage, rob, and murder."

"How do you know, Ada? And stop that crying, or I'll leave," Hart demanded, leading her to a shady place under the oak and seating her on the ground. She seemed near to hysteria. Something had frightened her and that was a fact.

As Hart sat down near her, she reached for his hand, which he promptly withdrew. A flicker of disbelief clouded her face. Hart's temper began to rise. *She thinks she can still manipulate me,* he thought, gifting her with a wide smile. *This could be entertaining.*

"Ada, for the last time, get on with it," he instructed, settling a few feet away from her. "I've other business today."

"Business?" she stammered. "Oh yes, business. Well, for some time I've been hearing people come and go at the oddest hours from Crapewood. And then a few weeks ago, I came home to visit Mama and the same thing happened. Only this time I caught a glimpse of them. A crude-looking man in rough clothes carrying a long rifle came sneaking along the boxwoods near the side entrance, right under my window. I saw him plain, but I don't know him."

"He stood for a while as though he was waiting. Then someone from the house must have come out the door because I saw him motion toward Natchez—you know, swing his arm in that direction. Then I heard voices raised in argument, hard and quiet like," she finished on a whisper.

"Where was Bruce?"

"That's what worries me. I don't know. We had retired early. I wasn't feeling well because of the baby," she explained. "When I turned to tell him what I had witnessed, he was gone—just plain disappeared. I hadn't heard a sound of his leaving."

Hart considered what she had told him. A strange, rough-looking man sneaking along the grounds late at night did sound ominous. "Was that it? You didn't see or hear anything else?"

"There was something else. At least, I think there was. I could have sworn I saw a hooded figure gliding along above the privet hedge. You know, sort of above ground," Ada added, a spiritual tone to her voice.

"A hooded figure?" Hart asked. "Do you mean wearing a cloak of some kind with a hood?"

"Yes, that's it. A cloak with the hood pulled around the head."

"Is there more?" Hart asked, his interest heightened.

"No, nothing. When I mentioned it to Bruce the next morning, he told me I was imagining things and suggested I take something to make me sleep at night." She paused, quite out of breath.

"Did he explain where he disappeared to, as you put it?"

"No, he didn't. He just laughed and said he'd gone downstairs for a glass of milk to help him sleep. But, Hart, I went to the kitchen as soon as the rough-looking man left, and Bruce wasn't there."

"Is that all?" Hart's mind played with the possibilities. He knew his brother well. There had been numerous scrapes, times when Hart had been summoned to Natchez under the hill to fetch Bruce home. But Bruce had never involved himself in political affairs. In fact, he had stated on several occasions that politics and things political were too much work and if he must work, it would be profitable to him. Perhaps he had found profit in politics after all.

He'd have to give Ada some answer, or he'd never get away from her. "Did you say, Ada, that this same thing had happened at Crapewood?" This bothered Hart. Secretive comings and goings at home meant trouble for his own family.

"Oh, yes. Much earlier in the month, I believe. I remember because the veranda had just been whitewashed and I had to make certain it was dry before I could sit there late in the evening."

"How late?" Hart pressed.

"Well, I believe, it must have been around two in the morning— yes, it was. I had just heard the clock in the front hall chime two."

"And the same thing occurred?"

"No, no. This time someone from the house came across the walk toward the barn, saddled a horse, and rode off into the night."

"But you don't know who it was?" Hart's interest had grown with the second report of stealthy maneuvers.

"I didn't see."

"Where was Bruce?"

"I don't know. He was in bed when I came down to the porch. I didn't return to our room that night. It was so warm. I spent the night downstairs on the sofa," she explained.

Hart thought it odd indeed that late-night callers would visit two plantations some distance apart. Ada was right about one thing. There was, if one believed her report, something peculiar going on.

Ada was watching him closely. She remembered well the way his light hair took on the color of warm ashes in subdued light, the way his eyes tightened at the corners when he was thinking to himself. She had never thought of him as handsome; but with his long face, wide-spaced gray eyes, patrician nose, and wide, thin lips, he possessed an arresting visage. Elegance was as natural to him as breathing, yet so was brawling. His body had developed into sinew and muscle. She realized now, as she waited for him to speak, that he was a very special man.

"I see what you mean, Ada," Hart said finally. "It does seem strange. But there's probably a simple explanation. I'll check into it. By the way, have you mentioned this to anyone else?" He rose, offered her his hand, and helped her up.

"Only Papa. But both he and Bruce insist I'm dreaming or imagining things due to my pregnancy," she answered, sighing.

"I'll do some checking, just to set your mind at rest," he advised from the saddle. With that, he edged Blister out from under the tree and turned him toward home.

"Bye, Hart, thanks for coming. I hope we can be friends," Ada called, as Blister moved into a trot. "I need a friend," she added quietly, watching until he was no longer in view.

She stood for a long time where he left her, then turned slowly and started toward the house. He was so distant, so cold. She had watched his eyes as she told her story. He was not sympathetic, simply interested. It must be that girl from the dance, that Lessie Lord. Otherwise, Hart wouldn't be treating her so coldly. It must be that girl.

She had wanted the fun, the parties, the gay social life that Bruce offered her in Hart's absence. She had them, but at what cost? She hadn't planned on a family. Now she would be forced to seclude herself until after the baby came. She was not at all certain that she could tolerate that.

*****

36

"Mr. Hart," Ash called when he saw Hart walking across the lawn toward the kitchen door.

"What are you doing out here so late, Ash?"

"Waiting to speak to you," Ash answered matter-of-factly. "I have a note from the governor. It was brought by messenger this afternoon."

"Thanks." Hart took the note, ripped open the seal, and read the contents. "I've received word there's a squad of British soldiers camping at Chickasaw Bluffs, about two hundred miles upriver from here. Lends credence to our suspicions about a planned takeover." The governor's seal had been affixed to the outside of the note.

Hart handed the note back to Ash, who had been standing by. "Burn it right away," he directed, continuing into the house.

CHAPTER 3

Nate stretched his young limbs across the soft sand, resting himself on his left arm, his right fist holding a large multicolored shooter. With his lips pursed, his right eye closed, he shot the marble toward others within the circle. Marbles scattered, his eye opened, and he sat upright.

"Tarnation!" he exclaimed, not satisfied with the results of his planned strategy.

"Nate Lord! Be 'shamed of yo'self. You know better than to blaspheme," Ozzie called, rocking her way from the clothesline in the back of the house.

"*Tarnation's* not a bad word, Ozzie. You ask Lessie," Nate answered, looking her square in the eye. He'd had enough of this bossy woman. She had been on his trail ever since he and Lessie arrived at the farm.

"Sounds like one t'me," Ozzie insisted, hands on hips, jaw set. "You march right into the house and wash up f'r supper, or you'll be eating the hind leg o' the chicken."

"That's all right, Ozzie. I like the hind leg of the chicken, anyways," Nate sang as he danced around her, his hand cupped to his mouth.

"Nows you stop that, boy, right this here minute!" Ozzie demanded, grinning in spite of herself. "This here ain't no Injun village."

Ozzie proceeded toward the house, war whoops and dancing surrounding her every step. When the two of them reached the rear porch, the door opened.

"Nate, stop that. Let Ozzie alone and come and wash up," Lessie corrected, taking hold of his collar and leading him toward the washbasin on the table inside the kitchen. "You've had a busy afternoon, I see. There's not a clean spot on your entire body."

"Yup," Nate supplied, perfectly satisfied with himself.

"And don't say yup, Nate. You know better," Lessie corrected again. It seemed to her that every word she spoke to Nate was a censure of some kind. She hated to be hard on him, but he was so determined at times that it scared her.

"Cousin John says 'yup,' Lessie," Nate answered matter-of-factly.

"Cousin John is a grown man and the master of this house. He may say what he chooses. You may not," she returned, her voice commanding.

"What's all this ruckus?"

Lessie and Nate turned in unison to see Cousin John standing in the doorway.

"Lessie's bossing me around, again," Nate answered, seating himself at the table and pulling a platter of popovers toward his plate.

"Hold it, Nate," John directed. "You will wait until the others are seated before you eat."

"I'm hungry, Cousin John. Why can't I start now?"

"It isn't done, my boy. You must, at certain times, sacrifice your will to good manners. This is one of those times," John instructed, winking at Nate as he pulled out his own chair. "As a point of fact, there are many such times in a man's life."

Nate pushed the platter back, dropped his hands into his lap, and grinned at his cousin. He liked his adult cousin very much. He was always referred to as a man by John. It made Lessie's bossing and Ozzie's fussing easier to accept. He wouldn't always be nine years old. One day, he would be a man.

When Cousin Joan and Lessie had seated themselves and the blessing had been asked, supper was begun. The cousins talked amiably together. A discussion of the spring flood, which had been the worst anyone could remember, was lightened by Nate's comment that it had been good for worms. Everyone laughed.

"We had a difficult time going round about the lowlands coming here," Lessie added, "there's still an awful lot of flooding. We were extremely lucky to be with a party of teamsters with oxen. Most of us were stuck in the mud more than once. Nate and I could barely put one foot in front of the other most of the way. When the postmaster's horse and cart got stuck, the oxen pulled them right out. I don't ever remember such a winter and spring."

"I don't, either," Joan agreed.

"I've noticed something very strange, Cousin John. The sun doesn't seem as bright as it should for this time of year. Have you noticed?" Lessie asked. She was in the habit of walking for a while each afternoon. The sun was barely warm, its shadows pale beneath her feet.

"I have noticed. Its lack of intensity is being discussed everywhere," John answered.

"My garden is not growing. I don't know what to do about it. Do you suppose lack of heat from the sun could have anything to do with it?" Joan interjected as she passed a bowl of jambalaya to her husband.

"Could be, I suppose," John returned, considering the extreme change in the weather. The sun had been paling for some time now, little by little. Then there was the flight of the squirrels and other animals who seemed to be driven by some unseen force. Even the passenger pigeons flew aimlessly, searching for direction.

The scientific organization in town was studying the phenomenon, believing the lackluster quality of the sun was due to the approaching comet's path between the sun and earth. Letters recently arrived from Europe foretold its imminent arrival. But the association had voted not to give out the news to the local papers until they had confirmed their suspicions.

"What do you think is causing it?" Lessie asked, more to relieve her mind than to get an answer. She doubted if any mortal knew the answer.

"I suppose the more learned scientists have theories. But I doubt if even they are certain," John replied. "At any rate, whatever is causing this freak weather is far away and won't threaten us. So, we need not worry."

"Good," sighed Joan, signaling for Ozzie to bring dessert, which tonight was rice pudding, a favorite of John's.

"I think something big is covering the sun," Nate suggested, giving his young mind free rein, "and then it will fall to earth and kill us all."

"Nathaniel Lord!" Cousin John, corrected. "We'll have none of that talk."

"Well, I do think so, anyway," Nate whispered, his head hanging.

"Let's talk of things less morbid, Nate," suggested Lessie. "You know, we'll soon embark on an adventure of our own." An adventure which, when she allowed herself to think of it, frightened her far more than the waning sun.

Nate's young face brightened measurably. "How long will it be, Cousin John, before we leave. I can't wait."

"Not for a while yet, Nate. You can't travel the trace at this time of year. One must wait until autumn, when the land is dry and the rivers and streams easier to cross," John explained.

"Not till fall! That long!" Nate exclaimed. Then when John answered affirmatively, "Oh, hang it all!"

"Nathaniel, please refrain from using vulgar expressions," Joan instructed, motioning for them to rise. Supper was finished. She wanted to retire early. "John dear, I think I'll go upstairs early this evening. You don't mind, do you?"

"I'm not going to bed," Nate informed, slipping past Lessie and heading for the front door. He'd found a spot in the soft sand near the drive where doodlebugs had dug into the ground. He planned to dig them up. He'd never actually seen one.

John moved toward his wife, pulling her into a warm embrace. "Of course not, love. I won't be long myself. I want to discuss something with Lessie. Then I'll be up."

Ozzie was removing the dishes as John took Lessie's arm, leading her into the parlor. She was glad for a chance to speak with him privately. There were so many things she didn't know—needed to know—before leaving on their planned trip to Nashville.

When they had entered the lamp-lit parlor, they seated themselves near the windows, where some small breeze wafted the sheer curtains.

"Would you care for a glass of port?" John asked, pouring one for himself.

"Thanks, no, Cousin John," Lessie replied, waiting for him to pour his drink. She could hear Nate outside singing the doodlebug song. Ozzie was rattling pans in the kitchen with the sounds of frogs and cicadas harmonizing, otherwise the evening was still, quiet.

John settled himself deeply into his worn chair, took a sip of his port, and studied Lessie from underneath his thick eyelashes. She was so young yet, he thought, to be sent on such a perilous journey. And Nate? Nate was a handful, even here in safe surroundings. He'd be impossible in the wilds. That's why he'd decided to enlist aid for them. He had grown to care for his two young cousins and felt it was his duty. Lessie had shown courage in bringing them this far alone, walking most of the way from Mobile in the company of the teamsters and the new postmaster, who was to be stationed at the Stand.

He had learned, after their arrival, that Nate had several minor scrapes along the way, managing to escape unscathed. But the Trace was different from the already navigable road from Natchez to Mobile—different and much more dangerous.

"Lessie, due to the difficulties which I personally know you'll find along the Trace, I've made arrangements for someone to travel with you and Nate as far as the Stand. You've never met the man, but I assure you he is well respected for his intelligence and ability in a fight. At the Stand, you will doubtless find others going on to Nashville. You should wait until a large party forms before leaving."

He watched her as he spoke. She relaxed perceptibly. The worried look in her eyes, which had disappeared only once since their arrival (at the MacAlpin soiree), was replaced with one of surprise, expectancy.

"I'm so pleased, Cousin John. I'd been so worried about Nate. And to tell the truth, I'm frightened. I've never traveled anywhere, except here. I don't know what to expect, what to watch out for, anything," she returned, feeling joy creep into her voice at the prospect of assistance.

"You won't have to worry about a thing now, Lessie. This traveling companion I've hired is Samuel Shute, a well-known woodsman. He fought in the War of Independence, earning a reputation for fearlessness and ingenuity."

"I've wanted to discuss our Nashville trip with you for days, Cousin John, but hesitated because I had no idea how to begin," Lessie replied.

"You need not go at all, you know. Joan and I have grown to love you both. You could make your home here, with us," John suggested, still hating the idea of their traveling over the trace.

"If only we could accept your hospitality," Lessie answered, wishing it might be so. "But as you know, Papa had arranged with our grandmother Lord that we go to her in the event of his death. I feel we must go, at least for a while. She is alone now too. She may need us with her."

"Yes, I understand all that. And you're right, you should honor your father's wishes in the matter. But if ever you or Nate need asylum, need a home, it's here with us. Remember that," John instructed, his voice gruff.

"You and Cousin Joan have been so kind to us. We feel you are our family already. We'll remember, Cousin John, and thank you always for caring," Lessie replied, tears filling her eyes. She knew Nate was excited about the trip to Nashville, but she wished—oh how she wished—it might not be necessary.

Silence filled the room as Lessie dabbed at her eyes with her handkerchief. John took a long pull on his cigar. After a few puffs, he continued.

"In that case, you will leave the first of October in the company of the postmaster, Sam Shute, and others. The postmaster's wife is very ill and cannot withstand the arduous journey. I sent out word that a party was forming to travel the Trace. We've already had several queries."

Sam's agreeing to accompany Lessie and Nate immediately upon being asked had surprised John, but he had been greatly relieved about allowing them to continue their journey. He studied the slim young girl before him as she rose and pulled back the curtains, searching the grounds for Nate. She was mature beyond her years and possessed none of the bantering, chattering, giddy attributes of so many of her peers.

"Thank you, John," she offered as she moved toward the door. "I think I'll sleep soundly tonight, for the first time in weeks, due to your kindness and support. We can't thank you enough for what you've done for us. Please accept this as a token of our love for both of you," she said, coming across the room and bending to kiss him on the forehead.

"You are family, my dear, and entirely welcome," John replied, rising as she turned to leave the room.

*****

It had grown dark. Lessie could not see Nate at play. She called to him several times. When he didn't answer, she left the porch and walked along the drive looking for him.

Shadows claimed the drive's edge. A mockingbird sang its night song just above her head. She paused to listen. It was as quiet as though the woods were devoid of all life, except for the mockingbird. It sang again. Suddenly, she turned and strained to see farther along the drive. Someone was coming on horseback. She could see a single rider through the twilight gloom. She stepped back, careful of being run down in the gathering dark. When the horse neared her position, it was reined to a stop. A remembered voice spoke.

"Why hello, Cousin."

Then long legs slid from the saddle, and Hart MacAlpin was standing in front of her.

"I must say I hadn't expected to see you out here in the dark." He stood quietly, his manner easy, relaxed.

"Good evening…Cousin," she returned. "I'm looking for Nate. He came out to play after supper, and I can't find him. I've called, but he doesn't answer."

Hart's eyes searched the area in front of the house for a moment or two, then he took Lessie's arm and led her back toward the porch, his horse following behind them.

"I must find him before it gets any darker. I'm worried he may have gone into the woods."

"We'll find him, don't worry," Hart responded, noting the anxiety in her voice. "Young boys are apt to forget the time. He's probably here on the farm somewhere and doesn't realize how dark it's become."

"He was here in the drive the last time I looked, just before it became dark. I can't imagine where he could have gone—and so quickly. It's so easy to get lost in the woods, and Nate has a penchant for mishaps." If she couldn't see him, she worried. It was that simple.

"You come and wait on the porch where there's some light from inside the house, and I'll mount Blister and circle the house and farm buildings till I find him," he offered, assisting her to a seat in front of the parlor window.

Lessie watched him mount his horse and move off. When he had ridden out of sight, calling Nate's name in resonant but demanding tones, she became nervous again. Nate was not answering. Where could he be?

*****

An enveloping silence stilled even Blister's breathing as both horse and man poised expectantly, waiting. Hart began to worry. The boy didn't answer, and unless he was deliberately hiding, something must have happened to him.

He moved Blister nearer the barn, dismounted, and tied him to a fence post. The family and farmhands had not been aroused. Hart hoped to find him without causing an uproar. The look in Lessie's eyes as he had insisted she wait on the porch tugged at him.

He entered the barn where a lantern lit the area just inside the door. It would do. He took it from the wall, left the barn door open, and remounted Blister, who shied from the light cast by the lantern.

"Whoa, boy. It's okay, steady," Hart murmured, as he turned the horse toward the front drive. He intended looking along the road and in the woods on each side of the road. When he circled the house, he saw Lessie standing on the walk leading to the porch.

"Go back to the porch. I'll find him. Don't worry," he added as he urged Blister into a slow trot. He began to call the boy's name more loudly.

Hart's intuitive caution had risen. He had the same uneasy feeling he'd felt on the pampas just before the onset of trouble. The lantern served as a beacon in the black night. It also outlined him and his horse as easy targets. When he reached the road, he turned toward Natchez. If the boy had wandered away, he'd likely go where he could see the most light. And Natchez was well lit until late in the evenings.

Blister trotted on, his steps certain, while Hart continued to call the boy's name. As they approached a bend in the road where a connector turned south away from Natchez, Hart pulled up. "Whoa, boy, whoa," he whispered, for he had seen a bobbing light not far ahead, on the road south. He slipped his right leg over the saddle horn and slid to the ground. Someone, or some party, was traveling through the forest up ahead, just off to the left of the road, as though they didn't want to be seen.

His pampas sense signaled danger. He'd have to investigate. That meant getting closer without being heard or seen. He tied Blister to some brush just off the road on the opposite side and extinguished the lantern. Then he began a careful, circuitous path toward the still bobbing light.

When he was within a few yards of the now illumined patch of woods, he crouched, listening and watching from behind a large tree. The boy was there. Two men held his arms as he twisted frantically to loosen their grip.

"You better let me go. My Cousin John will have your hide if anything happens to me," his shaking but determined young voice was saying. "Let me go. I know the way home. I'll not say I saw you."

"Saw us? You saw us doing what, boy?" The voice came from the larger of the two men, who had swung Nate around to face him.

"Why, nothing…I didn't see you doing nothing. I just meant I wouldn't say anything if that was what you wanted," Nate answered, his voice steadier now as he gazed upward. "You don't want to make trouble for yourself. Do you?"

Hart waited. *Good for you, Nate. That's the way to talk to them. You sized them up well. But if they don't buy it, I'll have to intervene.* He edged closer, his North & Cheney flintlock pistol loaded and ready in his right hand, his dirk poised in the other.

As Nate's squirming ceased, the other man dropped his arms but stood ready to grab him if he attempted to escape. This one was shorter, his back was stooped, and he wore a mane of long dirty hair, which at one time must have been red. The taller of the two concealed his hair under a wide black felt hat, which he had pulled low over his ears. His stance bespoke strength and agility.

"What do you think, Zeke? Should we let this young calf go?" the black hat asked.

Zeke grunted, obviously having trouble deciding exactly what he thought. "Makes no mind t'me."

Hart could see Nate glance carefully around, seeking a route of escape. The boy was keeping his head, thinking all the time. Hart had decided to create a ruckus in the cedars to draw the men away while he moved around to Nate's position when the black hat spoke again.

"I agree with the boy, Zeke. Such a boy as this will be missed immediately. All hell could break loose around here. We've had our fun. That's all it was, boy. You remember that. We were just funning with you. We're trappers, not robbers. You can go now," he finished, pointing toward the road. "Run, boy!" he shouted as Nate's lithe form disappeared up the road, running like a young colt.

As the two men gathered up muskets and packs, preparing to move on, Hart watched. They could be the two that Sam had mentioned. If so, he'd have to agree with Sam. They were not trappers. As they moved on toward Natchez, he returned to Blister, mounted, and rode off after Nate, catching up to him about a mile down the road toward the farm.

"Whoa, young Nate," he said, circling Blister around the boy, who was still attempting to run. "I'm a friend of your Cousin John. Don't be frightened of me. I know your sister, Lessie, too."

Nate stopped his attempts to get around Blister and stood still, looking up at Hart in the darkness. He didn't know this man. But if he knew Cousin John and Lessie, he must be a friend. "What's your name?"

"Hart MacAlpin," Hart answered, leaning downward in the saddle so the boy could get a look at him. "I've been out looking for you. Lessie's worried."

The two of them stared into each other's faces for what seemed to Nate a long time, then he asked, "Can I ride up behind you? I'm awful tired."

"Why, sure you can," Hart responded, his heart going out to the boy. "Here, take my arm, and I'll swing you aboard."

Nate reached up his arm and was soon hanging onto Hart's shoulders as Blister bore them back toward Wellsley Farm. When they emerged from the night onto the lawn of the farm, Lessie was standing where Hart had left her.

"Thank goodness, you found him."

"Lessie, I was captured by two men. They didn't hurt me, though. They said they were funning with me," Nate burst out, aware of the worry he had caused. "I'm fine," he assured her, as Hart swung him onto the ground and dismounted himself, tying Blister to the hitching post in front of the house.

"You nearly scared me to death, Nate. Don't you know how I worry about you? Why do you do these things?" she asked, keeping her voice low. She didn't want to explain another of Nate's "adventures" to her cousins.

"I didn't mean to get lost, Lessie. I was just following a mother raccoon and her cubs. It was dark and I went in the wrong direction. Then I saw a light and thought it was from here. When I got to it, it was the two strange men. I tried to run, but they caught me. They let me go," he added.

"That's right," Hart intervened. "I don't think they meant him any harm. They were just surprised by his appearance."

Lessie looked at Hart, then at Nate. "You go and wash up, Nate. I'll speak to you later when I come to tuck you in," she added, pushing him gently toward the front door.

When Nate had disappeared along the front hallway, she turned to Hart again. "I can't thank you enough. I was so desperately worried. Nate has these—little adventures—often since our father died. I don't know how to cope with him."

"You're doing all right. He's a fine young fellow. I was watching him just before the two men turned him loose. He was thinking on his feet, told them he'd be missed and that the whole territory would be on their trail. I enjoyed watching him handle those two," he added, offering Lessie his arm, then leading her to the bench by the front door.

"Thank you," she said again as he released her arm, seating himself beside her. "I don't know what I would have done if anything had happened to him."

"You're entirely welcome, Cousin," Hart responded. "Now to the reason I rode over here in the first place. I wanted to speak with John. But I guess, since you're out here alone, he's gone to bed."

"Yes, they both have. Joan was tired, so they went to bed early," Lessie replied.

"Another time then," he said, his eyes holding hers. "Are you still planning to travel to Nashville in the fall?"

"Yes, we are. Our grandmother has offered us a home, and she may need us with her. She's getting on in years," Lessie answered, returning his gaze. "Our grandmother has a working sugar business. She started it on her own after our grandfather died. She makes a living. We intend to help her."

"I see. Still I wonder at John's allowing you to proceed with such a dangerous undertaking. It isn't like him at all," Hart mused, as much to himself as to the girl.

"He discussed the trip with me earlier this evening. He's hired a traveling companion for us, a Mr. Shute. I feel much safer now," Lessie was saying, as Hart emitted a low laugh. "Is something wrong?" She asked, thinking it impolite of him to laugh at her cousin's attempt to insure her safety.

Hart suppressed his laughter immediately. "Sorry. I was laughing at my assumption that John was lax in his guardianship. I should have known better. I've known Cousin John since I could walk and always found him trustworthy. Of course, he would ensure your safety to the greatest degree possible," he finished, still amused with himself.

"Then you know this Mr. Shute?" Lessie asked, feeling safer all the time.

"Yes, I know him. He's a crusty old bird, but you listen to him. He'll get you and Nate safely to Nashville."

"I don't believe he is going past the Stand, as Cousin John called it," Lessie supplied.

"That right? Well, you'll find others there who travel the distance to Nashville all the time. You'll have plenty of company. It's the distance from here to the Stand that is the most dangerous," Hart counseled.

"This evening has been a revelation," Lessie sighed, relieved that Nate was once again safe and that they would be supported and protected during the long trip up the Trace.

They sat side by side in silence. Hart wondered at his attempt to meddle in John's affairs. He'd been worried about Lessie and her young brother since she confided her plans to travel the Trace. His earlier talk with Tchula had convinced him that the danger of attack by robbers or Indians under the influence of British money was greater now than ever before. He'd intended getting John's views on the political scene tonight. He'd wondered if John had knowledge of the secretive movements of the stranger wearing the black hat. It would have to wait.

He glanced at the girl sitting beside him. She too seemed lost in thought. It would be a shame if anything happened to her or her brother.

"It's getting late. I'd better go and let you go to bed," he said, rising.

"Let me thank you again," Lessie entreated. "Both for tonight and for your interest in our welfare. I feel secure in the knowledge that both my cousins care about our safety."

"As I said before," Hart returned, "I was happy to be of assistance." He took her arm and walked with her to the door. "Good night, Lessie."

"Good night, Hart," she replied as she closed the door behind her.

Hart stood for a moment, aware once again of a strange sense of loss as she walked away from him. No other woman had ever affected him that way, not even Ada. He slowly unhitched Blister and prepared to mount. Still considering his growing reluctance to separate himself from this slender young cousin, he walked Blister slowly down the drive. A cousin she was, he reminded himself—but by marriage only.

*****

Moisture dripped from the live oak just off the veranda. The sweetly pervading scent of the tea olive, which was in full bloom, assailed William Smythe's nostrils.

He had ordered his breakfast brought to the courtyard off his bedroom. Being an Easterner, it had taking him several years to become acclimated. Now he had grown accustomed to rising early, working during the morning hours, resting in the middle of the day, then finishing his work at his leisure in the late afternoon. He had settled in nicely. He enjoyed his life.

The most satisfying thing he possessed at present was this house on Broadway. His courtyard had a magnificent view of the Mississippi River, which offered various vistas as the barges, rafts, and steamboats plied her waters. The house had originally belonged to a Spanish Grandee. The facade sported French-lace ironwork and arched carriageways. He had furnished it with fine mahogany furniture that he had sent up from New Orleans. He had also sent back to New York for some of his family's possessions. It felt like home. But as he had thought before, he needed something else. He needed a wife and the money to keep her and his home well.

"Here's your breakfast, sir," Robert said, placing a plate of poached eggs, toast, and jam in front of him. "We've got melon this morning, sir. If you want some."

"Thanks, Robert. Just bring more coffee, will you? And increase the amount of chicory when you grind next time. I've developed a liking for the flavor," William ordered, folding his morning paper and placing it on the table.

As he ate his breakfast, watching the large crow that sat on a limb of the oak near the veranda, his mind turned to business. He had made a slip the other day. The governor had almost caught him in a lie about where he'd been. He'd have to be more careful in future. If things worked out as he'd planned, he'd be in a position to manage his home very well and soon.

He stopped chewing as the thought struck that Lessie Lord might be the right wife for him. He had been struck by her pristine beauty at the dance a few weeks back and she was a cousin to John Wellsley.

There was a man William planned to cultivate. He was extremely wealthy. But for reasons of secrecy, he'd have to stay away from Wellsley Farm, at least when Nate was present. In a few months, it wouldn't matter if he was recognized. He'd be in a position of governmental authority.

"It's time for you to go to the office, Mr. William," Robert said from just behind him. "I'll clear away and then bring your buggy around front."

"Good," William replied, moving inside to wash and shave.

Observing himself in the mirror above the washstand, he thought again how fortunate he was. Less than an hour later, he was in his office adjacent to the Governor's. Able Hand was waiting for him.

"Well? What have you got?"

"I've just heard that a party is being formed to travel the Trace in October. Thought you'd want to know," Able advised, his voice huffy. He recognized ridicule when he heard it. "But if you're not interested, I'll be going."

"No. Wait," Smythe said, his voice more civil. "What more do you have?"

"Just that Hart MacAlpin and that friend of his, Tchula, have the Choctaws helping them trace two hunters who came through here last summer. That worth anything to you?" Able didn't know exactly what Smythe was up to, and he didn't care as long as he was paid well for the information.

"We're aware of that," Smythe replied, then hesitated before speaking. "We need to know MacAlpin's movements daily. Can you manage that?"

"Maybe," Able said. "I'm a busy man, you know. Have my own farm to worry about. It'll cost you extra."

"You'll get all that's coming to you. We've already paid you plenty. Just watch him. We're not worried about Tchula on his own, but MacAlpin could cause real trouble."

"You ought to be," Able returned, his eyes steely.

"Ought to be what?"

"You ought to worry about the Chief Tchula," Able said.

"Why? He's just a minor chief, of little importance," Smythe insisted, irritated by Able's continued presence.

"He's related to Pushmataha—and that's very important," Able stipulated, a smile lifting his usually somber countenance. "I'll be back when I have something to sell."

*****

Hart sat on the weathered wooden bench in the gazebo, hidden almost completely by enveloping wisteria vines. Tchula was late.

"You there, Ishto Impa?"

"Yes," Hart replied.

Tchula entered and sat down opposite Hart. "You know this Able Hand who plays fiddle?" Tchula asked.

"Yes, of course. He was here the other evening," Hart answered, puzzled.

"Brave tells me he visits the governor's office much. Saw him counting money when he left yesterday," Tchula informed.

"That's interesting. You say he visits there regularly?"

"Yes. Brave says he's seen him many times coming out of the side entrance," Tchula explained.

"We'd better continue to watch him. Since I received the note from the governor about this Captain Bean at Chickasaw Bluffs, I've become convinced they plan to take Natchez. We're so isolated here. And with Natchez in British hands, they'd have a direct path from Canada to the Gulf. There may be many locals involved in this scheme. We can't be too careful, Tchula. And we've got to work quickly," he finished. "Have you anything else?"

"Nothing. We watch all trails. We watch this man Able Hand. I report back soon," Tchula stated, moving silently into the brush behind the gazebo.

"Good luck," Hart said, watching him disappear into the woods.

CHAPTER 4

An owl hooted twice outside his bedroom window as Bruce pushed his feet into his boots. He glanced toward the bed where Ada lay sleeping. He was careful not to make enough noise to wake her. She could be an interfering female, he thought, watching her breaths come in short quick wisps. He studied her face in the veiled light from the window. She was beautiful. She was beautiful and interfering and a great deal of trouble.

Finished with dressing, he carefully slipped from the room and headed downstairs, through the kitchen and out the back door. He had slipped out this way for years. Once again, he made his escape without notice.

Now that Hart was back, he'd have to ride his own horse, a large chestnut gelding. The horse was a decent mover but lacked the style and spirit of Blister. He'd always felt slighted by his father's gift of the chestnut. He knew why he'd received a horse half the worth of his elder brother's. His father had insisted that Bruce change his ways—ways his father called wasteful and lazy. But horse or no horse, Bruce had no intention of changing his ways.

When he'd saddled up and walked the chestnut out of the barn and across the back lawn, he mounted and trotted him through the woods in the direction of Natchez and Silver Street. He had a job to do. But first he wanted something to drink and a few minutes of the particular company he enjoyed.

It was past two in the morning, but lights glowed from upper windows along Silver Street and from small slits around the sides of floating houseboats tied to the pier. Bruce headed in the direction of the large rough-sided one, which sported the most light. Flatboat Fannie's never closed.

"Lost your way?"

Bruce turned quickly, shocked at the voice. "I might say the same for you," he sneered, turning to face Hart.

"I'm not married and caught entering a bordello, Bruce. Don't you think it unwise?" Hart kept his voice low, calm.

"I think it's none of your business, Brother," Bruce said, drawling the words out slowly, indolently.

"Maybe not," Hart returned, ignoring the vehemence in his brother's voice. "Just don't pass out and have me summoned to haul you back to Crapewood."

"Not likely," Bruce shot. "I've learned to hold my liquor, thanks, and to take care of my own business." He turned on his heel and proceeded up the boardwalk toward the entrance of Flatboat Fannie's. As he entered, he glanced back toward the street. Hart had disappeared.

Bruce handed his hat to Fannie, whose voice shook the rafters as she called for Imogene to come forward. Bruce had enjoyed Imogene's company for several years. His marriage had not changed that. He smiled, abandoning all thoughts of Crapewood, as she handed him a drink.

A few minutes later, he was back aboard his horse and moving in the direction of Brightway Plantation. He still had plenty of time. If his suspicions were correct, he could make a hefty profit. But they had to be caught in the act and know he was on to them.

Bruce had been watching Brightway for some time. The things he had seen were incriminating. He chuckled to himself as he thought of Hart's reaction if he learned what was going on. His elder brother might be his father's favorite, but he lacked a good deal of savvy when it came to dealing with people. *In that respect, I'm way ahead of him,* he thought to himself.

When he reached Brightway, he stopped in the shelter of one of the outlying farm buildings, came off his horse, and lit a cigar. He planned to wait and see what occurred between his father-in-law and the two strangers he had followed the other evening.

His father-in-law was a retired British officer, having retired just before the start of the Revolutionary War with the rank of colonel. That saved him. That and the fact that he married into a prominent Natchez family. Otherwise, he wouldn't have survived the war. What he was engaged in now, Bruce thought, a feeling of elation gripping him, could be profitable to them both. But first, the colonel had to be made to see reason—the reason being that unless he paid Bruce a certain sum, he would most likely be stood in front of a firing squad and shot.

He stubbed out his cigar when he saw movement near the smokehouse. Two men were approaching on foot, their horses being led. *Stand quiet*, he warned himself. He didn't want to be noticed until he had Albright cornered. Then he'd have the upper hand, and everything should fall his way.

The two men stood in the shadow of the smokehouse for what seemed to Bruce close to an hour. Finally, another shadow broke away from the main house and moved in their direction.

Bruce felt an urgency unlike any he had ever known. His palms were damp with perspiration, and his chest felt as though an anvil lay upon it. For a fleeting moment, he felt a desire to run. But as he watched the now three shadows move off into the woods behind the smokehouse, his courage was revived, and he moved stealthily after them.

He felt cold through and through. His hands had stopped sweating. He loaded and primed his pistol, holding it ready in his left hand. Then he crawled out to the edge of a bluff overlooking the ravine where the three men had stopped. He watched them from an observation point concealed by low growing scrub. After a brief discussion, the two strangers moved off at a trot.

Bruce had left his horse back at the farm, feeling it would be safer to follow them on foot. He moved nearer the edge of the bluff to get a better view of the direction the two backwoodsmen had taken when he kicked loose a small stone. It rolled down the face of the bluff, stopping almost at Sheffield Albright's feet. Albright was at once alert. He shouted after the two men to hold up as he pulled his pistol.

"There's someone up there on the bluff. We've got to find him!" he shouted, moving toward the face of the bluff as he spoke.

"Right," came the reply from one of the men as he turned his horse directly up the incline. "I'll go around this end. Zeke, you go around the other."

"S'posing it's Injuns. We'd best light out," Zeke yelled back.

"Do as you're told," Black Hat instructed, spurring his horse up the slope.

Bruce had thrown himself to the ground as the stone rolled down the slope. Sweat covered him again as he tried to think of a way out. He'd have to reveal himself and carry out a bluff. That was the only way to save himself and perhaps walk away a richer man in the process. He raised himself from the ground and walked into the yellowed light cast by a determined moon.

"Hold on, Colonel. It's only me, Bruce MacAlpin."

"What are you doing out here?" the colonel asked angrily.

"Trying to catch up to you, sir," Bruce answered, his tone as respectful as he could devise at the moment. "I've some business we need to discuss."

"What kind of business do we need to discuss at four in the morning here in the wild?"

Albright now stood directly in front of Bruce. The other two men stood behind him, their pistols high. Bruce recognized the one in black and was about to say so when the colonel spoke again.

"I'll ask you again, Bruce. What in the devil are you doing out here?"

Bruce swallowed, a bitter taste in his mouth. He could feel sweat oozing from his pores. "I thought I could be of some help. I've known for some time what you—and these two men—are doing. Perhaps I can help. We could make some kind of deal."

"A deal? With you?" Albright chuckled. "Why would I want to make a deal with you? You're a gambler, a nonproductive spendthrift, and a wanton chaser of petticoats. The saddest day of my life was when my daughter was silly enough to marry you when she could have had a man like Hart. A damn fool she was, and I think she now knows it."

Bruce felt blood drain from his face. He'd never known how his father-in-law thought of him. He'd no idea that Albright knew of his visits to the gambling houses and bordellos of Natchez. He should have known, he supposed. He'd never kept his life a secret. He'd a right to do as he pleased and had always been rather proud that he did just that. But he'd better keep to the issue, make Albright keep to the issue at hand.

"Well, sir…I know what you've been doing…and I know this man. I'm seen him around Natchez…and—"

"You shut your mouth!" Sheffield spat. "If you think you're going to horn in and ruin everything the way you've ruined my daughter's life, you're in for a surprise."

"You just hold it right there," Bruce returned angrily. "You've no call to talk to me in that manner. You're fortunate that I married her at all. I—"

The colonel swung his right arm backward, preparing to punch Bruce's face. Zeke lurched sideways to avoid the colonel's backward swing, squeezing the trigger of his pistol. It went off in a blast of light and noise.

The shot dropped Bruce where he stood, stunned amazement contorting his features, blood pouring from the hole in his chest.

"That's capped it," the man in black wheezed through tight lips. "We were supposed to keep low. Now you've killed the son of one of the leading citizens. If what I hear about that older brother of his, that Ishto Impa, is true, we're in trouble."

"Hang the MacAlpins," the colonel gasped, his face a sick shade of gray. "If Hart had stayed here and married Ada, none of this would have happened. Natchez can well do without Bruce. He was everything I accused him of and more," he continued, studying the body of his son-in-law. "But you're right about his brother. We'd better hide the body."

Sheffield Albright didn't know what he was going to do. He watched as his two confederates covered Bruce's body with several dead branches, then threw cedar limbs over it. When they had finished, they mounted and rode off, leaving Sheffield to erase as many tracks as he could from the moist earth. *That should do it*, he thought.

Even Hart's friend Tchula would have difficulty figuring out who or how many men or horses had been here. He then walked slowly down the slope of the bank and brushed out the tracks there.

Afterward, he returned to Brightway and entered the kitchen where he asked the maid for coffee. He felt cold through and through. He wondered if he would ever be warm again.

"Nice morning, Colonel," Leatha said, handing him his coffee.

"Yes, it's going to be after all," Albright returned. *And it would be*, he promised himself. *It would be all right for Ada too. She could have Hart now*, he figured. He doubted if Hart was over her.

He had often wondered at his luck in producing a daughter with Ada's looks. Her mother had certainly been no beauty, and age had not improved her looks. But she had other credits, like money and position. And he had no illusions about his own looks. It was a wonder, indeed, he mused, that people as plain as he and Mildred could have a daughter like Ada.

"You want something to eat now?" Leatha was busy at the fireplace, placing iron pans on the rack above the coals for making breakfast.

His appetite failed him. He finished the last drops of hot coffee and got up from the table. "I'm not hungry," he said as he left the kitchen and crossed the hall toward the stairs.

*****

Heat seared his brain as Bruce stirred underneath the layer of limbs. It took him long minutes to remember where he was. He'd been shot. Strange, he didn't feel any pain. He was very cold.

The soft sound of a quiet step reached his ears. He attempted to turn. He was covered with cedar. The limbs were not heavy. He pushed several away from his face. Someone was standing over him.

"You! What are you doing out—"

The blow, which came suddenly, silenced him. In a matter of seconds, he was dead.

Only the raspy breathing of his murderer was heard above the stillness of death. After a moment, the figure walked away, swallowed up immediately in the dark.

*****

Hart stretched his arms above his head as he rose from the bed. He moved languidly over to the window and looked out, noting the pale layer of sun washing the outlying fields. His thoughts turned to the events of the previous evening.

His accidental meeting with Bruce on Silver Street had worried him deep into the night. His brother's continued philandering was hard to swallow. Several of the men he knew, old and young alike, visited Silver Street at some time in their lives. But Bruce had been a regular. Hart had met this Imogene years before when he'd been summoned to the flatboat to carry Bruce home. As he prepared to dress and go downstairs, he wondered at Bruce's marrying at all. But Ada did have her charm.

He glanced out the window to check the weather again as he finished dressing. The weather was important to almost any movement a man made. He frowned. The lawns should have been glowing in brilliant morning sunlight by this hour. Instead, there was only a jaundiced yellow light laying across the damp grass.

"Morning," Hart said, entering the kitchen.

Cleo glanced round from the skillet of pan fried steak she was about to place on the table. "It'll be just a minute. We got steak and eggs this morning. Them Orpingtons of Miz Flora's is laying their hearts out. We got plenty of eggs."

"Good. How about making some of those tea cakes of yours? The ones with the handprint on them. Big as saucers, as I recall," Hart teased, knowing it pleased her that he enjoyed her food.

"I'll just do that." Cleo smiled at him over the top of the coffee pot. "You do look better these days. I'm glad. Don't you think so, Miz Flora?"

Flora, who had been watching their exchange as she ate her own breakfast, agreed. "Yes, Cleo. He's not the same young man who returned from the pampas. What do you suppose is responsible?"

"I'm certain I don't know, Miz Flora," Cleo answered seriously. "But I like it."

"I like it too. I like it very much," Flora said to Hart as he began to eat. "Perhaps you know what has happened to lift your spirits in such a noticeable way."

Hart placed his fork on the table and stared at the two women. "What are you two babbling about? I'm simply rested from all that traveling, and I'm glad to be home, that's all."

"Um hum," the women said in unison.

"You two had better spend some time apart. You're beginning to merge into one voice," he said, laughing. "But all jokes aside, anyone fortunate enough to have you two in the kitchen to greet him on rising would be an idiot not to feel good. And I do. I feel great this morning," he finished, realizing it was true.

"What are your plans for the day?" Flora asked, rising and assisting in the removal of the dishes. "Didn't you say something last night about visiting the Albrights?"

"I did. I've something to discuss with the colonel," Hart answered, finishing the last bite of steak and pushing back his chair as he did so.

"Is it a secret?" Flora continued, not understanding why her son would want to visit the home of his former sweetheart.

"Now, Mam, don't worry. I'm going there on business. It has nothing at all to do with anything else," Hart said, crossing the room and giving his mother a brief kiss on her forehead.

As he walked from the room, the two women stood watching. Then Flora turned to Cleo. "I believe him," she stated. "We'd better finish here and start our berry-picking. Hart enjoys blackberry jam."

"Miz Flora, we have more than one man in this house. Why don't we pick some of them berries for them too?" Cleo suggested, a twinkle in her dark eyes.

"I hear you, Cleo. But he was away for so long. Give me a few more months of doing just for him, then I'll settle down to normal," Flora directed, leading the way from the house with a large basket in her hand.

*****

Tchula and Hart met at regular intervals in the old gazebo at Crapewood. The late-evening shadows served as cover for their discussions. But this morning, they had changed their meeting place. They met at Saint Catherine's Creek, near the Trace. A few weeks earlier, they had formed a plan for secretly following the men and determining their supply point in the hope that where their supplies were, there would be the agent who was in the pay of the British.

Tchula gave Hart his report. Although his braves had not witnessed weapons being delivered, they had followed the red-haired man and two others to New Orleans. The men went directly to a well-known, but poorly respected, gunsmith where they left with long boxes tied to each side of a mule.

"If we could catch them delivering or even storing the weapons, we'd have a good case against them. We must catch them in the act." Hart spoke slowly, considering the enormity of their crime against the colonials. Whoever was responsible was without conscience.

"Yes, Ishto Impa, we'll catch them. Our watchers lost them after they left New Orleans because of heavy rain. Washed out all tracks," Tchula said. "Men caught riverboat. Braves no go on boat."

Hart considered their problem for a moment or two. "Who do you think is behind it?"

"I think same as you. They go near only one man's property more than others," Tchula added.

"Right. I'm afraid I do agree with you. But I cannot understand why he would do it. He has everything he could want. What could be his reason?" Hart wondered.

"Perhaps he tell us when we catch him," Tchula stated, rising from where he squatted on his heels.

"Still, if he is arming the renegades, he's receiving money from someone else. He's not the type of man to take a chance with his own money," Hart continued.

"Maybe so," Tchula agreed. "We find who Black Hat is, we find answer."

"I've seen him somewhere, seen that posture of his, the way he moves. But I can't remember where," Hart said. "We've got to catch them delivering weapons."

"We do that, Ishto Impa. Soon," Tchula promised.

"I sent the colonel a note yesterday informing him that I would be calling on him this morning around ten o'clock. I plan to question him," Hart finished as he started Blister down the road toward Natchez and Brightway Plantation. "Watch your back," he called to Tchula as Blister picked up speed and rounded a bend in the road. People were dying as a result of someone's treason.

When Tchula first informed him of the war going on right in their own backyard, Hart had considered it possibly a small flurry of vengeance by the Indians. He soon learned through Tchula's trackers and various stories he heard at the inn and along Silver Street that a war was in progress, well hidden, carefully manipulated and silent, but still a full-fledged war.

As he approached Natchez, he turned Blister toward the tavern, intending to speak with Sam Shute if he was there.

*****

On entering the tavern, Hart spotted Sam sitting exactly where he had been on the first occasion, enjoying a large plate of food. He moved toward him, as Ed Boles hailed him and asked what he wanted to drink.

"Coffee, Ed, strong and black. I've had my breakfast, thanks. Morning, Sam, thought I might find you here." He seated himself.

"Morning," Sam replied, wiping at his mouth with his sleeve.

"I'm surprised you're still in the area. Thought you'd be traveling toward the Stand by now. Isn't that where your family lives?"

"It is, until I move them somewhere else." Sam placed a marker in the open Bible lying near his plate.

Sam read his Bible daily and took it seriously. He also took good care of his family, just like the good book said to do. And the best way he knew to take care of them in this territory was to move them often. He didn't like his enemies to know where his family was. They might take it into their heads to harm them. It had been done to others.

"I remember your ways, Sam, and appreciate them. I haven't forgotten how it was the summer you saved Tchula and me from the

Harpes. They're gone now, but there are others just as deadly. I know they threatened your family. But I came here for information about the strangers, not your family."

"Staring at me with those caustic eyes won't get it," Sam responded, chuckling. "I do believe you could stare a coon out of a tree. But this old coon ain't impressed."

Ed Boles chortled as he placed Hart's coffee on the table. "Looks like you've met your match, MacAlpin," he said, moving back toward the bar.

"I'm certain of it," Hart agreed, taking a drink of the coffee.

"Lay all that aside, and I'll tell you what I have," Sam suggested, waiting until Ed had returned to his counter.

"Fine," Hart agreed, easing back in his chair.

"First, I suppose you've been told that John Wellsley hired me to escort his cousins as far as the Stand in the fall, October," Sam said, carefully pushing his plate and cup back on the table and crossing his arms across his chest.

"Yes, I know about that," Hart agreed.

"I accepted the job because of two things. One, my family is there. None of this tramping around in winter for me. Two, I've discovered a bit of news, which leads me to think one of the strangers has a family there."

Hart sat forward in his chair. "Got his name?"

"Nope, not yet. It seems he mentioned a woman there on several occasions. Then he went on to say that he had a son. Thought I'd check his story. Maybe he lies low there from time to time," Sam concluded.

"That's a possibility. And a good one, Sam," Hart agreed, considering what little they had to go on. "We've been doing some checking of our own. Tchula and his braves followed the short one as far as New Orleans. He and two others carried long boxes from the gunsmith's."

"Where'd they take 'em?"

"We don't know. A heavy rainstorm wiped out their tracks and covered up all noise of their movements during the night. In the morning, they boarded the riverboat. The braves lost them."

Hart's last statement prompted silence from each of them. Sam's information concerning one of their women, and possibly a son, was really all they had. The colonel's involvement seemed certain but had not been proven. They'd have to do more, continue to follow, watch; and when the opportunity presented itself, seize the culprits in the act of passing arms to the Indians.

The governor had sent word of his deep concern for the continued safety of the families outside of Natchez. He had suggested the possibility that Natchez could come under attack if the outlying farms were sacked and urged Hart to increase his surveillance with the hope of immediate reprisal against the man, or men, responsible. As he studied Sam's thoughtful face, Hart made a decision.

"Sam, I've decided to travel the Trace this fall, secretly. You and Tchula will be the only men who know where I am. Tchula can move between the two of us easily since the Choctaws move about the forest at will. You watch the road, I'll ride a few miles ahead or behind. Agreed?"

"Agreed. That's a good idea, I reckon. That way, we'll be aware of any movement and"—Sam smiled his wizened smile—"you'll be able to watch out for Ms. Lord and her brother."

"That hadn't entered my mind."

"Maybe not," Sam returned, his smile reaching the grooves along his nose. "But it was probably hidden in there somewhere."

"Why do you think I'm interested in Ms. Lord?"

"There's been talk ever since that soiree at your place. I heard you two really hit it off dancing together."

"She was a guest, new in the area. I was being a good host." Hart spoke carefully as he rose and pushed his chair under the table. He didn't want the public making arrangements for him.

"I'd say you succeeded. She's a pretty thing," Sam said, the grooves along his nose growing deeper with each word.

"I'll be in touch, Sam," Hart fired as he moved toward the door, accompanied by Sam's chuckle.

*****

During the ride to Brightway, Hart considered his interest in Lessie. For the first time, he was drawn to a woman almost magically without intention. In the past, even with Ada, he had dallied with their affections. Ada had, as he now remembered, been the one to continue their relationship until he had finally fallen in love with her. Or was it love, he wondered. When she married Bruce, he had felt doubly betrayed.

This interest in Lessie, if that was what it was, was something new in his life. The girl would not be considered beautiful by current standards, but there was about her an aura of beauty, a glow of femininity. She was thin, plainly clothed (due to her circumstances, no doubt), and headstrong.

She should have better sense than to travel the Trace without an army along. *But she feels she needs to be with her grandmother*, he reminded himself. He liked that. She was loyal, unlike some he could name.

"Good morning, Mr. Hart," a voice said from inside the door of Brightway. "The colonel is expecting you. But he says for you to wait here on the porch. He'll be down directly."

Hart swung around, aware of the effrontery of this greeting. He'd always been invited inside. "Thanks, I'll be delighted to wait—on the porch," he said, smiling broadly. "Just inform the colonel that I've something urgent to discuss with him, will you?"

"Yessir," the voice replied.

Footsteps receded toward the interior of the hallway, and Hart was alone on the porch. He moved across to a high-back twig chair and sat down, still wondering about the colonel's bad manners toward him. He had noted the sad state of Mildred Albright's flower garden when a step sounded on the brick floor behind him. He turned to see the colonel approaching.

"Morning, Hart. What brings you way out here? It's been a long while since we've had the pleasure of your company," the colonel said, seating himself across from Hart.

Hart studied him for a moment before answering. He seemed wary, poised on the edge of his chair as he was, his fingers drumming the arm rest.

"I thought we should talk, Colonel. Perhaps you can shed some light on a problem that concerns us all."

"A problem? What problem is that?" the colonel answered, watching Hart closely, his nervous fingers still drumming the arm of the chair.

Hart glanced at his hand, letting his eyes rest on the moving fingers. The colonel immediately ceased the drumming.

"You know about the recent raids on the outlying farms. The murder of families, pillaging of their belongings and burning of their buildings, don't you?" Hart asked the question slowly, stressing each point, watching to see what the colonel's reaction would be.

"Dastardly business, of course. Yes, I do know about all that. They haven't come close to Natchez yet, though. Have they?"

"They seem to be moving in a wide circle, ever closer to Natchez. We believe Natchez is their main goal once they wipe out all outside help. Have you any idea who could be behind it?"

The colonel squirmed in his seat, stretching his legs in front of him, before replying with a question of his own. "What makes you think I'd know who's behind it? You just said the Indians were sacking the outlying farms. You evidently know more about it than I do."

"I know very little. Someone ought to seek out the leader who is funding this war. That's what it is, don't you agree?" Hart probed, carefully watching the colonel's eyes, the way his face tightened at the mention of war. Perspiration covered his forehead.

"I repeat, why do you ask me?" The colonel rose, his face red with emotion. "I don't know what you're up to here, Hart. But I advise you to think carefully before accusing your neighbors of starting wars. I haven't heard anyone else call these raids a war."

The colonel moved toward the door, preparing to end the discussion, leaving Hart sitting where he was. Hart rose and followed him.

"I'm not accusing you of anything, Colonel. This is a dangerous business for everyone involved. If you know anyone who may be involved, you'd be doing them a favor by insisting they cease these activities at once." Hart turned and walked toward Blister, mounted, and rode away without looking back.

He was certain the colonel knew more than he was telling. His nervousness in the face of Hart's questions left no doubt. *You'll have to tread softly*, Hart warned himself. *Albright is well respected and has many influential friends.*

*****

Deep in thought, his mind turning over the various consequences if Albright was involved and found out, he rounded a corner and almost rode Blister into an oncoming buggy.

"The road's wide enough for both of us," an authoritative voice shouted from the buggy. "You should watch how you ride."

"Warning noted," Hart stated, bringing Blister alongside to make his apology. Lessie Lord was sitting next to the man from the soiree, William Smythe.

"Please forgive me, Cousin," he continued. "I was deep in thought. I didn't hear you coming."

"You're forgiven. We were just startled when you kept coming right at us," she replied, as her escort whipped the reins, urging his horse forward.

Lessie's sudden appearance in the company of another man rattled Hart momentarily. He'd never considered competition. *Why not?* he questioned. Every available man at the dance had been seeking time with her. That sobering thought settled his problem concerning his relationship with her. She'd have plenty of opportunities. He turned Blister around and moved toward home.

"Well, old boy," he said aloud, "better him than me."

*****

"Do you know Hart MacAlpin well?"

"Only slightly," Lessie answered, placing one hand on her bonnet to keep it from flying off. Mr. Smythe had prompted their horse to a canter after leaving Hart on the road. She didn't like riding so fast in a light buggy. "Could we slow down? I'm about to lose my bonnet."

"Certainly. I guess I was angered by MacAlpin's nearly running us down," Smythe replied, slowing his horse to a walk.

"Thank you," Lessie returned, shifting her position to a more comfortable one. "I'm certain he didn't mean it."

"Are you? How?"

"How? I don't..." Lessie began, then armed her thoughts. "He appears to be an honest and kind man, that's all. I don't think anyone like that would deliberately attempt to run us down."

Smythe laughed. "I see you're his champion," he stated matter-of-factly. "However, I don't really believe he was attempting to run us down."

"Good. Let's talk of something else, shall we?" Lessie directed. She didn't want to discuss Hart with anyone. Their brief relationship was so undefined she didn't know how to think of it.

"How about filling me in on the local goings-on? I stay so busy serving as emissary for the governor that I seldom get a chance to discuss local happenings with anyone," Smythe asked as their buggy rolled on toward the farm.

"I don't think I can help you there," Lessie said. "I've only been here a few weeks. Nathaniel and I are leaving soon for Nashville."

"I must say, I'm surprised," Smythe returned. "How are you going?"

"Up the Trace with a large party of travelers," Lessie responded.

William Smythe glanced at the lithe young woman beside him. He had about made up his mind to court her. His position on the governor's staff would be ascertained if he married one of the pillared folk, preferably rich. Of course, there was the problem of the boy.

"I see. Your family is visiting in Nashville then?" he quizzed.

"Not our cousins, John and Joan Wellsley, just Nathaniel and I. We're going to live with our paternal grandmother," Lessie continued, hating having to explain her position once again.

"I see," Smythe mused. And he did see. Lessie was not the heiress he had thought her to be.

They spoke very little for the rest of the drive to Wellsley Farm. As they turned in at the gate, he marveled at the well-kept lawns, at the cleanly swept paths among the flowering shrubs surrounding the house.

"What is that delicious scent? I seem to find it everywhere I travel around here," Smythe asked.

"That's sweet shrub. See that row of flowering bushes with the small dark-red blooms?"

"Yes. So that's what it is. Do they bloom all the time?"

"On and off throughout the summer. But if the weather stays warm, they'll bloom even longer," Lessie explained. The captivating scent of the sweet shrub was her favorite of all the sweet scented plants she had grown up with.

"I am favorably impressed with your cousin's home. It reminds me of one I once knew," Smythe said. "We didn't have this wonderful perfume everywhere. But the houses are similar."

"It is nice," Lessie answered, looking at the house with new appreciation.

As the buggy pulled up to the front door, Lessie prepared to descend, gathering her voluminous skirts around her.

"Let me assist you," Smythe stated, reaching up to help Lessie down. "It has been a marvelous pleasure to accompany you this afternoon, Ms. Lessie."

"Thank you, Mr. Smythe. It was good of you to offer. It allowed Cousin John to attend to some matters here," Lessie divulged, moving to enter the house. "Would you care for a cup of tea before you leave?"

"Thank you, another time," Smythe said, bowing as he turned to climb into the buggy. "Another time."

The buggy moved away as Lessie watched from her position on the porch. He was a nice enough man but very restrained.

"That you, Lessie?" Joan called from the parlor.

"Yes," Lessie answered, walking through the hall and entering the room.

"Tea, dear?" questioned Joan, sitting before the tea trolley.

"Yes, please." Lessie sighed, sinking onto the cherry-colored damask sofa. "I could use some. We discussed plans for the church interior for hours. I was never so tired of listening—or talking—in my life."

"Now you know why John sent you. He absolutely hates to get involved in anything of that sort. And since you kept insisting you wanted to help out—"

"Well, in that case, I'm glad I went. I like knowing I took a tiresome job off his shoulders. Umm, this tea is good."

"How did you like Mr. Smythe, dear? John told me that he's on the building committee and a great favorite of the governor. Said he wanted to meet more of the local people and learn how things are handled. He's bought one of the old Spanish houses on Broadway, I believe."

"Oh? I didn't know. He did complement the farm. Said it reminded him of a place he once knew," Lessie replied.

"Did it? How nice," Joan said, sipping her own cup of tea.

"I don't suppose I'll see him again," Lessie announced, resting her saucer and cup in her hands.

"Why is that, dear?"

"I told him Nate and I were leaving for Nashville soon."

Joan made no comment. She had done all she could to persuade Lessie to stay on at the farm. "Let's go and rest before dinner. You look as though you need it."

"I do," Lessie agreed, moving toward the stairs.

CHAPTER 5

Hart spent the rest of the day visiting farms near Natchez. Most of the farmers had heard of the attacks, were well armed, and had posted scouts. But some showed antipathy at being advised to protect themselves. They assured Hart they were well equipped to handle their own affairs and any trouble that came their way. He hoped they could. They'd be outnumbered.

He found his father waiting for him when he arrived back at Crapewood. He was in a state of anxiety.

"I'm glad you've returned, Son. Bruce is missing. No one knows where he is."

"Missing? Don't you mean absent? He's done this kind of thing before, as I remember," Hart replied.

"Nay, not absent. He didn't come home last night. Ada says he left in the middle of the night. Adam searched everywhere for him this morning," Angus explained.

"Don't worry, Father, he's probably all right, just sleeping it off somewhere. I saw him late yesterday, uh, in the evening, in Natchez. I think I know where he is." If Bruce had stayed out this long, he'd be impossible to deal with. He'd better take Adam along. "Where's Adam? I'll take him with me. We'll bring him back. Don't worry," Hart added.

"He's eating supper. He missed his lunch and has been searching for Bruce in and around Natchez. I think you can leave off there and look elsewhere for him," Angus returned, pulling his thoughts into constructive channels.

"We will, Papa. I'll go and grab a sandwich, and we'll be off." Hart spoke over his shoulder as he departed the room, heading in the direction of the kitchen. When he entered the room, Adam was just finishing a sandwich and glass of milk.

"Make one for me, will you, Cleo? I'll pour myself a glass of milk," Hart said.

"Are you ready?" Adam asked, finishing his sandwich.

"Yes. Just let me finish this milk. I'll take my sandwich with me," Hart replied, sitting his empty glass on the table. "Get a lantern and a blanket, will you, Adam? We may need them," he amended. "Where's Mam, Cleo? Has she eaten?"

"No, sir. She began to worry so about Mr. Bruce she began to feel faint. We sent her up to bed. Now don't you worry about her, Mr. Hart. I'll look after her. She'll be find, just fine," Cleo instructed, stopping Hart with a glance of her brown eyes, when he started for the back stairs toward his mother's room. "What she needs is for you to bring Mr. Bruce home. Then she'll be up again."

"All right, Cleo. I'll leave her in your capable hands. Just take care of her, understand?"

"Of course, I do. I's been looking after her since before you was born," Cleo retaliated, her eyes wide with indignation.

"I know. I just don't want anything else to happen." Hart took the sandwich she held out to him and started for the barn. Blister was tired from the day's outing. He took his father's horse.

Adam was waiting, sitting in his saddle, a blanket tied on behind him, a lantern hanging from the saddle horn. "Where do you think he is?"

"I really have no idea. I thought I did. But Father said you had searched Natchez and Silver Street. That right?"

"Yes. He wasn't at Flatboat Fannie's, if that was what you meant," Adam answered.

"It was," Hart replied, mounting his horse and moving from the barn. "I saw him there last night after midnight."

"What were you doing there?"

Adam's question caught Hart off guard. He hated to lie to his younger brother. He had great regard for him. He was becoming a fine man, intelligent, moderate in his youthful pursuits, and industrious.

"I'll tell you later, Adam. Right now, just let me say I wasn't visiting the flatboats along the waterfront." Hart prompted his horse to pick up speed. "We'll go over to Brightway first. He may have been there."

"Nope," Adam shouted above the sound of pounding hooves. "I was there this afternoon. The colonel said you had been there this morning, but he hadn't seen Bruce. He assumed he was at home."

Hart reined his horse up short, dirt flying from his skidding hooves. "He hasn't been to Brightway?"

Adam pulled his horse to a stop. The two brothers stared at each other for a long moment.

"Where in the devil is he?" Hart voiced his anxiety slowly, a feeling of doom settling around him. He could see the same sentiment in Adam's eyes. "Well, come on. We've got to find him. He'll be all right," he added, more to ease Adam's worry than his own.

They stopped at every house along the road, rousing the inhabitants, asking if anyone had seen Bruce. No one had. He was well known in the area. Anyone who had seen him would have recognized him. So the brothers decided he had not rode back toward Crapewood from Natchez. After they scoured Natchez, they met at the tavern.

"He hasn't been here for several days," Ed Boles informed them, placing a glass of ale before each of them. "Drink up. You may be out all night. You'll need it."

"Someone's lying to us," Adam spoke quietly, nursing his glass of ale.

"I agree. Someone must have seen him after he left Fannie's," Hart replied.

"Adam, you ride a mile or so south on the Trace. I'll ride toward Brightway. We'll meet at the intersection where the road forks toward Mobile."

"Right. What am I looking for other than Bruce?" Adam asked.

"Signs of someone passing. It's getting late. You'll need the lantern to scan the ground. I'll borrow one from Ed and do the same. Fire three shots if you find anything, then one shot every five minutes until we meet. I'll do the same. The shots will guide us to each other. Just pray that we find him in time."

Hart took the lantern Ed held out to him as he finished speaking, and they left the tavern, each riding toward the south, one in an easterly direction, the other toward the river.

As Hart rode along toward Brightway, he considered the whereabouts of the two unknown backwoodsmen. He had a vague idea they were involved in Bruce's disappearance. It was the only probable explanation. As willful as Bruce was known to be, he was liked by the local men. If something had happened to him, it would most probably have come from an outsider, someone new to the area.

The old mare was still strong and covered the distance between the tavern and the perimeter of Brightway in a few minutes. Hart sat back in the saddle as he pulled back on the reins. The mare stopped immediately, standing quietly while he studied the lay of the land. Clouds had obscured the brilliant moonlight, leaving gloom in their wake. He decided to skirt the main house and move along a bridle path through the woods toward the river. If Bruce had been anywhere about the main house, someone would have seen him and reported to Crapewood.

The backwoodsmen had been tracked through here by Tchula's braves just before they left for New Orleans. Hart loaded and primed his pistol, returning it loosely to its holster, then he did the same with his rifle. When he finished, he laid the bola around his saddle horn and stuck his dirk through his belt.

A heavy layer of clouds filtered the too-brilliant moonlight, darkness settled through the woods thickly, obscuring his vision. Steadily the mare moved along the trail, her breathing relaxed. Hart relaxed as a result. Horses sensed danger. If the mare could move along here undisturbed, danger was not present.

A few minutes later, she put up her ears. Hart could feel her muscles tighten. They were moving into a shallow ravine just west of Brightway and just east of the river. Suddenly the mare stopped, stamped her foot in an agitated manner, and tossed her head. Hart dismounted, tied her short to a tree, and moved ahead silently, his pistol ready in his hand.

In the fog-filled dark, he could barely make out shape and form. He was now in the ravine, moving toward an overhanging cliff. The ground beneath his feet had recently been cut by horse's hooves.

His foot caught on a limb lying in his path, and he bent to disentangle himself. He was searching for the end of the limb in order to pull his foot free when his hand touched something cold covered by cloth. He rested his fingers there. An awful awareness filled his senses. It was Bruce. He knew it just as surely as he knew he had touched human flesh.

Slowly, he moved his hand along the length of cloth. He felt an elbow, and his fears were realized. He pulled at the brush, lifting some of it away from the human form below. His brother lay on his back, his arms outstretched, his body ashen. A gaping hole occupied his left shoulder. His forehead had been battered. Hart swore beneath his breath as he rose and moved back toward the mare to get the lantern. Once the lantern was placed by Bruce's body, he raised his rifle and fired three shots. Then he got the blanket from the roll behind his saddle and covered Bruce.

Almost immediately, he heard approaching hoofbeats as Adam came along the path behind him. When he saw Bruce's body lying gray in the glow of the lantern, he glanced quickly at Hart. Hart shook his head. Adam moved to wrap Bruce's body in the blanket without a word. The two of them placed it behind Hart's saddle, draped another blanket over it, then mounted and rode toward home.

Daylight was creeping among the upper branches of the forest as they turned down the long drive to Crapewood. Hart saw his mother standing near the hitching rail, watching anxiously for them. He was bringing Bruce home dead. Although he and Bruce had never enjoyed each other's company, the pain he felt at this moment was consuming. He pulled up at the rail, dismounted, and gathered his mother in his arms, just as his father came out the door.

When his father saw the body, which Adam carefully laid on the porch, he bent to his departed son, and the anguish he felt poured from his heart. At the sound of her husband's voice, his mother cried out, then collapsed against him. He scooped her up and carried her inside the house, calling for Cleo as he climbed the stairs toward her room.

"Cleo, get Mam's smelling salts. Put a blanket over her and stay with her. Don't leave her for a minute. Do you understand?" he demanded, anger seething within him—anger that Bruce, even in death, should bring more pain to his family.

"Yessir," was all Cleo could manage. She had never heard him speak in that tone of voice.

Hart left the room as soon as Cleo arrived with the smelling salts, rejoining Adam and his father on the front porch.

"Come, Papa, let's bring him into the parlor. You hold the door. Adam and I will carry him," Hart said, gently pulling his father away from Bruce.

His father walked into the parlor behind them, signaling for Hart to place Bruce on the sofa. When they had placed him there and covered his body with a brocade cloth they took Angus's arms and led him to the opposite room.

"Where'd you find him?" Angus asked.

"He was in a ravine near the river, south of Brightway," Hart answered, leading his father to a chair and gently pushing him down onto it. "Sit there. I'll pour you some brandy."

"How did he die?" his father asked, accepting the drink which Hart held out to him.

"He was shot at close range. There's a bad gash on his forehead. I don't know which of the wounds killed him," Hart added.

"Shot at close range? How? Who would do something like that?"

Hart knew the question. He had wrestled with it on the ride home. Whoever shot his brother was someone Bruce knew and *trusted*. He had known almost everyone in the area. He presented no threat to anyone. *Or did he?* Hart thought suddenly. *And why strike him a killing blow? Was he struck first then shot? Or was it the other way around? Maybe Bruce had posed a threat and, because of it, had been murdered by someone he knew well.* Hart shied away from the idea forming in his mind. He couldn't believe it. But Bruce was found very near Brightway.

In the morning, the doctor came from Natchez to examine Bruce's wounds. After spending some time with the body, he spoke to Angus, Hart, and Adam. "I can't determine which wound killed him. Either could have. They were administered within a few minutes of each other. He'd lost a lot of blood. I figure he was struck after he was shot."

"Struck after he was—who would do something like that?" Angus questioned, his face gray.

"Many men would," the doctor said, climbing into his buggy. "I see things like this almost every day."

"I've seen the same," Hart declared. "I won't rest until we find and convict his killer."

"That goes double for me," Adam added, handing the buggy reins to the doctor.

*****

On July 27, 1811, Bruce MacAlpin was buried at Crapewood in the family cemetery. He was the second member of the MacAlpin family to be interred there, the first having been Angus MacAlpin's father, who had also been called Bruce. The given name went far back in history, as did the MacAlpin family in Scotland. Now there were two Bruces buried in the Crapewood cemetery. One had died of old age after eating a hearty meal and downing a pint of ale. The other had died alone, and much too young, at the hands of a murderer.

Ada Albright MacAlpin was the epitome of the proper nineteenth-century bereaved widow. She kept her head bowed during the funeral, dabbing at her eyes with a handkerchief edged in black lace. Hart watched her from across the grave.

Her pregnancy was well hidden underneath the layers of black crape, which she wore fitted tight through the shoulders and eased through the waist. Buttons trailed from underneath her neck to the hem of her wide skirt, which swung as she moved. Hart could imagine her discomfort with the high neck and long sleeves, which were finished with a ruffle. As a child, she had complained of the restriction such garments caused. As a young widow, she displayed them to advantage.

When the family gathered at Crapewood after the funeral, she presided like a queen, seating herself in a straight-back chair and accepting the condolences of the mourners. She had changed to a black satin dress that bared her shoulders. Her enormous dark curls fell softly against the porcelain skin of her neck.

Mildred Albright hovered nearby, offering refreshments to everyone. Her chatter buoyant, she moved among the mourners, her demeanor more elated than bereaved, Hart noted.

While Hart was assessing Mildred's unusual behavior, Sheffield offered Angus and Flora their continued solicitations, saying they needed to leave but would return tomorrow. When they departed, Hart's eyes returned to Ada.

He was amused at the expressions on the young men's faces. They walked a tight rope between expressing the proper face of sympathy for Bruce's family and the more honest emotion of male admiration. When this byplay ceased to amuse him, he left the house, saddled Blister, and rode toward town.

He was barely on the road when he saw a buggy approaching. He slowed Blister's pace, then halted him opposite the buggy. "Good afternoon, Lessie," he said, bending low in the saddle.

"Good afternoon, Hart," she returned, bringing the buggy to a stop. "I'm so sorry to hear about your brother. We've had a siege of sickness at the farm. That's why Joan and I missed the funeral. I hope you understand."

"Certainly. John explained when I saw him. Don't think anything about it," he added, dismounting and taking her arm as she moved to leave the buggy.

"How is your mother and father?" Lessie asked when she was standing beside him.

"They are, I regret to say, numb with grief. It will be a long time before they get over Bruce's death."

"I am so sorry," Lessie said again as she looked up into his eyes—eyes that mirrored his own pain.

Her eyes, filled with sympathy as they were, held his in sweet custody. Before he knew what he was about, he bent his head and kissed her. It was but a token shared between them, but it unleashed in him hunger such as he had never known. He jerked his head away suddenly, full knowledge of his unplumbed feelings engulfing him.

Lessie reached up and touched his cheek. "Don't worry. I understand," she said as she prepared to enter the buggy, her back to Hart.

"I'm sorry," he said as he assisted her to her seat. When she turned toward him to say good-bye, he gripped her hands in his, hating to relinquish them. "I shouldn't have done that...I—"

"No, no. Don't apologize. I truly do understand," she added. "Now I must be off. I want to visit your folks and return to the farm before dark." She flicked the reins, and the horse moved off.

This is a fine state of affairs, he thought, as he mounted Blister and started off toward the tavern in Natchez. *I'd determined not to involve myself with any woman. Now here I am, head over heels for a woman I hardly know. I'll keep my distance. It's only when I'm near her that I'm so possessed.*

He didn't appreciate that thought. He never intended being possessed by any woman again.

He kicked Blister. The horse jumped, almost unseating him, then lunged into a canter as though the devil himself were after them.

*****

Ada had risen and walked to the front door when she heard the buggy. She was disappointed to discover Lessie Lord stepping from the carriage, wearing the latest-style afternoon dress of amber-colored silk with matching brocaded slippers. On her simply dressed blond hair she wore a Devonshire mob with point on the forehead made of fine Brussels lace trimmed with amber-colored ribbon.

"Good afternoon, Ms. Lord," she said, restraining the urge to ask her where a pauper would acquire such finery.

"Good afternoon," Lessie returned. "Please accept my sincere condolences and those of my cousins, John and Joan Wellsley."

"How quaint of you to repeat John's gift of sympathy," Ada proclaimed, leveling her dark eyes at Lessie.

Lessie could feel heat rising to her face. She had not expected to be received with such maliciousness. Her voice even, her eyes looking down into Ada's, she retaliated. "Good manners require one to repeat the condolences of family who are not present if one is asked to do so, and I was. Joan instructed me to offer you both hers and John's sympathies. I'm certain you wouldn't consider Joan Wellsley quaint."

"Naturally not. You would do well to heed her instruction," Ada spat, her dark eyes flashing. How dare this upstart attempt to instruct her in manners.

Lessie laughed, a tinkling, light laugh, tossed her blond curls and proceeded ahead of Ada into the parlor, where Angus and Flora MacAlpin were seated side by side on the sofa. She approached them as Angus rose to meet her and Flora put out her hand in welcome.

"Please know how very sorry we are. You have all our sympathies," Lessie said, her heart breaking at the sight of their ravaged faces.

"Thank you, Ms. Lord." Angus assisted her to a chair near his wife. "We're pleased that you came."

"Yes, my dear. We do appreciate your visit, and we know all your hearts grieve with us. Tell Joan that I'm well and ask her to visit as soon as she's able. I'd love to see her." Flora sighed as she uttered words of welcome for this winsome young cousin of John's.

She continued to study Lessie as she sipped the glass of sherry which Angus had insisted she drink. The girl was beautiful. Her beauty was serene, charming, in a quiet way. Flora saw the way Ada was watching her. *There's jealousy there*, she thought. *Jealousy for this quiet, calm girl with the intelligent eyes.*

"Tell me, Lessie, did you meet Hart as you drove up? I believe he left for town just a few minutes before you arrived," Flora asked, amazed to see color creep underneath the creamy skin of Lessie's cheeks.

"Actually, I did. We chatted for a minute or two as we passed on the road," Lessie replied, aware of the warmth in her cheeks. She wondered if Hart's kiss was stamped there. She could feel it still. As she smiled into his mother's eyes, she received a shock. His mother knew.

A rustle of petticoats turned their attention to the doorway. Two young women entered. Flora held out her hands to them.

"Come and kiss me. I'm so glad to see you. It's good of you to come," she continued, as they crossed the room and kissed her lightly on each cheek.

"We could do nothing else, Aunt Flora. This is a tragic thing, a tragic thing," the smaller one said.

Lessie recognized the girls from the dance at Crapewood. They were cousins of Hart's. His father's dead sister's grandchildren by her twin daughters, or so Joan had told her. They lived near Washington on a small farm that had been left to them by Viola's father.

"Viola, Callie, you know Lessie Lord. She is John Wellsley's young cousin from Mobile. She's staying with them for a while," Flora offered, as the newcomers settled into chairs placed for them by Angus.

"I'm certain we haven't met," Viola said, turning her eyes away from Lessie as though the sight of her was distasteful.

"Of course, we have," Callie interjected. "You remember. She's the one Hart danced with at the soiree. You know, we discussed her beautiful skin."

"Oh shush! I don't remember anything of the sort," Viola commanded, still looking at Flora instead of the object of their discussion.

"But I remember you, Viola," Lessie said steadily. "You were the two who stood behind the potted palm, discussing the guests behind raised fans."

"What! How dare you!" Viola cried, glancing at last at Lessie to see the look of amusement in her eyes.

Flora couldn't help a small laugh, in spite of the heavy mantle of grief that clothed her. "This won't do at all. Viola, you owe Lessie an apology. Lessie, my dear, I'm afraid we are often unkind to newcomers. At least, some of us are. We don't mean to hurt. I'm sure you understand that." She pleaded with her eyes as she finished, not wanting the confrontation to continue.

"Of course. I'm the one who should apologize. Viola just didn't remember me, that's all." It wasn't all, and she knew it. But it was better not to cause a problem here today. The MacAlpins had enough to endure. She rose and turned to leave. "I must be going, anyway. Thank you for your courtesy to one who comes virtually unknown," she said, as Angus rose to escort her to the door.

"Come again, dear, and soon. I would very much enjoy a visit with you," Flora responded, a genuine smile touching her eyes.

"I'd like that," Lessie replied.

"And don't pay any mind to Viola," Callie instructed, rising and walking out with Lessie. "She's been head over heels for Hart since they were children. Only she won't admit it."

"Callie," Viola hissed, attempting to withdraw into the chair on which she sat. "No such thing!"

"Not true, Viola. You'd better 'fess up. It'll do you good." Callie was enjoying baiting her.

"Callie Warren! You just wait until we get home. You'll be sorry," Viola seethed, her face a flaming pink.

"As I said, Lessie. Don't pay her any mind," Callie continued as though Viola was not present.

Lessie smiled. "Don't worry, Callie. I'll heed your advice. And thank you," she finished, holding out her hand.

"I hope we see more of you, Lessie," Callie invited, holding the door for Lessie as she left the house. Then on the porch, just as Lessie was stepping into the buggy, she added, "By the way, have you heard we're going to Nashville, too?"

Lessie was astonished! "No. I hadn't heard," she replied, lifting the rein into her hands. "But that's wonderful, Callie. We'll have time to become friends."

"My thought, exactly," Callie said. "I've inherited some property near Nashville from my father's people. I must personally attend a reading of the will before I can claim anything. So we're going, too."

"That will make our trip much nicer," Lessie said, prompting the horse to move. "We'll talk more later."

I wonder if she and Hart are seeing each other, Callie thought, as she reentered the house. Then she giggled, a soft girlish giggle. He certainly seemed mesmerized at the dance.

"Callie Warren, I never! If you ever do that to me again, I don't know what I'll do...but I'll do something. Believe me I will," Viola cried, as Flora attempted to quiet her.

"You asked for it, Vi. That is a really nice girl. You shouldn't let your jealousy get the better of your good sense," Callie retaliated, seating herself beside Flora on the sofa.

"My what? My jealousy?" Viola sputtered, her face now crimson. She stammered and hissed, searching for something to use to rebut Callie's assumption that she was jealous. But she couldn't think of anything. Callie knew her too well.

"Now, girls, I won't have any more of this. Stop it this instant," Angus ordered. "This is no place and no time to bicker."

"I'm sorry, Uncle Angus." Callie sighed, feeling guilty. He was right. This was no place and no time.

"I'm sorry too," Viola said finally, a hint of malice sharpening her words.

As the afternoon wore on, the sound of horses' hooves and buggy wheels ceased, and the family retired to their private grief. Callie and Viola left for home. Flora was afraid for them to travel alone so late in the day, so Adam escorted them. Flora and Angus went to their room, refusing supper.

Ada moved to the porch. She sat in a chair near the door, waiting for Hart to return. Lessie's appearance had piqued her. She needed to settle things between herself and Hart. She had married one MacAlpin. Now she intended to marry another. She was as certain of it as she was of her charm.

Ada waited for what seemed hours. She attempted to doze for a while but was bothered incessantly by mosquitoes. She knew she should be inside under netting. But she wasn't giving up just yet. The mosquitoes were merciless. Finally, she rose and walked inside to find Hart coming from the rear of the house.

"Where have you been?" she demanded.

Hart stared at her, at the small welts on her bare shoulders, at her griefless eyes. "Why do you ask?"

"I've been waiting for you all evening on the porch. The mosquitoes nearly carried me off."

"I'll say it again, Ada. Why were you waiting for me?"

Hart was tired; he had wrestled with the problem of who could have killed Bruce all evening. He was feeling irritable.

"Why? Why? That seems to be all you have to say to me these days, Hart." She moved up against him. He backed away, and she moved up again until she had him pinned against the stairs.

"Cut it out, Ada. You should be ashamed. Your husband was buried today." Hart's voice crucified her with full intention. "You never did care about anyone but yourself, did you?"

"You…you…arrogant…MacAlpin! How dare you talk to me like that! You went away and left me. You're to blame for what I've become. A widow, carrying a child I don't—" She stopped short at the look in his eyes. She had said too much.

"Finish it, Ada. A child you don't?" He paused, letting the incriminating phrase hang her.

"Oh…oh…Hart, let's not fight. You mean so much to me. More than anyone," she began, but he thrust her away from him and started up the stairs.

"That's a howl, Ada. You have never known what you want. And that's the truth of it. I'm only amazed I didn't see it years ago," he said, as he climbed the stairs to his room.

Ada was left standing against the bannister, a flush on her cheeks and the beginning of fear in her heart. Things were not going the way she planned.

*****

Hart slept little that night. He lay for hours thinking about Bruce, about the possibility that the colonel may be involved in the gunrunning, about Ada and how his feelings for her had finally changed. He couldn't believe he'd ever been so naive as to think she loved him. When he could finally settle his thoughts on that score, he would find Lessie's lovely visage floating through his dreams. Try as he would, he could not get her out of his mind.

When morning finally came, he jumped up, thrust on his clothes, and headed downstairs. He had settled two problems during his tossing and turning. He was free from Ada's twisted ideas of love.

And he'd decided he must speak to the governor personally. He doubted his and Tchula's commission to find the gunrunners was a secret, anyway. There were few secrets in Natchez.

"Where're you going without your breakfast?" Cleo cried from the doorway of the kitchen as he walked through on his way to the barn.

"Not today, Cleo," was all he said.

When he and Blister were on their way to Tchula's summer encampment, he felt better. Better to take positive action of some kind than to muddle around in suppositions.

"Welcome, Ishto Impa," called Achukma from near her cook pot. She was placing large pieces of fried fish on a store bought platter. "You eat?"

"Thanks, no, Achukma," Hart responded. "Some other time. Is Tchula here?"

"He inside, you wait," she answered. She walked across the open compound and entered their quarters.

The walls were upright saplings tied together with rawhide strings. The roof was made of horizontal saplings covered with a thick layer of thatch held down by more logs. She knelt on the dirt floor and touched Tchula on the shoulder.

"Ishto Impa here."

Tchula turned over and looked at his wife. To him, she was the most beautiful maid he had ever seen. He smiled at her. "Offer him food."

"I did. He no want," she informed him in their language before rising to return to her cooking, pushing her shiny black hair away from her forehead as she walked.

"Living the good life, I see," Hart joked as Tchula came out to meet him. "Not your usual style to sleep late."

"Out late, hunting turkey. Had good luck. You take one," Tchula offered, showing Hart the mound of birds piled near the cook fire. "All village share. There's plenty."

"Thank you, I will," Hart said, picking up one and tying it onto his saddle. "We need to talk. I have something I want us to do today."

"Talk," Tchula agreed.

"I think we ought to visit the governor. He may have new information, new ideas, about this uprising."

"Fine, we go," Tchula agreed again. "I'll get horse."

*****

The Governor greeted them warmly, insisting they be shown into his office as soon as they arrived.

"How good to finally meet you, Hart. And, Chief Tchula, it is good to see you again."

"Thank you, Governor," Hart replied. "We appreciate you seeing us on such short notice. We felt it urgent that we talk."

"I see," he said, his eyes regarding them intently. "William, have you met Chief Tchula of the Choctaw Nation and his friend Hart MacAlpin?"

"I haven't had the pleasure of meeting the chief, Sir. But I did have the pleasure of attending the party that welcomed MacAlpin home from Argentina," Smythe answered.

"That's right. I missed that one. Heard it was a good one," the governor stated. "Well, gentlemen, what is it you wish to discuss with me?"

Hart glanced at William Smythe, who was standing beside the governor's handsome mahogany desk, his right hand toying with a quill.

"Perhaps we could speak in private?" he asked.

"By all means. Smythe, you don't mind, do you? You have some mail that needs your attention, I believe," the governor directed, dismissing him from the room.

"Of course not, sir. Call, if you need me," he submitted, walking toward the double oak doors.

As he passed the chair where Hart sat, he glanced at him. Hart was struck by the hostility he saw in the man's eyes. They had only met twice, once at the dance and once on the road. He'd no idea what generated such wrath on Smythe's part but was willing to return it. The man just didn't fit.

"Governor, we're having the devil of a time tracking these gunrunners. Can't you give us any additional information? Anything at all that we can use to ferret them out?" Hart stated abruptly.

"I felt it was something like that," the governor said, sitting back in his chair, assessing them. "Your last report stated that you had trailed them as far as New Orleans where they bought guns. But you lost them before they could be seen disposing of them. Is that correct?"

"Yes, it is. We know one of them as Zeke, no last name. The other I call Black Hat. I have no other way of identifying him. Our primary concern right now is whether or not you suspect any of the pillared folk as participants—anyone of means living in the Natchez area?" Hart declared.

"Evidently, you suspect someone. Who?" the governor asked.

"I'd rather not say, at present. I hoped you had more to give us," Hart replied, not willing to mention his suspicion of Albright until he had more proof.

"I see. Well, you have my complete support. As soon as you find proof of some kind, come again. I'll alert the local militia to take orders from you at your request."

"Fine," Hart agreed, rising. "I take it you don't suspect anyone in government of having a hand in this treason?"

The governor laughed shortly. "I suspect everyone I know and, certainly, the British sympathizers among us. The problem is, we don't know all of them. There may be some who are closeted, doing their work under cover of nationalism," the governor explained, rising and shaking Tchula's hand, then Hart's. "I expect you two to find them and bring them before a trial."

"We're traveling the Trace this fall in October. We hope to capture one or both of them dispensing the guns to the Indians. If we get one, we should be able to find the other," Hart explained.

"I wish you good luck," the governor said, then paused. "Have you been able to learn anything about who shot your brother?" This he directed to Hart.

"We've had no luck there, either. I personally believe there must be a connection between his unexplained murder and the gunrunning. I plan to find out who did it and bring him to trial."

Hart's voice was edged with ice as he spoke, his gray eyes cold. The image of Bruce's body lying so near Brightway stayed permanently before him, as though frozen there. Someone who knew him had shot him and then covered his body to hide it. Someone they all knew and trusted. Of that, Hart was certain. Whether or not that same person, or persons, had bashed him over the head was yet to be determined. But he wouldn't rest until he exacted retribution for his family's sake.

"I wish you good luck in both your quests," the governor said again as Tchula and Hart left his office.

*****

"You think governor frank with us?" Tchula asked, mounting his horse and waiting for Hart to mount his.

"Yes. He doesn't know any more than we do. We'll stick to our plan. We'll catch them eventually. I just hope it's in time to stop some of the killing."

Hart mounted Blister and turned his head toward home. Tchula rode away toward his village.

It was late in the evening when Hart finally arrived at Crapewood. Ash hailed him from the hallway as he entered the house.

"Mr. Hart, I've something I think you ought to know."

"Yes," Hart replied.

"I hated to say anything before—before Mr. Bruce's death. But now he's gone, I think you should know that he often slipped out of the house late at night and rode over toward Brightway."

"Why?"

"I don't know. But since his body was found over there, I thought—you know," Ash finished, his eyes earnest, his voice low.

"I see. I'm inclined to agree with you. There must be some connection between Brightway and his death. But don't let on to anyone, will you?" Hart replied, sitting on the bottom stair and removing his boots. "We're looking into it."

"Yessir. But there's more. I followed him down under the hill one evening, then over to Brightway," Ash continued, his voice earnest. "The strangest thing happened. Kinda scared me. Somebody else was following him."

"What!" Ash's last statement had brought Hart up short. "Someone else was following him? You sure?"

"Yessir. Somebody wearing a robe—with a sort of...hood over their head. I couldn't see who it was. But they cut in between me and Mr. Bruce just after we left Crapewood, heading toward Silver Street."

"Did you recognize the horse?" Hart asked, remembering Ada's description of a hooded rider.

"No, sir, I didn't. Course, it was dark, you know. Couldn't see much of anything," Ash explained.

"What happened?"

"Nothing, as I could tell. When Mr. Bruce left. When he left Silver Street, the rider was there again, moving along in the shadows, following him out toward Brightway."

"You've done well, Ash. We've had another report of the same thing. We're looking into it. Keep your eyes open, will you?" Hart directed as he stuck out his hand to shake Ash's.

"I will," Ash returned, moving to blow out the hall candelabra. "If you need me, you know I'm available."

"Right. And thanks," Hart said, climbing the stairs to his room.

CHAPTER 6

Hart sat his horse, waiting at the intersection of First and Main Streets for the new minister to arrive. He'd been requested to stand in for his father at the groundbreaking ceremony to build the new church. He waited impatiently. He had work to do but was glad to see at least some of the Natchezians looking forward to life after the comet. Many people had fled. Some were simply waiting. Keeping busy was better, he supposed. And Natchez could use a new church.

Natchez was growing, burgeoning under the influx of settlers from the East and Canada. Hart had been astonished at the bustle and activity when he arrived home. A few years earlier, the town consisted of six streets running in one direction and seven in the other. Now there were numerous others, forming a square grid, extending for many blocks.

Money was being made from hemp cordage, tobacco, cotton-seed oil, cattle, and lumber. Retailers sold imported wares and luxury items from Europe. Vast fortunes were being compiled from cotton, which had become white gold in the pockets of the landowners. Due to improvements in the ginning process, gins with the new screw press could produce five hundred pounds of processed cotton fiber a day. The more prosperous merchants and landowners could purchase anything and everything they wanted. The world's markets were only as far as New Orleans. From there, anything was possible.

He folded the newspaper that he had been reading earlier and placed it inside his coat pocket. The minister was late. He could feel the facial scar tighten with his growing annoyance. Waiting, for a man of his energy, was near torture, and in his black wool mourning coat, the heat was becoming unbearable. Dismounting, he walked Blister into the shade of a grove of trees. There he positioned himself against a knurled trunk and continued his perusal of Natchez.

Newly erected buildings and the more imposing facades of enormous mansions could be seen from anywhere one stood. It was no longer the Natchez of his youth, populated with known individuals whose families had been there since the French and Spanish occupations. It was now a growing metropolis with banks, churches, schools, newspapers, a scientific association that boasted a giant telescope with which (he had just learned from the newspaper) the astronomers had announced the approach of the great comet. His fears had been substantiated.

The whistle of rapidly moving buggy wheels interrupted his thoughts. He moved out toward the road to find the minister tying his horse to the hitching rail in front of the lot where the church was to be built.

"Good morning," Hart said, moving toward him with long strides. "I'm Hart MacAlpin."

"Saddler James is the name," he replied, wiping at his perspiring forehead with a handkerchief. "I asked for this posting. I don't think I would have if I had known about this insufferable heat."

"Could be you won't suffer long," Hart suggested, thinking of the giant comet. "What can I do for you?"

"As your father has probably advised you, we will be receiving supplies in a few minutes for building our church. Most of the lumber, nails, and windows have been donated by your family. He suggested you supervise the unloading and make a record of anything damaged that should be replaced," Saddler stated, putting away his handkerchief. "Let me say how grieved I am personally by your family's loss. If building the church was not so urgent, I would not have asked you to come out so soon."

"I understand," Hart returned, as the sound of heavily loaded wagons reached his ears. "I see them coming now."

"I wonder where Ms. Lord can be? She's to attend the ceremony in place of the Wellsleys. I do so prefer people to be on time. It makes life so much easier."

"Did you say, Ms. Lord?"

"Yes. She's a very nice young woman. I met her the evening of my arrival when the Wellsleys had me to dinner." Saddler considered the meal as he spoke. He had enjoyed himself immensely. Natchez, except for the climate, might turn out to be livable.

"I agree. She is a nice young woman," Hart replied, wondering how he'd manage when pressed with her company for the next few hours.

"Here she is now, I believe," the minister said, walking toward an enclosed carriage that had come to a stop near his buggy. When the door opened, he continued. "Good morning, Ms. Lord. Mr. MacAlpin is waiting. We can proceed with the ceremony immediately."

"Mr. MacAlpin? Oh, I see," she said, smiling when she saw Hart. "It's young Mr. MacAlpin."

"And the ever lovely Ms. Lord," Hart said as he approached her. "It seems we're destined to serve together."

"Here, Ms. Lessie," Abbey, one of the Wellsley's house maids suggested, as she emerged from the confines of the carriage, "I'll take that hamper."

"Fine, Abbey. We'll set up over there under those trees," Lessie directed, pointing toward a group of beech trees on the north side of the lot.

Lessie was wearing a day costume of white corded and yellow-striped muslin, cut on the bias, with two ruffles around the skirt, long sleeves, and a square neck. She was altogether fetching, Hart thought, as he watched her charming the new minister with her calm beauty and soft words.

"Ms. Lord, if you and Hart will walk this way, we'll begin the groundbreaking ceremony so that we can start work immediately," the minister said, waving toward a group of local townspeople who were hurrying forward, some carrying tools and supplies.

Hart took Lessie's arm and led her to a cooler spot underneath an aged cedar. Finally, Saddler James was ready and the ceremony began. He read a brief verse from the book of Solomon, asked God's greatest blessings upon the building of his sanctuary and those who would worship therein. The gathering was dispersed, with the exception of Hart, who would stay to supervise the unloading of supplies, and Lessie and Abbey, who had come prepared to open picnic hampers for the workers at the noon meal.

The morning's work progressed well, and by noon, the ground-floor rafters were raised over the rock foundation. The crew was voicing sounds of hunger, glancing often toward the board and sawhorse tables, which Hart had helped to set up. Lessie, who was busily placing platters of food and napkins on the tables, was looking lovelier than ever. Her light hair was escaping from around the small hat perched on her head and curling about her face.

Hart felt a plummeting pain as he watched her, busy and oblivious to his attention, directing Abbey to spread a quilt on the ground. He had decided to stay away from her. But Providence seemed to have other ideas. Always in his mind, she now seemed destined to plague his presence. She would hate that thought, he knew. She would hate being in anyone's way. He moved toward her.

"Lessie, what does John think about the comet?"

"He discussed it with the family. I don't think he has made any plans, if that's what you mean." She placed a chocolate cake on one end of the table, picked up a knife, and sliced it in thick slices.

"It is. The whole town is in an uproar. People are trying to sell their stock, get rid of their crops, and so forth. Some are beginning to hoard everything they can get their hands on. The merchants are growing short on supplies. Salt and sugar are at a premium. If your cousins need any, they'd better get it now." Hart watched her face as he explained the growing hysteria around them. "Most of us are attempting to live normally," he continued. "We expect the comet to move away in an outgoing orbit. But no one really knows."

"We've praying for that. John says we can always go over to the salt domes and dig salt if we must. But thank you for warning me. I'll tell John," she said, turning to face him from across the food-laden table. "What does your family think?"

"Mam doesn't have time to worry about it with Ada ailing. My father has moved some of our stores to a root cellar. If something should happen, we should be able to manage." He couldn't bring himself to tell her they might not survive.

The table between them, he could only resent his need to be nearer. "I want to wish you well, sweet cousin, on your journey," he began. He intended telling her good-bye. Instead, he said, "I may see you in Nashville. I have business there later this fall." He moved around the table, picked up her hand and touched it briefly with his lips. "I'm off. There's a great deal of work to be done before the weather turns."

He watched a question flicker in her eyes before she replied. "Good-bye, Hart. Take care."

He tipped his hat and turned toward his horse. Once again, leaving was treachery.

*****

As he rode back toward Crapewood, he turned his thoughts to the approaching comet and its possible threat to their lives and property. The approach of the comet explained the strange behavior of the weather and the unseasonal migration of millions of birds and animals. The paper had mentioned the possibility of earthquakes in its wake. Even if the comet didn't strike the earth, its passing could be disastrous.

He and his father had attended a town meeting a few days ago to discuss what precautions could—or should—be taken to ensure some measure of safety for the Natchezians. Other than saving as many dried foods and meats as each of them could manage, there didn't seem to be anything they could do. The people of the territory were living in a state of purgatory—awaiting they knew not what while the rampaging Creeks and Chickasaws, under British leadership, were eliminating as many of them as possible. Natchez and the territory faced a double threat, one from nature, one from man.

He and Blister were moving at a walk along the road when a sound brought him instantly erect in the saddle. He listened. A slow smile creased his face. It was Tchula. The sound had been a rough version of the *yarrup-yarrup* sound of the Flicker. They had used it as their signal since childhood. He pulled Blister to a stop and waited.

Tchula burst through the undergrowth and rode toward Hart, a mean-looking rifle clutched in his fist.

"Where'd you get that?" Hart asked, before Tchula was abreast of him.

"That why I stopped you," he answered. "This gun was given me by Choctaw brave. Said a man wearing a black hat and coat had offered him this gun and English money if he would convince a band of braves to help fight the greedy colonials. Said he would come back later and sign them up."

"They probably mean to arm as many of your people as they can before they attack Natchez," Hart stated, considering Tchula's news. "Did your brave say where we could find this Black Hat?"

"No. He follow Black Hat to edge of Natchez. Lost him when he turned down alley. He very near, I think, like Chickasaws. Many hide in woods."

"You'd think the Chickasaws would be running or hiding in the face of the comet's threat. Why aren't they?"

"They believe Tecumseh's prophecy. This comet is coming to help them wipe out white men," Tchula explained. "I believe you, Ishto Impa. Comet will destroy all men."

"If it hits earth, it will destroy a great area, cause great fires, floods, earthquakes. It could, because of its size, possibly destroy the earth. Our only hope is that it will begin its outward orbit before it gets much closer. According to the newspaper this morning, it is already affecting the tides."

"What we do?" Tchula asked, fear for his people gripping him. He now fully understood the threat to his family and his world.

"Go about our business as usual. Tecumseh may find his prophecy coming true, or he may not," Hart continued. "In any case, we can stop some of his killing."

Hart prepared to turn Blister toward home. "By the way, have you received reports of someone else following Sheffield Albright or the others? Anyone?" Hart asked. "I've been told that someone else was seen following Bruce on several of his late night trips."

"Not heard anything," Tchula answered, a question in his eyes. "You know who it is?"

"Don't have a clue. But I suspect this person may know who killed Bruce. He was seen following Bruce the evening he was killed."

"That strange," Tchula replied. His braves had been watching Brightway. They had not mentioned another rider. "I'll check," he said. "Send message by runner," he continued, referring to the two runners who always followed after him to carry messages to and from his camp.

*****

The summer of 1811 passed swiftly. Those planning to travel the Trace with Sam Shute and party were busy buying supplies and arranging their affairs for the extended trip. Angus and Flora MacAlpin had their hands full taking care of Ada, whose health seemed to be failing. Crapewood stood suspended in time, enveloped in a mantle of sorrow. Hart came and went from the lumber mill, the commissary, and occasionally assisted Adam with farm business. Each of the brothers buried himself in his work, talking little, falling into bed immediately after supper in the evening.

Bruce's death and their father's sorrow, coupled with the necessity for him to stay with Flora and help her support Ada, had left a tremendous burden of supervision and management to them. Hart had forgotten how hard his father worked. Money was never made idly, he had learned, and big money owned its recipient.

He saw Lessie only once after the groundbreaking ceremony. She had smiled and nodded when she found him staring at her in church as she sat with her cousins in their pew. After the service, he immediately withdrew. He was standing by the buggy, waiting for his mother to finish speaking with the minister when he felt a tug at his arm.

"Hey," a young voice said.

"Hey, yourself," he replied, recognizing Nathaniel Lord, who stood at his elbow, looking up at him.

"You waiting on somebody?" The boy's eyes studied him carefully as he spoke before they turned toward his sister, who was just emerging from the church.

"I'm waiting on my mother. She's just coming this way," Hart replied.

"Oh," Nate returned, his face closing a bit as though he'd been disappointed.

"Had any more adventures, Nate?" Hart asked, attempting to change the direction of Nate's thoughts, which he suspected were aimed at him and Lessie.

"Nope. Well, not hardly," Nate answered, kicking at the dirt with the toe of his polished boot. "I nearly fell in the well the other day. But that was an accident."

"What happened?"

"Nothing much. Just that old Lucifer. You know, Cousin Joan's black cat. He had my ball. I was trying to get it back from him, and I slipped. But I caught hold of the rope and bucket and hung on. The brake was on."

Hart attempted a straight face as he asked. "Who pulled you out?"

"That Ozzie did. She whupped me good. I don't like her much."

"Even though she saved your life?'

"I'd have gotten out okay by myself. She needn't have bothered."

"Are you certain of that? Suppose the brake had slipped while you were trying to climb out. What do you think would have happened?"

The lean, young features lacked all expression as the boy's eyes studied Hart. "I hadn't thought about that."

"Think about it. And think next time before you act, before you place yourself in a position to get hurt. You never know. There might not be anyone around to help you."

Nate flashed his snaggletoothed smile. "I will. I'll think first next time."

The two of them were still talking when Lessie called Nate away. Nate joined her, and they drove away with their cousins.

"What's the matter, Son? You look as though you've lost something," his mother said.

Hart had been unaware of her approach. He took her arm and helped her into the buggy.

Flora glanced at her son's face. The look there confirmed her suspicions. He had lost something, whether he wanted to admit it or not. She smiled and patted his outstretched hands, then settled back into the soft leather of the cushioned seat. Youth was sometimes so hard. She was glad all that was behind her.

As they turned away from Natchez, riding along tree-shaded roads toward home, Hart spoke. "I'm going to be away for a while. Tchula and I have some business that needs our attention."

"I know," she replied.

"How do you know?" he questioned, surprised.

"I am usually aware of what's going on with my family. Adam told me that a party was being formed to accompany Lessie and Nate up the trace. I assumed you'd be among them."

"I won't be. I'll be leaving much sooner."

"Oh. Then you and Tchula will be leaving right away?"

"Yes. We'll be leaving before dawn tomorrow. We need to get an early start."

"I see. If you feel you must, you must. My love goes with you both," Flora added, patting his hands again, much as she had done when he was small.

"Thanks, Mam. I hate leaving right now, with Ada ill and you and Papa still grieving. But it must be done." He slapped the reins, and Blister picked up speed.

"Don't worry about us. We'll be fine," Flora stated, seeing the worry in his eyes.

"But I do worry. This comet is larger than any known to approach earth. Most believe it will eventually turn in an outward orbit. No one knows for certain. It's hard to go ahead with my plans with that thing hanging over us."

"I know. I'm finding it difficult to get through the day, to make any kind of plans. We're storing what we can. Angus even had some of the hands dig a cave shelter in the side of a bluff near the rear of the house. But it might not do any good at all," Flora stated thoughtfully. "All we can do is wait and pray. People are praying around the clock."

"While you're at it, pray for the group traveling the Trace, will you?" Hart asked.

"They're already on my list," his mother affirmed, patting his hand once again, "as are you and Tchula."

They were soon home, and Cleo had a cold lunch waiting for them on the dining room table. "The mister done ate. He's gone over to Brightway to talk with the colonel," she informed them as they seated themselves.

"Did he say why?" Hart asked, curious.

"He didn't, and I ain't the one to ask," she answered, placing cups of tea beside their plates. "Miz Ada didn't eat yet, though. Said she wasn't hungry. Wanted to see Mr. Hart when he got home?"

Hart glanced at his mother, who looked up as Cleo spoke. "I'll see Ada, Cleo, immediately after I finish lunch."

"Yes, ma'am, Miz Flora. I'll be glad to tell her," Cleo sang, departing the room with a look of triumph in her eyes.

Hart said, "I don't think she cares much for Ada."

*****

The sun was not yet up when Hart and Tchula arrived at their prearranged meeting place on the Trace just north of Natchez. Each had a packhorse carrying supplies. Hart carried his rifle, dirk, bola, flintlock pistol, and the letter from the governor that William Smythe had delivered in the guise of an invitation to dinner at the capitol. The letter authorized any legal authority, including the territory militia to assist Hart at his request. It had not been opened, but Hart felt certain that Smythe knew its contents. His manner had been casual, offhand, as he handed the letter to Hart, but his eyes were hard, his back rigid. When he had gone, Hart wondered at his response to the man. As usual, it wasn't good.

Tchula, too, had come well armed. He carried his bow and arrows, tomahawk, knife, and the rifle that Black Hat had given his brave. Hart had brought rice, bacon, cornmeal, a small bag of flour, coffee, and some of Cleo's tea cakes. Tchula had beans, hominy, cornmeal and molasses. He had also brought a supply of chicory for coffee. He preferred it. They were as well provisioned as possible.

"Where's your blowpipe?" Hart asked.

"Rifle much better," Tchula replied, sighting along its barrel.

"You ready?"

For answer, Tchula turned his horse across the trail and moved into the brush, heading north. Hart moved to the opposite side and followed a stream in the same direction. They planned to meet about twenty miles up the trace the first evening, making LeFleur's Bluff in a few days.

Hart's first and only visit to LeFleur's Bluff was after the episode when he and Tchula had been attacked by the Harpes, Micajah and Wiley (known as Big Harpe and Little Harpe). They had been terrorizing the Trace for several years. Sam Shute had been in the woods nearby and heard the yelling. Hart owed his life to the man. He had intervened just in time to keep Hart from losing his head to Big Harpe's knife.

Tchula had come away unhurt. Sam had suffered a minor cut on his arm as he swung at Harpe, knocking him down. Everything had happened so quickly that Hart had trouble believing it had been real—until he looked in the mirror of a morning and saw the long, thin scar. Sam and Tchula had bandaged Hart's face as best they could, insisting they ride for LeFleur's Bluff. They spent a week there. When Tchula and Hart had been able to return to Natchez, they learned the Harpes had been captured and that Big Harpe's head had been severed and placed on a pole as a warning to others like him.

*****

On the first evening, just about dusk, Hart crossed the Trace and met Tchula at the prearranged spot. Tchula had a small fire going. Curls of smoke drifted up through the surrounding trees.

"Is that wise?"

"No tracks on this side for three miles. Yours?" Tchula asked.

"The same. It looks as if they rendezvous farther along the Trace." Hart glanced at the piece of meat Tchula was placing over the fire. "What's that?"

"Rabbit. Got it with my bow. You hungry?"

"Very."

The two of them sat cross-legged near the fire and finished off the rabbit, then moved to tether their horses under the overhanging boughs of a cedar before bedding down underneath it.

Hart walked over to Blister and reached inside a leather sack tied to his saddle horn, pulling from it two large cloth-wrapped items. "Here, try this," he said, handing one to Tchula. "Save the bits of cloth. Cleo insists I return them to her for use again."

Tchula unwrapped his, a wide smile spreading all the way to his eyes. "This good. I remember from when we were boys. What you call them?"

"Tea cakes," Hart answered, munching on his, his mouth full.

"You have more?" Tchula asked when he had finished his exceptionally large one.

"I do," Hart replied, handing him another one. "This tree should screen us well. I don't think any man or animal has ever set foot beneath it," Hart said, pushing his way underneath a pungent cedar while holding his tea cake carefully.

"Just so," returned Tchula, wedging himself in alongside. "Many people come now. Not so before. Not long till footprints everywhere, I think."

Hart considered Tchula's point. "It's likely," he agreed, pulling his blanket over him as he positioned himself in the dry underbrush.

The day had been long. Tomorrow would be the same. The weather had decided to cooperate for a change. Although the sun was jaundiced all day, there had been no rain. If there were people in the forest, he and Tchula would find sign.

He turned over on his side, preparing to close his eyes. He thought of Lessie and Nate, of his parents and brother. He couldn't help worrying about them. It's better this way. Better to let them go about their lives normally for as long as possible. But going about his life normally had put him many miles from them.

*****

"Ada, you've got to get up, get some exercise. Lying here day after day isn't doing you any good," Flora stated as she stared down at Ada's wan face. "Dr. Van Cleve says you need to move around more, get your appetite back."

"He hasn't done one thing to make me feel better," Ada retorted, refusing to stir from her prone position on the bed.

Flora sighed. She didn't know what to do with Ada. She refused to move to Brightway, insisting she needed to stay in Bruce's home. Flora knew the real reason she stayed. She wanted to be near Hart. But Hart was gone, and Ada didn't even know it. Perhaps she should tell her. Maybe then she would get up and busy herself sewing clothes for the baby.

"Ada, you know you should busy yourself making lovely things for your baby." Flora watched Ada's eyes widen. "You do want the baby to have nice things, don't you?"

"I suppose. But you and Mama are making so many things. And I can't sew or embroider as well as you two. So I'll just let you take care of the baby's wardrobe," Ada said, still without lifting even an arm from the bed.

"No! I insist you make some of the baby's things. You really should, you know." Flora whipped back the covers and spoke in her sharpest tone. "Now get up and get dressed. I insist."

"Oh, all right! If I must, I must," Ada spat, her temper short. She had begun to dislike Flora. Until Bruce's death, she had not known what strength Flora possessed. She was definitely not the retiring, amenable woman she had always thought her to be.

"Good," Flora said when Ada was standing before the mirror and toying with her hair. "Wash and dress. Then come downstairs for dinner. We're having crayfish, red beans and rice, and a wild strawberry cobbler for dessert. All your favorites."

"Ugh." Ada shuddered, glancing at Flora in the mirror. "Sounds simply awful."

Flora ignored Ada's attempt to continue their confrontation. Leaving the room quietly, she went in search of Angus. She'd seen him return from Brightway from Ada's bedroom window. Something

104

had to be done. Ada was near skin and bones. If she didn't start eating—Flora didn't want to think about it.

She found her husband on the front lawn, walking with his hands clasped behind his back as if in deep thought. She had seen him like this many times. Once he had told her that walking cleared his thoughts, allowing him to channel them to good purpose. She felt she knew what was worrying him. It wasn't the farm, the mill, or the store. He saw her approaching and held out his hand. She took it, placing her arm through his. They continued walking, both silent.

Finally, Angus spoke. "How is she?"

"Worse than yesterday, I'm afraid. Angus, the doctor said he could not find anything wrong with her. Yet she refuses to eat and behaves as though the sight of food is sickening to her."

"Don't fret, Flora. We'll help her if we can," Angus responded, sensing the helplessness his wife felt. "I know you're worried about the baby and about Ada. Could this be simply morning sickness?" he asked.

"I don't think so. I've never heard of it lasting all day. And she doesn't throw up, Angus. She just won't eat."

"I see. I discussed her problems with Sheff today. He and Mildred are as confused as we are. Mildred wants her to go home. Sheff says leave her where she's happiest, especially now that he's going to be away from home. But is she happy here?" Angus had been considering that question before Flora joined him.

"No, Angus, she isn't. You know, it just occurred to me. I don't think Ada has ever been really happy. She was all pins and needles when Bruce was alive. They quarreled often. Bruce spent many nights away, as I'm certain you know." Flora paused, looking up at Angus.

"Yes, I know. But there's just so much a father can do with a grown son. Bruce was Bruce. He made his own rules. I pray he didn't bring about his own death."

Flora squeezed her husband's fingers. "I'm sure that was not the case, Angus," she replied, more to ease his grief than from her own belief or knowledge. She had lost Bruce a long time back.

"Where is Sheff off to? You said he was going to be away," Flora asked.

"Turns out he's going up the Trace with the Shute party. Said he had urgent business in Nashville," Angus answered.

"Imagine that," Flora returned, perplexed.

"By the way, Mildred asked if you had seen her pelisse, the brown velvet one fastened with Brandenburghs. Said she thought Ada had borrowed it," Angus stated, his mind still on Ada's puzzling decline.

"No. But I'll look around the house for it," Flora offered.

The two of them walked a while longer then returned to the house. As they entered, Flora asked. "Should we tell Ada that Hart has gone, that he may be gone for a long time? Do you suppose knowing she can't see him would bring her around?"

Angus considered the question, then spoke carefully. "I don't know. That's the trouble. It could be the wrong thing. But I agree, we must do something. Let's tell her," he said at last, a long sigh preceding the words.

*****

"Where is she?" Flora stood in the middle of Ada's room, turning slowly, looking in every corner.

Angus said nothing but turned on his heel and left the room, calling orders to Ash. "See that my horse is saddled immediately. Did anyone in this house tell Miz Ada that Hart had left for Nashville?"

"I'll ask," Ash replied, moving immediately to carry out Angus' instructions.

That woman was more trouble, Ash thought, hurrying across the grounds toward the stable.

*****

Sheffield Albright stood in the middle of the road in front of the tavern, making suggestions as to where each person should ride in the caravan about to start up the Trace. He was going to Nashville, to the bank that had originally financed his plans to settle in Natchez and raise cotton. There he might be able to raise the emergency funds he needed.

The last few years had dwindled his cash reserve. His poor payment of debts had cancelled what credit he had in Natchez. His hope that Bruce MacAlpin might take over as his plantation manager when he married Ada had turned sour almost immediately. Bruce had laughed in his face when approached about the job. He didn't work on the farm at Crapewood, he had said. He certainly wasn't going to start at Brightway. That was the beginning of Sheffield's contempt for Bruce. It had grown almost daily since.

As the eldest man in the group and a one-time army officer, he had been put in charge of the caravan. He'd been surprised that Sam Shute made no objection. But when it was put to a vote, Sam had voted with the others.

"Let's go," he yelled at the top of his voice.

The entourage began to move slowly northward along the Trace toward Washington, St. Catherine's Creek, Lefleur's Bluff, and points north to Nashville. He mounted his horse and rode back along the line, speaking to each person, reminding them to keep their distance from each other but not to lag behind.

The sun was casting its apathetic glow sparsely among the leaves. The air was cool and dry, a pleasant change from the humid, damp summer.

Lessie and Nate rode directly behind Albright, their horses pulling Cousin John's enclosed buggy. He had insisted they take it. He wanted them to have ample room for supplies and a dry place to ride in rainy weather. They could return the buggy on their first visit home to Natchez, he had said, when he saw them off at the farm.

Lessie felt she was indeed leaving home. She couldn't keep back the tears as she whipped the reins and the buggy rolled down the drive, perhaps for the last time. She and Nate were heading into the unknown, away from all they had grown to love. She was leaving more than her cousins behind. She had been thinking of Hart MacAlpin all morning. Would she ever see him again?

Immediately behind them was the open buggy carrying Viola Vespar and Callie Warren. The postmaster was next, his old horse trudging along as though already tired. Then came Able Hand on Joe; then Sam Shute, who, to Lessie's surprise, made no attempt to grasp the reins of leadership. He rode quietly in the rear, his hawk-like eyes scanning the woods on either side of the Trace, even though they had hardly put Natchez behind them.

She held a tight rein on fear. The fear that had plagued her since her father's death, that had followed her every step of the way from Mobile to Natchez. The fear that something awful could happen—that something awful would happen.

She glanced over at her brother. He seemed content, now that they were on their way. They had the leather flaps raised, allowing the cool autumn air around them. He smiled at her as he turned on the seat, gazing first one way and then the other. He was happier than she had seen him since they left Mobile. Perhaps everything would go well. Perhaps nothing awful would happen to any one of them. She lifted her head in a silent prayer that it might be so until she heard a horse approaching at a trot. She turned to see Sam Shute behind her.

"Everything fine, Ms. Lessie?" he asked as he pulled his horse into line beside hers.

"Yes, thank you, Mr. Shute. We're doing fine," Lessie replied.

"My wife's the only person calls me Mr. Shute," he said, grinning. "You'll meet her at the Stand."

"Yes, Sam," she returned. She felt better. Sam Shute had a way of making one feel protected, she thought, as he wheeled his horse and returned to his place in line.

"I like Sam, almost as much as I like Hart," Nate commented. "Why didn't Hart come with us?"

"I don't know, Nate. I suppose he had work to do," she answered.

"I thought he liked you, Lessie," Nate returned, his mind moving much like the jumping bean he carried in his pocket.

"I'm certain he likes us both," Lessie answered. "But he has his own affairs to take care of, Nate. He's probably very busy helping his father and brother now that Bruce is gone."

"I don't know as I believe that," Nate returned.

Lessie considered Nate thoughtfully. She didn't know that she believed that, either, especially after—well, Hart MacAlpin owed them nothing. He and his family had been exceedingly good to the

Lords during their stay in Natchez. *And that,* she thought, *is probably that.*

*****

The household was in an uproar. Ada had not been found. Angus and Ash had set out in different directions, both in buggies, hoping to find her and bring her back. They each knew she was in no condition to make her way through the forests or along the roads. She hadn't taken a horse or carriage.

"Where can she have gone?" Flora asked herself over and over again. "Cleo, are you certain she said nothing to you?"

"No, Miz Flora. I done told you. I didn't see her since right after lunch," Cleo replied, her own eyes reflecting worry.

"Well, we'll just have to wait. They'll find her, I'm sure," Flora continued, just as Adam walked in.

"Mam, what's all the fuss. Someone said Ada was missing?" He came to her, his eyes questioning.

"Yes. She simply disappeared. We have searched high and low, just everywhere. She's gone." Flora almost cried the words; she was so worried.

"Where's Papa?"

"He and Ash have set out in different directions looking for her," Flora sighed, a sudden premonition assailing her. "I'm afraid they won't be in time, Adam. I'm afraid they won't be in time."

"Mam, it's no fault of yours or any of us. Ada has always done as Ada chose to do. You go upstairs and rest awhile. We'll take care of things," Adam urged, pushing her toward the stairs. He glanced at Cleo as he finished speaking. She understood and moved to accompany his mother.

He sprinted toward the back hitching post and mounted Jubal, his large dun-colored stallion. He had an idea where Ada had gone. He had found her there before.

Jubal's speed was a matter of record around Natchez. Adam and Jubal won any race they cared to enter. He was flying across the open fields between Crapewood and St. Catherine's Creek. There was a spot there where he, Hart, and Ada had spent long summer afternoons swimming. Adam had found Ada there several times during the last few years. She would be sitting on the old log they had used for diving, staring before her as into another world.

He saw her immediately when the creek came into view, but she was not sitting. Something was wrong. He urged Jubal on at a high gallop. They skidded to a stop near the water's edge, and Adam jumped from the saddle letting the reins hang.

"Ada! Are you all right?" He bent over her, lifted one hand, and felt for her pulse. She was cold—so very cold. Gently, he turned her over and laid her on the soft grass. She was as still as death.

He had no way of carrying her back to the house except aboard Jubal. He lifted her in his arms and placed her in front of him across the saddle, holding her head up as best he could. She moaned as they began to move forward. The terrain was rough. She moaned again.

It took less than thirty minutes to return her to Crapewood. She had made no other sound. Her skin was pale and cool to the touch. When they trotted down the drive, his father met them. He and Ash lifted her down and carried her inside, their faces haggard.

"How is she?" Flora asked, coming from her room in her dressing gown. "Oh no!" she exclaimed when she saw Ada's wan face. "Quickly, get the doctor, and go fetch Mildred Albright. We must hurry."

The doctor arrived ahead of Mildred Albright. He checked Ada's pulse, her eyes, and felt her clammy skin, then pronounced an imminent miscarriage.

"We already know that," Angus argued. "Tell us if she will live. Will the baby live? Do you know?"

"Of course not, Angus." Dr. Van Cleve had treated the two families involved for years. He could speak frankly to them. "We could lose both of them."

A general cry went round the room, Mildred Albright's bringing alarm to Flora. "There, there, Mildred. The doctor didn't say for certain. There's a good chance she'll make it."

"We'll do all we can," the doctor stated. "Come with me, Cleo. I'll need you. The rest of you stay out of my way," he commanded.

"Come, Mildred, we'll wait in my sitting room," Flora suggested, taking Mildred by the arm and leading her away. "Angus, why don't you and Adam find yourselves a glass of brandy. You look as though you need it."

"We'll all need to be strong until this is over," Flora continued. She didn't want this for Ada or for her child.

It had grown dark. Ash had served sandwiches and tea, which no one touched, when the scream reached their ears. They had gathered in the parlor, hoping the long hours meant Ada was surviving and that she would not lose her baby. It started slowly, growing in pitch and volume until the women covered their ears in horror and empathy. The men stood transfixed. Silence followed the scream—cold, deathly silence.

No one moved for a moment or two. Angus looked at Flora. They both knew. Then Mildred Albright started for the stairs, running.

"Flora, stay here," Angus ordered, his voice a low growl. "Adam, stay with her."

As old as he was, he took the stairs two at a time. He wanted to see the baby, see if it was all right. He pushed open the door of Ada's room to find Mildred on her knees by the bed. She was weeping, long hysterical sobs. The doctor had wrapped the baby, a boy, in the knitted blanket that Flora had finished only hours before. The baby was dead.

Dr. Van Cleve held the small bundle in his hands. Cleo reached to take the child from him. Angus moved forward. He lifted the cover and examined the baby.

"We'll call him Bruce," he said, taking the child from the doctor and holding the lifeless form near his heart.

"The cord was wrapped around his neck," Van Cleave informed them before accepting a glass of brandy from Cleo. He needed it. He'd never witnessed a labor so hard and so long. He hoped he never would again.

Angus put out his hand to the doctor. "We know you did your best, Warren." Nothing could be said to bring back the dead or to ease their suffering. His recent loss had taught him that. But there was something to be done for the living.

"Flora, we must force some hot soup into Ada. Make her eat something. She's gone too long without proper food."

Flora's face was perfectly calm as she retreated to the sofa against the wall and sat down. The baby was dead. Bruce's child was dead. The words rang in her ears. Somehow she felt responsible. If she hadn't forced Ada to get out of bed, forced her to get dressed, she might not have run away. She placed her face in her hands and wept.

"Adam, bring your mother's medicine. Cleo, fetch Ash. Then reheat those warming irons and get some soup. Hurry!" Angus ordered, feeling relief in charging others with action.

"Yes, sir," Adam replied, moving quickly to do as his father had instructed.

"I'm here," Ash said from the doorway.

"Ash, bring up the baby's new cradle," Angus instructed. "We'll place him there. Then go and bring that cherry wood from the commissary, in the storage room. You know, the piece I was saving to build a chest."

"Yessir, I know," Ash replied. "I'll be right back," he finished, leaving the room.

Two days later, a small grave was dug next to Bruce's. Ada's baby was buried there, wrapped in fine cotton lawn and placed in the hand-carved coffin that Angus and Ash had made from the prized cherry wood.

CHAPTER 7

There it was again, the unmistakable sound of horses' hooves. Thuds vibrated the earth, signaling their presence several miles ahead to the perceptive ears of Tchula. He had dismounted and stretched himself over the deep-rutted road, his ear to the leaf-strewn soil. Now he raised himself and signaled for Hart to listen.

Hart had heard nothing but slid off Blister and put his own ear to the ground. Tchula was right. They were coming at a steady gait.

"How far back are they?" Hart asked.

"Not far. We get off road and wait?" Tchula suggested, as Hart remounted Blister and, for answer, edged his way up the bank and into thick brush. Tchula turned his own horse across the road on the opposite side, moving into a stand of catalpa and haw trees.

Both men remained motionless. They were well hidden, screened as they were by autumn colors, their canvas suits blending into the background like a fawns coloring. Even Blister's dappled gray form melted into nature's mantle. Only Hart's green bonnet suggested color left over from summer.

It was October 10, according to Hart's reckoning. Nature was discarding her foliage, preparing to wait out winter's cold before sprouting summer's green. Hart had spent many hours waiting like this, sitting under cover of a thick cedar or spreading oak, watching for a turkey or a white tail to make its offering. He and Tchula had hunted often together, supplying both their homes with venison and turkey.

But the comet had caused a strange silence this year. Birds and animals alike had changed their habits. They had food enough. The spring flood had left the lakes and rivers high, so there was water enough. But still they moved, crossing the treetops or the forest floor according to their kind.

The great Shawnee, Tecumseh, had forewarned of this strange occurrence by issuing his brother's prophecy that a darkness accompanied by a wailing and moaning of the earth would fall over the land if the alliance that the Shawnees sought did not solidify. And it had not. The Choctaw mingo, Pushmataha, a relative of Tchula, had defeated Tecumseh in an already famous battle of oratory at the meeting of the tribes on the Tombigbee River last spring. He had affirmed that the Choctaws would never kill one white man to gratify another. Now it seemed that Tecumseh's prophecy of doom was to give him the last word after all, at least among the superstitious.

The way Hart saw it, the hunting was poor because the days were unnaturally dark. The approaching comet, massive as it was, had come between the sun and earth, casting a pale shadow in daytime, a more brilliant light than the moon at night. No wonder the wood's inhabitants were confused.

The sound of voices caused Hart to pull his thoughts back to the road, just as the Natchez caravan came into view. The colonel was riding in the lead, with Lessie and Nate following close behind in a closed buggy. Callie and Viola were next. Then came the mail carrier, a medium-sized man, gaunt in worn boots, black hat and coat. A well-packed mail pouch hung across his horse's back. A tin trumpet swung from his saddle horn. Sam and Able Hand rode into view next, with Tchula's two braves bringing up the rear. A larger party would have been better. However, a few men who could handle guns and knives were better than many who could not.

He turned his attention back to the head of the line just before Lessie and Nate passed from view. Lessie was engaged in amused conversation with Nate, who was hanging out the window on his side.

"Nathaniel Lord, if you don't turn around and sit down, you'll probably fall out and be trampled to death." Keeping Nate in hand was becoming tiring. They had been traveling for more than a week now, and he was becoming more and more difficult.

"No, I won't, Lessie. I'm holding on to the edge of the window. See?" Nate was enjoying looking backward as he rode, watching the erect, straight-faced Choctaw braves. He wanted to see them use their weapons.

Hart signaled Tchula to stay hidden as the group moved past their position. As he did so, Lessie's head turned sharply in his direction, her eyes seeking the origin of the sound. A shaft of sunlight ignited her hair into brilliant flame, giving rise to memories that Hart was trying to bury. He watched as she gazed toward the thicket where he hid. For a moment, it seemed their eyes met. *She must possess a sixth sense equal to Tchula's*, he thought. If she hadn't seen him, she had felt his presence. When the sounds of their passing had ceased, he moved down to the road, emerging from the forest just as Tchula did.

"They gone now," Tchula advised.

"I thought for a minute Ms. Lord had seen me. She looked right at me," Hart replied.

Tchula allowed a rare smile to crease his face. "She not like your bird call, maybe."

Hart emitted a short laugh. "Probably not."

"She pretty ohoyo," Tchula continued. "She *pakahle*."

"I agree," Hart returned, moving Blister into the woods again. She did resemble a flower, with the sun lighting her hair.

Tchula had that matchmaker look on his face, Hart thought, as he moved northward through a thicket of beech. He'd made no secret of the fact he felt Hart would be better off with a good wife in tow. They'd had a heated discussion about that very thing just the other evening as they prepared to bed down near a small stream. Tchula began to talk of Achukma, his wife. She was, as her name designated, delightful. It was obvious he missed her and his boys. When it seemed he intended reminiscing into the wee hours, Hart had interrupted stiffly, insisting they needed sleep and that he had more important things on his mind. He now regretted his tone. But Tchula would not let well enough alone. He had been behaving like a mother hen of late. Hart knew he meant well. Choctaws were family people. Tchula simply could not accept the idea that Hart intended to remain a bachelor.

Matchmaking or not, Tchula had been doing his job. He'd found track the day before—seven ponies and three horses with shoes. The interesting thing was they seemed to be following the slight trail left by Hart and Blister, moving along at about the same speed.

"We circle back and find out who it is?" Tchula asked.

"Good idea. They could be bandits. Or they could be the gun-runners. They may have been sent to eliminate us."

"Maybe we get rid of them," Tchula returned, anxious to have it out with them.

"Let's circle back. Ride easy. When you find track, try to circle in behind them. We'll follow them," Hart suggested, as he and Tchula turned south again.

Several hours later, Hart crossed Tchula's track, which ran parallel to a stream flowing southwest. Tchula was moving northward again along the stream. There were signs of other horses moving into the stream a few yards up. Hart followed.

"Ishto Impa?" the voice spoke softly from a short distance in the brush across the stream.

Hart halted Blister. "I hear you."

"They move into stream, go north. Following group from Natchez now, not us," Tchula advised. "We go?"

"Yes," Hart replied immediately. "I hope we're in time."

*****

Dusk had fallen as Hart and Blister moved along through the quiet woods. Blister was picking his way quickly, Tchula following, when the shot rang out through the forest. Hart signaled for Tchula to stop. They sat their horses, waiting, anticipating another shot. When none came, they urged their horses onto the Trace and moved carefully.

"Too dark now to hunt. Could be ones following us. They catch Natchez group," Tchula commented.

"Right. Something must be wrong," Hart said, feeling the numbness of fear. It was a sensation he remembered well. Once acquired, it stuck like gumbo.

"You worry about group?" Tchula's question penetrated his numbness.

"Yes." He knew the deadly silence that often accompanied mayhem. "They can't be far ahead. The shot sounded close."

Within minutes, they had discovered what was left of a small campsite. They searched for members of the Natchez party. Hart's throat felt constricted as he moved carefully among the brush. He prayed he didn't find what he knew he must. Then he did. A body lay sprawled across a fallen tree, a prophetic hole in its chest. Tchula came up behind him just as he bent to examine the man. It was the new mail carrier.

"I feel a pulse. Let's see if we can bring him around," he urged, motioning for Tchula to help him lift the man. They positioned him carefully on the ground.

"Can you talk? Where are the others in your party?" Hart asked, his voice strained, fear clawing at his mind.

The mail carrier's eyelids flickered, then closed. He spoke in an uneven breath. "Many warriors, silent…white men. Ran! Sam told women to run. Don't know. Short red-haired man kept hollering for MacAlpin to come out and fight…"

"He's dead," Tchula said quietly, while deep in the western forest, the sound of a tin trumpet split the night.

"Chickasaws?" Hart whispered.

"Many," Tchula grunted.

"How many?"

Tchula got up and walked around the campsite, then spread his hands. "Seven braves, three horses with shoes."

Hart nodded as the sound of the trumpet rang through the night again, screaming victory for its possessor. What could the British be thinking? It wasn't enough that all normal trade had ceased to flow from the colonies for years. Now they were responsible for the massacre, or possible enslavement, of innocent travelers in this remote corner of the new country through the manipulation of the Indians by some hidden foreigner wearing a red coat and brass buttons. He had come to think their brains were made of brass. Once set, they didn't seem able to change the pattern of their thinking. Couldn't they see cooperation would net them much more than bloodshed? His father was right. This nation would go to war again. And he, for one, was beginning to think it a good idea.

If they were to find any of the party alive, they'd better move. Tchula signaled that he was looking for track. It would take him longer in the dark, but he would find it. Even in the shadowy entanglement of dense growth, he could find signs of man's passing. He was walking bent forward from the waist, leading his horse, scanning the ground before him.

Suddenly he motioned off toward an open space near the campsite. A buggy lay there, overturned, the horses gone. It was Lessie's. Hart rode forward and dismounted, his heart pounding. She wasn't there; neither was Nate. They must have been carried off, he thought, as he searched through the brush. It was a good sign. At least they must be alive.

Tchula bent to examine an indentation in the soft earth near the buggy, then rose and mounted his horse, starting off at a trot. Hart followed. The trail moved along a small stream across low country toward the west. After a few minutes, Tchula halted, glanced back at Hart, and motioned toward the underbrush.

Hart froze, letting his eyes search the thicket of vines and trees. Something had gone in there and recently. He prepared to move on, pointing westward, when a small sound reached his ears. Tchula heard it too.

Blister stood quietly as Hart slipped from the saddle, his dirk ready, the bola hanging loosely at his hip. Tchula began to circle round the thicket as Hart moved slowly toward the opening. Briars pulled at his sleeve as he lowered himself to the ground and looked inside.

"What in the name of—" he began, as a pair of eyes met his, eyes filled with horror until they saw him, then they began to fill with tears.

"Tchula," he called as he sprang forward, grasping the girl by her bleeding arms and pulling her from the confines of the vines. "Tchula," he demanded. "Come around here." When he had Lessie in his arms, he held her close, placing her head against his shoulder, murmuring words of comfort as she tried to tell him what had happened. "Hush," he said softly. "Hush, it's all right now. We're here. We'll help you."

"Oh, thank God!" she cried. "Thank God, you found me." Then as he was reassuring her, she pushed away from him and looked into his eyes. "We must hurry! We must. They've got Callie and Viola. I don't know where Nate is."

"What happened to Sam? And the braves?" Hart broke in.

"I don't know! I saw Sam strike down two of the Indians before he was struck on the head from behind," Lessie began. "After that, we were all running. The postmaster? Did you find him? Is he alive?"

"No. I'm sorry. We found him just before he died," Hart answered, his mind racing ahead. "Able Hand? What happened to him?"

"Mr. Hand? No, no, I didn't see," she began, then suddenly went limp in Hart's arms.

"Tchula, get a blanket and some of that brandy I carry," Hart directed, lowering himself to the ground and cradling Lessie's limp body in his arms.

When Tchula brought the desired items, Hart wrapped Lessie as tightly as he could in the blanket, and Tchula held a small cup of the brandy to her lips. She sipped it at first and then almost gulped the warm revitalizing spirit into her mouth.

"We must go. We must find them," Lessie whispered, her voice weak. She grasped Hart's hand, attempting to right herself.

"No, Lessie. You must get warm before we can continue our search. You're in shock. You won't be of any help if you collapse on us," Hart said, resisting her attempt to rise.

"I'll rest here for a minute or two," she said, sinking into the folds of the blanket.

Hart watched her breathing become stronger, then moved aside to speak with Tchula.

*****

Nate was cold. He was hungry. He was alone in the dark woods. He had run for a long, long time. He had run until he could not hear the screaming, the sounds of fear, or the eerie sound of the tin trumpet. The Indian had it. He had seen the painted face grin as its owner shot the mail carrier and took the trumpet. His skinny frame shook with the remembrance—shook with the remembrance too that Lessie was probably dead. Large tears rolled down his grimy cheeks, dropping silently between his feet.

Someone would come, he told himself. But he didn't think they'd be able to find him. He rubbed at his wet eyes, drying his cheeks with his hand. He sat perfectly still, exactly where he dropped until he dozed. Suddenly he awoke with a start. He knew what he must do. He must feed himself and find his way through the woods carefully until he came to civilization. He had learned that word from Lessie. She used it often in an attempt to teach him the difference between barbaric and civilized behavior. He thought he understood now.

It was dark here in the forest, but a faint light cast streaks among the trees, like reaching fingers. He noticed a particularly large tree with spreading lower branches near where he sat. He moved to it and climbed into the crotch made where three giant boughs separated. He made himself as comfortable as possible. His fatigued young body slowly relaxed as the weight of exhaustion closed his eyes.

*****

Hart looked down at Lessie, where she sat wrapped in the cocoon of his blanket, her eyes closed. They had to move, to keep searching for other survivors, but he hated to subject her to the horrors of what they might find.

"I'm not asleep," she said, opening her eyes. "Is it time to go?"

"Yes. You'll have to ride double with me," he answered, offering his hand to assist her to her feet. "The trail splits here. It looks like they separated."

She took his hand and was soon aboard Blister, sitting sideways in front of Hart. Tchula took the lead as they moved off, carefully following the telltale signs of recent flight.

They had been carefully picking their way through the night for what seemed hours when Tchula grunted and held up his hand. They stopped.

A large animal was moving across their path. Moonlight glittered off its black coat as it plodded slowly into a thicket of cane off to their right. Lessie sighed as it disappeared into the dark. She had been holding her breath.

"It's all right. Bears don't see well, and we're down wind of him. He didn't know we were here," Hart explained, nudging Blister forward as Tchula moved off again.

Lessie offered no reply, simply turned her head in the direction they were traveling. She was most uncomfortable, but it couldn't be helped. She was sitting with her left leg wrapped around a high saddle horn and her right one dangling. She held on to the horn through the folds of her riding skirt with both hands. It was the only way she could maintain her balance. The saddle was a Moorish one, wide and soft. She hoped Hart was seated better. The saddle held them both with no room to spare.

"Uncomfortable?" Hart asked.

"A little."

"We'll rest as soon as it's light," Hart explained. "Are you feeling better?"

"Some," Lessie answered, turning to face him. Their eyes met momentarily before Hart prompted Blister to pick up speed. Even in the darkness, Lessie could see the honesty that now lay in Hart's. He was not, for the moment, avoiding her.

"I'm sorry this happened. I feel—" Hart began.

"Don't blame yourself. You warned me. If it's anyone's fault, it's mine," she said, her eyes steady.

After a moment, Hart continued. "Did you recognize either of the white men with the ambushers?"

"No. No, I didn't. I really only saw one of them. He kept calling for you to show yourself. He was...not very tall...and was red haired, I believe," Lessie answered, allowing her mind to recall the horror.

"I've seen a man like that. The night Nate was lost in the woods. That ties him and the man in black to the gunrunners. They must have been sent after Tchula and me," Hart stated.

"Gunrunners?" Lessie questioned.

"Yes. We feel they're behind the pillaging going on in the territory."

"I'd heard something about the killing. John discussed it with me, hoping to change my mind about traveling the Trace. I should have listened to him and you," she whispered, her thoughts for Nate.

"You felt you had to go to your grandmother. John and I understood that," Hart replied, then added, "We'll find them."

Lessie could only nod her head in acceptance. She turned her face forward again and tried not to think of Nate.

*****

Just as a pale wash of sunlight filtered the gloom of daybreak, a horse whinnied directly ahead of Tchula. He pulled up abruptly. It was standing in a small clearing, wet lather foaming over its body. Lessie recognized it at the same moment Hart did.

"That's one of the Wellsley's," they said in unison.

Hart dismounted, groping his way through the cane along the narrow path that they were traveling until he came to it. It stood perfectly still but turned its head in welcome.

"Hold on. We'll get you out of this cane," he said, allowing the low pitch of his voice to soothe the animal as he pulled the restraining vines from it.

"Was someone riding it?" Lessie called.

"No. The horse has run a long way. She's dragging her traces," Hart returned. He knew Lessie was thinking of Nate, that possibly Nate had been riding her. No sense letting her think Nate would be found this easy. He might never be. But Hart intended to try. He never should have let them travel the Trace.

Nate had been on foot, Lessie remembered. He'd wondered off from camp, and Sam had gone into the woods to look for him. Nate had been told repeatedly to stay within the camp. He had disobeyed and caused Sam to go after him. She couldn't tell Hart that, not when she might never see Nate again.

Hart took a bit of dry grass and began to rub down the horse, speaking softly to it all the while. They needed this animal. Perhaps an hour or so of feeding on some grass and a bit of water would fix it up.

"Tchula, let's move on through this cane. Ms. Lord should stay aboard Blister until this horse has time to rest. We'll stop as soon as we're out of here," Hart directed.

Tchula moved off again; Lessie and Hart rode after him, leading the tired horse. They soon came to a small stream. Crossing it, they stopped to rest, just as the sun made its proper appearance, pale though it was.

*****

Viola cowered behind Callie when the painted Indian loomed over them. He grabbed Callie's arm and pulled her to her feet, examining her hair and clothes. She slapped at his hands, pushing away from his grasp. He seemed to find her attempt to free herself amusing. He pushed her down next to Viola again.

"What will they do with us?" Viola's voice penetrated Callie's anger.

"How should I know?" Callie answered, her voice trembling with rage.

"I'm so scared, Callie. I don't think I can stand it."

"Of course, you will. Don't be a ninny, Vi. We'll get out of this somehow. There are white men here. Surely, they won't let these... these savages have us," Callie continued.

"Look at the colonel!" Viola whispered, pointing toward the campfire around which most of the Indians were now crouching. "What is he saying to them?"

"Heaven only knows," Callie answered. The colonel held some power with the Indians. She could see that. And the red-haired man hung on his every word.

"Callie, I'm so hungry and thirsty. Do you think they'll give us anything to eat?"

"Heaven only knows," Callie returned again. She was hungry too. She could smell food cooking on the spit over the fire.

*****

"When this meat is done, see to it those women are fed. And give them some water," the colonel issued the order, hoping his small role in claiming the territory for England would empower him to control these heathens. "I don't want them hurt. Do you understand?"

The tall, muscular chief nodded his head in agreement but watched the colonel's eyes carefully. He recognized uncertainty there. This Englishman was working with the British but lacked the strength needed to deal with the captured colonials properly.

"You do understand, don't you, Chief?" the colonel asked, watching the chief's eyes blaze.

"I do," the chief said. He had learned a few words of English, enough so he could make out most of what was said to him—or in front of him. He intended learning more. He didn't trust whites, not even these British ones.

"You may keep the horses and all the bounty you found back there, but the women are to be set free. We do not make war on women or children. Do you understand?"

Again the chief nodded in agreement. But he didn't like it. He had use for these women, especially the little red-haired one.

"Good. We want the colonials out of this territory. But we do not want the women and children harmed," the colonel insisted, wanting to make certain the tight-lipped fanatic before him really understood their mission.

"You, maybe. Not others," the chief replied in hesitant English.

"What do you mean? Which other?"

"Leader. Man in black. He say kill all. Take all. All belong to us," the chief returned, a sly gleam in his dark eyes. This white man was no leader. He would get rid of him later. He trusted the man from Natchez who wore black. He knew how to make war.

"That man and these other men are simply servants," the colonel replied, using the word *servant* deliberately. Indians knew what servants were. They had always kept slaves themselves.

The chief stared at him before turning and walking away, his back ramrod straight, his mind made up. He would get rid of this white man.

The colonel watched the chief walk away. He had an enemy there, he realized. He'd have to be careful, at least until they reached Chickasaw Bluffs, where he'd have the security of a few soldiers.

He walked over to the two girls sitting on the ground near the tethered horses. "Are you all right?"

"What do you care, you turncoat!" Viola hissed, attempting to rise. "I saw you talking with that chief. You're in on this horrible thing."

The colonel put his finger to his lips, signaling for her to be quiet. Then he sat near them, offering them water from his bag. "I'm doing all I can to get you released. You must not cause any trouble. They may abide by my orders. But you can never be certain," he said, handing the water bag to each of them in turn.

"Drink it, Vi," Callie instructed. "You may not get more for a while."

After they had drunk their fill, Callie turned to the colonel. "Colonel—if I might truly call you that—what do we do now?"

"You may call me colonel. I served in the British army before the revolution. I am loyal to the crown and volunteered to help claim this territory for England. You also are English, even though you try to forget it."

"Actually, we are descended from Scots, not English. Oh, there may be one or two mixed in somewhere. But Scots we were. We are now Americans. We do not swear allegiance to the British Crown," Viola stated vehemently.

"You will, eventually, if you survive this ordeal. We'll soon take the entire territory. You will swear allegiance or be shipped out as slaves," he replied, his words certain, his eyes serious.

"You and your friends may find taking this territory harder than you think," Callie suggested, an even tone to her voice. She knew how to talk to a fanatic. She had dealt with Viola for years. "You keep saying 'we,' Colonel. Are there local people involved in this *venture?*"

"Ah, Ms. Warren, you are the one, aren't you? Yes, there are more of us. No, I will not tell you who." He laughed.

"I bet we'd know most of them," Viola hissed.

"I'm not at liberty to say, you understand. I would relish telling you who the principals are just to see your response," he thrust.

"Callie, do you think they're our friends?" Viola asked, horrified.

"Heaven only knows," Callie answered, her mind moving along to the possibility of their escape.

"Callie, if you don't stop answering me that way, I swear I'll scream," Viola almost shouted, her temper up again.

"Shush, Vi. What way? What do you mean?" Callie asked, her mind now on Viola.

"That heaven only knows answer of yours, Callie. I'm so tired of hearing it," Viola cried, sinking farther onto the grass. She was tired, more tired than she could ever remember. She had been forced to run all night. She wanted to sleep. But she was so hungry.

"That's all beside the point right now," the colonel said, rising. "You just stay quiet, and you may live to return to your homes."

*****

Sam had been cussing himself for miles. He had taken responsibility for the raid on his own shoulders. He'd been hired to take care of the young Lords, and yet he'd let this happen. That boy, Nate, would have some answering to do, too, if he was still alive. If he hadn't kept wondering off, Sam would have been aware of the approach of the raiding party.

As it was, he'd been sent chasing after the boy by his sister just as the ambushers broke from cover and charged the party. He felt his head. The swelling was getting bigger, the pain worse, with each jolt of his horse. Sam spoke to the elder of the braves in Choctaw. "How long?"

"Not long. Can smell smoke from campfire," the brave returned.

"We don't want to be seen or heard. You and Standing Oak move off in that direction. When I fire my gun, start firing yours. Don't miss," he instructed, moving his horse in a northerly direction.

He could smell the smoke now. He prayed he'd find the women and boy there and be able to reclaim them. He had been praying all the way; praying, and cussing his own stupidity.

*****

With daylight, Able moved. He'd been hiding in a deep ravine about a mile south of where the attack had taken place. His horse was fresh, having rested during the long hours of the night. Able tried not to think of the attack. He wasn't expecting it. He knew that Smythe and others were selling out the territory to the British, but he'd never expected to be caught in the middle of the actual fighting. He'd planned to be on the winning side. It didn't much matter which side that was.

As it happened, he'd been looking for a spot of grass for Joe, a little way from the others in the party, when the attack started. The firing of the gun had alerted him. But he didn't ride back to see what was taking place. Instead, he moved farther away to the south, into this ravine, and lay quiet, waiting. After the ear piercing blasts of the trumpet died away into the night, all was silent. He knew what that meant.

"I'll have to check," he said, out loud. There would be questions. People would ask how he happened to survive. The militia would ask the same. He'd need to do some serious thinking before he moved on to the Stand. Maybe he'd just go back to Natchez. He could say he felt ill and decided to return home. But even as he was attempting to convince himself to turn south, he headed Joe northward toward last night's campsite. He just couldn't bring himself to ride off without checking to see if anyone was left alive. He just couldn't do it.

What he found were the tracks of two men, one in moccasins, the other in boots, and a newly filled grave. He had no way of knowing who lay buried or who the two men where. Who could they be? Probably not members of the raiding party. They wouldn't stop to bury anyone. Then who?

He turned Joe northward for a mile or two, checking sign. What he found surprised him. The boy must have escaped capture. His footprints led off up the Trace. The soft sand was firm around the edges. It had not had time to dry. From the looks of it, the boy was alone. Following and looking after the boy would ease his conscience some, he figured, and give him an out with the authorities.

"Get up, Joe. We've a boy to catch," he said.

CHAPTER 8

During the night, Nate dreamed heavily. In his dreams Hart was telling him to think, Lessie was telling him to be careful, Sam was running after him through the brush, waving a stalk of yellow flowers. He awoke with a start, the hunger pangs in his stomach sounding their alarm. Artichokes! That's what Sam called the yellow flowers. He could eat the roots. The Indians ate them. There'd been lots of them along the Trace.

Now that he was awake and thinking, he remembered another yellow flower that Sam had pointed out. It held a much larger bloom. You didn't eat the roots of that one; you ate the seeds that hung loosely from the drying flower heads. A sunflower, Sam had said.

He walked away from the rising sun. He'd been walking away from the setting sun yesterday when he entered the forest. He supposed he should walk away from the rising sun now if he wanted to return to the Trace.

He tried to look for the approaching comet. In the daylight, it was just a brilliant blur in the faded sky. The light hurt his eyes. He hoped the comet wouldn't fall while he was alone in the woods.

He squinted toward the sun. He was still walking in the right direction, he figured. All of a sudden, he stepped around a clump of brush and tumbled headlong onto the Trace. The rough road was a narrow strip between high banks, made so by the heavy wagons and teams that traveled over it, or so Sam had said. Nate was glad to find it. It led somewhere definite.

"There they are," he sang out. He raced across the road and up the other bank to a thicket of yellow flowering artichokes, their blooms almost spent, their leaves drying in the autumn air.

It was their roots he wanted. With a pen knife his cousin John had given him, he dug at the roots of a particularly large one. Finally, he had it out of the ground. He stood up, holding the ugly, scaly-looking thing in his hand. He couldn't eat this dirty thing. Then he remembered. Sam had said to wash them or peel them some before eating.

He sat on the bank of the road and started peeling the largest of the roots with the penknife he carried with him, trying to decide which direction he should take as he peeled. Again, he checked the sun, just as Sam had taught him to do. He turned his right cheek to the warmth and started in what he hoped was the direction of the Stand.

He had to eat. And he had to have food to take with him. He took a tentative bite of the raw artichoke, chewing it slowly. It did have a sweet taste to it. But he would need many more. His shoulders sagged visibly as he turned back toward the artichokes and began to dig again. He'd dig up as many as he could carry. Then when he found water, he'd wash them all.

"I'll make out," he promised himself out loud, to the accompaniment of a crow's raucous call. But it took every ounce of will he possessed to continue digging at the artichokes. Finally, when he had nine or ten of them tied to a length of loose string he had found in his pocket, he took his stick and started up the trail. As he walked, he began to whistle. The sound he made was weak at first, almost a whimper. But the more he tried, the better he felt. Whistling as loudly as the crow had called, he moved off up the Trace.

The empty condition of his stomach finally brought him to a stop. He couldn't go any farther. Lessie had made him wear a jacket and short trousers for the trip. He peeled off his jacket and removed his white muslin shirt. He began to wipe at the now dried dirt clinging to the largest root with one sleeve of his shirt. When he'd removed most of the loose dirt, he removed a thin layer of the skin, not cutting as much of the root away this time.

"Not bad." He grunted between bites of the root. "Not bad at all," he said again. *If I could wash them,* he thought, *they'd be all right.* His father had always told Lessie that a little dirt never hurt a boy much. He'd soon know. He spat out the stringy parts. But he finished the largest root before he stopped. His stomach felt better. Strength was returning to his limbs. His headache was getting easier too. He could move on now.

The day wore on uneventfully for Nate. He was very tired by the time the sun was at three o'clock. He was thirsty, and he was hungry again. He moved to the side of the Trace.

Just as he was sitting down on the fallen trunk of a small tree, he heard the wild cry of a panther. It startled him so he dropped the roots and his jacket. The cry of the wilderness cat was one he knew well. One had stalked their party all the way from Mobile to Natchez. He had been told at the time that the cat was after one of the oxen or horses. The party had managed to evade his stealthy attacks, but they had not managed to kill him. Nate would always remember that sound.

He swung around wildly, seeking movement with his eyes, his senses. Where was the cat? The sound had been very near. Suddenly there was the surreptitious snap of a twig just behind the log where Nate had been sitting. Panic gave wings to his feet. He was off and running, leaving his food behind, each thought that of survival. Running was not good, he knew. But he had to reach some point of safety. He crossed the Trace and dashed up a small ravine. As he ran, he realized he was splashing through water. Here was water. But he couldn't stop to drink.

At the point of exhaustion, he saw through sweat-filled lashes a small cave just above him. He climbed the short distance, slipping and sliding until he reached the entrance. It was only a few feet wide, hardly room enough for him to wedge into. When he crawled inside and turned to face outward, he saw the cat. It was trailing him along the water-filled stream below. Panting and with icy fear griping him, Nate pulled the pen knife from his pocket and faced approaching death.

The sleek coat of the big cat gleamed as it moved stealthily across the stream, its eyes now pinned upon the cave where Nate hid. It crouched momentarily, eyes never wavering from their intended prey. Then it sprang, moving at a flash up the slope of the bank until its face was just outside the cave opening.

Nate's heart was pounding so heavily he could hardly breathe; his right hand clenched the small knife. The cat emitted a low growl, causing him to push farther back into the cave. His body was bent almost double, his legs hurt from their cramped position.

He heard himself praying. "God, please help me. There ain't nobody else."

The cat began to paw at the opening to the cave, its claws catching at Nate's shoe, almost dragging him out. He squirmed backward, kicking at the cat as he swung at its face with his pen knife. The cat cried, enraged by the sharp sting of the knife just below its nose. Nate felt his senses fading; he couldn't see well. He heard the sound of a gun. The cat jumped, then fell backward.

"Here now, young fellow, are you all right?" Able Hand shoved the dead cat aside and pulled the limp boy from his hole.

Nate opened one eye, afraid of what he might see. Then he opened the other. "Mr. Hand! Am I glad to see you!"

"I can see that," Able returned, assisting Nate to his feet. "You were putting up a good fight when I showed up."

"Yessir. That cat would have been too much for me. But I was fighting it off," Nate added, braver now that Able Hand was present and the great cat was dead.

"That you were, boy," Able agreed. "But what was that you cried out, just as I arrived on the scene? Something about nobody else?"

"Oh, you mean the prayer. I asked God to help me 'cause there was nobody else," he answered. "And he did! He did," Nate finished, amazed. "He really did."

"Well, he did...with a little assistance from me," Able added, grinning now at the astounded expression on the boy's face. "I'm told he often uses others to do his work."

"Where'd you come from?" Nate asked, adjusting his shoes and brushing dirt from his shoulders.

"I've been trailing you all afternoon. When the Indians attacked, I slipped into a ravine. When I thought everything was over, I decided to come back and see if I could help. I'm not much in a fight, you understand?"

"You find anybody alive?" Nate asked.

"No, son, I didn't. I found one grave. Someone else had been there and buried at least one body. Then I started up the Trace toward the Stand. It's the closest habitation, you know."

"I thought so too. But I wonder who buried the body and who was it they buried," Nate continued, his face long, worrying that it may have been his sister.

"Now, boy, don't make pain for yourself. Indians usually carry off women, make slaves of them. Your sister is probably still alive," Able argued, his hand on the boy's shoulder. "Our work right now is to keep us both alive and get to the Stand."

"Yessir," Nate said. "Thanks for saving me back there."

"Don't mention it, boy. Don't mention it," Able replied, starting back down the stream toward the Trace. "Here, boy, fill up this pouch with water. We'll need it later in the day. And here, take your jacket and these roots. I found them where you dropped them. We'll need them too."

"Yessir," Nate replied, lying down on the bank to drink his fill of the clear liquid before filling the pouch.

*****

Sam had left his horse a quarter mile back and approached the camp on foot, stealthily moving through the drying leaves and twigs. He was now in position. He waited. It would take Tchula's braves a few minutes longer to reach the other side of the camp.

He squatted on his heels, his body covered by the spreading branches of a wide sycamore. He'd wait until they had time to get where they wanted to be. When it was time, he moved downward off the slight rise where he'd waited until he was within fifty feet or so of the tethered horses. There was one of the chestnuts that had pulled the Lord buggy and the dun that had belonged to the mail carrier. The matched blacks that had pulled the other buggy were tied nearby.

Hand, Albright, and the boy must have gotten away, he thought. Then he recognized the colonel's horse. It was tethered beside the blanket topped Indian ponies. Carefully, he covered the camp with his eyes, seeking both victims and captors. He wanted a fix on where everyone was before he started what he hoped would be a rescue and, to some extent, retribution.

He raised his gun and fired one shot. A warrior dropped where he stood. Reloading quickly, he could hear the guns of Tchula's braves coming from two different spots on the adjacent hill. Two more dropped in midstride. The camp exploded into action.

Sam had seen the girls sitting near the tethered horses. He moved quickly, cut their bindings, and assisted each of them aboard a horse. "Where're the others?" he yelled, slapping the horses' rumps.

"We're the only ones!" Callie shouted, her horse plunging up the incline toward the cover of forest.

"Where's the boy? Ms. Lessie?" Sam Shouted after her.

She pulled the horse to a stop, turning in the saddle. "I don't know. The colonel is here. He's one of them," she cried, kicking her horse into movement, as an arrow shot past her head.

The camp had regained some kind of control. The chief was shouting orders. Braves were moving to their weapons, firing both newly acquired rifles and arrows at Sam. Tchula's braves had not exposed themselves but continued to fire into the camp. They were hitting their targets with a regularity that pleased Sam. He turned and fired as one shell barely missed his shoulder. The Indian who fired at him dropped. Then Sam was off at a run up the incline toward his own horse. When he reached the top of the hill, Callie was there, holding his horse's reins.

"My gratitude, miss," he grunted, bounding into the saddle. "Get moving."

Viola was sitting her horse, waiting near where Sam had originally left his, hidden far back in the brush.

"Vi, come on!" Callie called as she and Sam neared the spot. The three of them rode hard for as long as their horses could take the strain.

"Let's hold up a bit," Sam ordered, moving alongside Viola and grasping her reins. She was almost out of her saddle, leaning sideways with a death grip on her horse's mane.

"Quiet, miss," Sam ordered, patting her horse on the neck. "Shhhh," he crooned. "Easy, girl. We'll rest a while."

"We can't rest!" Viola cried. "We can't rest. We've got to get back to Natchez. We'll all be killed."

"Vi!" Callie corrected in her sternest voice. "Hush up! We're in Mr. Shute's hands. He knows best."

Her wet cheeks shinning with a new wash of tears, Viola whimpered. "He let us get captured in the first place."

"Viola, hush, I said," Callie repeated, getting down off her own horse and moving to Viola's. "Get off that horse and straighten yourself." Her near presence and the tone she used convinced Viola to follow instruction. Viola climbed down and stood holding the reins, remnants of sobs shaking her sparse frame.

Sam squatted on his heels, thinking. Tchula's braves should be catching up to them soon. They'd wait here. It didn't take long. Within minutes, sounds of approach were heard. It would be Chulhkan and Standing Oak. The rampaging Chickasaws would not have allowed him to hear their approach. Sam called to them in their language.

"We're here," they replied, emerging from the forest together.

"Good," Sam said, grinning at the two of them. "You made quite a war party. Now let's get these women to the Stand."

Callie urged Viola aboard her horse, then mounted her own. "But, Callie, should we go with them?" Viola asked, near tears again.

"Of course. They're the two braves Hart's friend Tchula sent along with us. We're safe with them," Callie insisted, mounting her own horse.

"Come on," Sam urged, taking the lead with the women falling in behind. "We'll reach the Stand before dark if we hurry."

Standing Oak and Chulhkan brought up the rear. Chulhkan pointed toward Viola and raised his brows, questioning the sanity of the strange white female. Standing Oak grinned, pointed to his head, and spun small circles in the air with his finger.

"Maledict," he pronounced. They both laughed as the group moved off toward the Stand.

- - -

The colonel crouched where he had hidden until all sounds of gunfire and pursuit had ceased. He had gotten himself mixed up in something vastly different from what he had in mind when he joined British efforts to take the Mississippi Territory for England, thereby connecting it with Canada.

The cause was a good one. The English had settled this continent and had a right to keep it for the crown. Natchez and the Trace would be better off with a well-trained British regiment to protect it. He had lain awake nights thinking of the money to be had from sending trade goods straight up the Trace without danger of robbery. The profits would be enormous. But his personal attempt to gain rank through service was beginning to fall apart. Not only was he afraid of being found out by the colonials, but this Indian chief, Bent Arrow, had turned on him. He was now caught between opposing forces. His outlook was bleak.

Eventually he moved from cover and found his horse. There were one or two others grazing nearby, previously owned by the now dead or dying Indians which had been shot from ambush. Whoever led the raid knew about Indian fighting. They had reclaimed the women and made good their escape.

Smythe had done his job of arming the allied Indians well but had failed to enlist the more independent Choctaws. No amount of reward seemed to interest them. Pushmataha was a wise bird, Albright thought, as he led his horse away from the others before mounting, so he would remain neutral. That way, he and his Choctaws would be no man's enemy.

"That should tell you something," he said out loud. "If Pushmataha refuses to cooperate and the militia at Nashville get wise to our actions, we've lost."

The colonel turned his horse northwest along a trail that led from their campsite toward Chickasaw Bluffs, where he would find allies.

*****

Hart rolled over, peeling back the top of his bedroll. Something had stirred his senses, causing him to wake. He straightened his canvass shirt, placed his bonnet on his head, and walked toward the small fire burning near the stream.

"Coffee?" Lessie asked, offering him a cup of the steaming brew.

"Yes," he replied, accepting the drink, holding the cup in both hands, enjoying the warmth. He had slept cold for most of the morning. "Have you any idea what day it is?" He finished the coffee and handed the cup back to her.

"The fourteenth, I think," Lessie said, pouring more coffee. "We've got pancakes and syrup."

"I don't remember when we ate last," he said, taking a plate of syrup-covered pones. They were warm, sweetened with molasses and quite good. "Have you eaten?"

"Yes. I ate one of the first ones. Tchula has had several," she replied, offering him more coffee from the small tin pot.

Hart watched her as he chewed. The sweet cakes and coffee holding his attention. "You've cooked on a campfire before," he noted, observing her smooth operations.

"My father used to take me along on short hunting trips. He owned a gun shop, you know. He would try out his newer inventions. If they worked well in the wild, he would make some for sale. He taught me many things."

"Such as?" Hart asked, intrigued.

"Oh, how to build a good fire. How to hunt and shoot well," she replied, her attention on the frying pan.

His interest was aroused. He didn't know any gentlewomen who could handle a weapon of any kind. There'd been some in Scotland and England who enjoyed a certain amount of hunting, but he'd never heard of any here at home. "You mean you can use a rifle?"

"Yes. Quite well, in fact," she answered, glancing at him to see how he would receive such news. Most of the young men she had known in Mobile considered it unladylike.

"I think that is the most intelligent thing I have ever heard a territory woman say. Natchez and Mobile may be growing, civilized towns, but they are bordered by some of the worst wilderness I have ever seen. A woman should be able to protect herself and others if it should come to that."

Hart's attention had been totally captured by her statement, his food forgotten for the moment. He considered her slender, almost frail frame, her graceful hands. Yet they were strong. They would do her bidding well. At that moment, his heart enveloped her completely. He wanted this woman in his life, for as long as Providence would allow, and nothing short of death was going to remove her from it.

He was about to speak when she glanced up at him, worry creasing her smooth brow, darkening her eyes. He knew the loss of Nate was uppermost in her mind.

"Don't worry so. We'll find him. He's a tough, intelligent boy," he said, rising and pulling her to her feet. "He's out there somewhere, making his way back to civilization."

At his words, Lessie released the tears she had been holding back. They were tears of sorrow for her lost companions, for the girls, for the possible death of the men who had traveled with her, but most of all, for her young brother, who had never had a proper chance at life. Great sobs whacked her slender frame as Hart's arms held her tightly, his words soothing, his lips kissing her forehead, her eyes, and moving, as her sobs ceased, to her mouth. Their embrace lasted for what seemed minutes.

"All right now?" Hart asked finally, still holding her head against his chest, his arms clasping her tightly.

"Better. I'm much better," she replied softly, raising her eyes to look directly into his. "Is this real?"

"I'd say so, my sweet pakahle. It's real, and it's going to last. You'll never escape me," he continued, kissing her forehead once again.

A hint of mischief came into Lessie's eyes. "Are you certain? You play hot and cold, Mr. MacAlpin."

"Guilty as charged," he replied. "I had decided to remain a bachelor for several reasons. But from the moment we met, my resolve weakened. I tried to put you out of my mind—and my heart. But it didn't work." Hart smiled at her, yet his eyes were serious. "When I was with you, I wanted you. When I was away from you, I couldn't stop thinking about you. I worried about you," he explained, caressing her cheek with his. "If that isn't real love, I don't know what is."

"It'll do," Lessie said, rising on her toes to kiss him on the mouth. "I just wanted to be sure you had finally made up your mind."

"And you? How do you feel?"

"I love you. I've known that for some time. But I have a responsibility to Nate, to his education," Lessie stated. "He must come first. And I've known the struggle you've been going through since we met on the road to your house," Lessie began but was stopped in midsentence by the pressure of Hart's lips.

"I'm not running now or ever again," Hart said when he could pull himself away from her. "And of course, Nate will come first. I wouldn't have it any other way. We'll plan for his education together."

A twig snapped. Hart thrust Lessie away and turned, his dirk in his hand. Then he relaxed, smiling. "It's all right. Tchula is playing one of his tricks.

"Come on out. I know you're there," Hart spoke, his voice raised.

"I not want interrupt," Tchula said, emerging from the trees just behind them and walking forward, his face solemn. He walked over to the fire and poured himself a cup of coffee. When he was safely squatting before the fire, his back to them, he allowed himself to smile.

Lessie and Hart looked at each other. Both of them expected some outward display of joy from Tchula. But there he sat, drinking his coffee, with his back to them as though nothing unusual had occurred. Hart shrugged, took Lessie's hand, kissed her gently on the lips, then moved forward.

"Find anything?" he asked, crouching beside his friend.

"No tracks west of stream. Found some moving to the east just upstream," Tchula answered.

"Let's pack up and move," Hart ordered, motioning to Lessie. "You'll ride the spare horse this time."

They rode for hours, sloshing through streams, climbing up steep inclines, and pushing their way through barricades of dense thickets.

Finally, Tchula held up his hand. "Just ahead, off to right. Smell old smoke," he whispered.

"I'll scout it out," Hart said, preparing to dismount.

"I go," Tchula insisted, moving off silently.

Hart and Lessie remained on their horses. It was somewhere near three in the afternoon. The sky was a dreary expanse of washed-out blue, the sun barely warm.

Hart considered Lessie. She was probably in need of rest. "Want to get down for a while?"

"Not unless you think it's all right," she replied, anxiety plainly visible on her face. "How soon will we know? About the captives, I mean," she added.

"Soon now. Tchula won't be long."

They waited. Lessie was sitting as quietly as she could endure. Her mind jumped between the prospect of finding Nate well and the awful doubt that she would. She would look at Hart occasionally, wondering what he was thinking. He seemed far away, his thoughts holding him.

Suddenly, he spoke. "He's coming back. Sit still until we know what he's found."

"Yes," she replied. Her mind agreed, but her heart wanted to race through the woods and see for herself.

"They all gone!" Tchula gasped when he emerged from the dense covering of the forest. "Big battle."

"Signs of captives?" Hart asked.

"Women were there, some horses with shoes. No sign of small boy," Tchula stated, his eyes on Lessie.

"Are you certain?" Lessie asked. She was not willing to accept this. Nate had to have been with the girls. She couldn't accept anything else.

"No boy. I'm certain," Tchula affirmed. "One man who travel from Natchez there. Heavy man on big horse. He go north alone after battle."

139

"What happened to the women?" Hart queried, knowing who the heavy man on the big horse had to be.

"Looks like Shute's footprints near where women were sitting. Looks like Shute took them," Tchula explained, his attitude proud. "He good woodsman."

"That's good news, anyway, Lessie. If Sam has the girls, he may have Nate. He would have been tracking them, he and Tchula's two braves," Hart replied.

"Chulhkan and Standing Oak there. They attack camp from different spots. Big fight. Horses ride off through woods. Shute with women," Tchula confirmed.

"Which direction?" Hart was determined to find them before dark.

"Toward the Stand, on Trace. We move after them?"

"Yes. Get mounted, and we'll move off," Hart said. "Here, Lessie, drink some water. We won't stop before we find them, or it gets too dark to travel."

They each drank from the leather pouch, then spurred their horses on, each thinking their own thoughts, riding single file as Tchula's eyes followed sign.

*****

It was near dark when Able sighted the Stand. He spurred his horse on. "There it is, boy. We've made it."

Nate strained his eyes to see ahead. "I don't see anything. How far is it?"

"Two miles, I'd say, just through these trees and over that far ridge," Able answered.

"You come this way often, Able?" Nate asked, still not seeing anything except dense forest.

"A few times. I don't say as I like traveling much. But it has its rewards from time to time," he replied, shifting his weight in the saddle.

"How?" Nate questioned again.

"That's for me to know, boy," Able said.

They rode on into the hazy afternoon. It was growing dark as they sighted the Stand. Nate's fatigue lessened when he saw the many pole and thatch huts, the brightly dressed Choctaws, the seemingly endless numbers of children, Indian and colonial, playing games or standing and watching the new arrivals. They passed an Indian guard who sat stonily on the ground as Able's horse walked into camp.

"There's lots of Indians here," Nate commented.

"That's right. This is one of their oldest villages and one of their winter camp grounds. They spend all winter here, hunting. There's good hunting for bear, dear, beaver, duck, goose, and good fishing, too," Able said. "But more important, they're friendly."

Nate was entranced with the spectacle before him. Some of the men were sitting cross-legged before small fires, carving on bows. Others were standing with weapons in their hands talking in their language. The women were coming and going from a small stream, carrying clay jars of water. A few children were splashing about in the stream.

Able spied a white man sitting with a chief near a small fire. "Come on, Nate. Get down off Joe, and we'll introduce ourselves to the Factor. I knew him from before he left Natchez."

After introductions were made, the two were fed a meal of wilderness stew, followed by small gourds of honey. When they had finished, they were shown into a large thatched hut where, they were told, the bachelor men slept.

Nate was very tired. He crawled into the blanket offered him and lay down immediately. But just as he was preparing to close his eyes, thankful that he was safe and among friends, he remembered Lessie, and tears slipped down his cheeks. He brushed them aside and pulled the blanket higher around his neck.

Before he slept, he heard a commotion somewhere on the compound. He sat up, wondering if the village was under attack. He moved to the door of the hut and peeked through. What he saw brought him headlong through the door and across the distance to the new arrivals.

"Lessie, Lessie! You're here. You're safe," he cried, joy lifting his voice.

"Oh, Nate! Thank God! Oh, thank God!" Lessie cried in return, as Hart helped her from her horse. She gathered Nate into her arms. "Where have you been?" she asked, still hugging him to her. "I've been so worried."

"I've been worried too, Lessie. You're the only sister I have. I thought the Indians had killed you," he replied, his eyes bright with unshed tears.

"I am so sorry, Nate. It's all my fault. I should have written to our grandmother and told her we simply could not make such a hazardous journey," Lessie said, realizing the fright Nate had suffered due to her desire to honor their father's wishes.

"It's all right, Lessie. We're halfway there, now. Have I got a lot to tell you," he added, his eyes bright now with anticipation.

"Later, dear, after we've settled our horses. You can tell me everything."

"Sure," he agreed, turning his attention to Tchula and Hart. "Did you find my sister?"

Hart turned from loosening the girth on Blister to look into the boy's face. "Yes, we did. How did you get here?"

"Able found me. We just got here ourselves," he added.

Hart saw Able Hand approaching from across the compound. He was glad to see the man alive and well. Three of the ambushed party were now in safe hands. Sam now had, according to all evidence, Viola and Callie in his custody.

"I'm glad to see you well, Able," Hart said, extending his hand.

"Likewise," Able returned, shaking hands with him. "We need to talk after I get Ms. Lord and her brother settled for the night," Hart stated.

"That's fine by me," Able agreed.

Hart handed Tchula the reins to their horses, then walked where Nate had joined Lessie. "Nate, have they fed you yet?"

"Yessir," Nate answered. "I ate good. Com'on, you and Lessie can have some too."

"That good, was it?" Hart laughed, feeling less guilty now that he had them safe at the Stand. "The Stand is known for its hospitality. So let's go and get some of that good food," he continued, taking

Lessie's arm and walking with them toward a large cook pot that was emitting steam.

"Hart, why is this place called the Stand?" Nate asked. He couldn't see anything standing except people and trees.

"It's called the Stand, Nate, because the Choctaw name for this particular village is Chahta Ahaya Moma, which means many 'Choctaw standing or present.' You understand?" Hart finished.

"Sure. That's great. Many Choctaw standing. What a name for a place. I like it," Nate sang, all evidence of fatigue or fear gone. He had Lessie back. And Hart had brought her. He was happy to turn his attention to the excitement of traveling over the Trace and his encounters with its inhabitants.

Lessie was feeling better. The three of them were together. She was thankful. "Is it all right to take the food without asking?" she whispered as Hart sought small gourds for each of them to fill with the hot stew.

"Yes. It isn't considered polite to be standoffish. Visitors here bring food stuffs and share it with the local villagers and are expected to help themselves to whatever is available to eat. We've arrived at a good time. Hunting must have been good. This looks like venison, rabbit, and possibly wild carrots. There may be some frog legs in there too," Hart advised, stirring the stew with the large gourd left for dipping.

"I'm sure we'll enjoy it," Lessie stated, handing Nate a filled gourd.

"I'm full, Lessie. I told you. It's good."

"All right then. Why don't you sit here with us while we eat. Or better yet, take some to Tchula," Lessie directed.

"Yes, I will," Nate said, balancing the filled gourd carefully as he went in search of Tchula.

*****

Lessie was allowed to sleep in an unoccupied hut. At first sight, she felt repulsed by the earthen floor and dried twig sides. But they seemed to be bug free, and she soon settled down on a blanket, her eyes sighting a watery moon through holes in the thatched roof.

A noise at the entrance startled her. It was Hart.

"I've come to see if you're comfortable," he whispered, moving inside.

"Yes, thank you. I'll be fine," she whispered in return.

"Come outside for a minute, will you? I want to show you something," Hart insisted, helping her from the blanket. Once outside, Hart pointed toward the darkened night sky. "Look. High above those tall trees."

"What is it?" Lessie asked immediately. "Is that the comet?"

"Yes," Hart replied, holding her hand in his. "It's getting closer every day."

Lessie thought she understood why he had called her outside to look at it. It was a beautiful sight, that moon-sized brilliant orb with its luminous tail arching across the horizon. It was strange to think of something so heavenly as a potential threat to them. She glanced at Hart. He was studying the sky, a question in his eyes. She knew he was preparing her in the only way he could. He wanted her to understand what might eventually happen as a result of the comet's approach to earth.

"The night sky is almost as bright as the day," Lessie commented. "Why are the days darker?"

"The comet is between us and the sun," Hart responded. "In the day, it prevents some of the sun's rays from getting past it to us. At night, the comet's own fire lights up the darkened earth."

"I understand," Lessie returned. "Don't worry. I don't believe it will strike earth."

"Why not?" Hart asked.

"I don't really have an answer for that," she whispered, gazing at the distant light burning its way toward them. "I just won't accept it, I suppose."

"Come on," he urged, tugging at her hand, leading her back to the hut. "Sleep well," he said, as she entered and moved toward her blanket.

"I'll do my best," she returned, smiling at him.

He looked at her. He had just shown her the greatest menace possible to her life, yet she remained calm and agreed to attempt sleep. She was the most rewarding woman he had ever known.

*****

"Were you with the others when the attack came?" Hart asked Able after Able had given a stumbling account of what happened the night before.

"I...no. I had gone into the woods to find grass for Joe. Everything seemed fine. Then I heard screaming and a shot," Able replied, his eyes watching Hart carefully for signs of disbelief.

"And?"

"And I started back for the others, but thought better of it. I'm just one man. And I'm not any good in a fight. Never have been. So I waited till I thought I could be of some help to them."

"You waited until you thought you could be of some help. You mean you didn't assist them?" Hart's eyes flashed with contempt for the large man before him. "You might have saved the post courier."

"I doubt that, Mr. MacAlpin. I doubt that. Most probably I'd of been killed too. As I said, I'm no man—"

"Right!" Hart shot. "You're no man in a fight! How about undercover, Hand? Do you do very well as a double agent?"

"What? What do you mean by that?" Able asked, his expression that of a trapped animal with nowhere to run.

"I mean that some of your more nocturnal activities have been found out. If you're caught giving information to the wrong parties, you could be hanged," Hart stipulated, his voice hard.

"That right? Well, I don't have anything to hide. I'm not worried," Able fired, as he turned on his heel and walked away.

CHAPTER 9

Lessie woke the next morning with a vague sense of discontent. The events of yesterday slowly filled her consciousness, causing her to glance quickly around the small hut, seeking Nate. Almost as quickly as fear had come, it was gone. Nate was safe. She was safe.

"Lessie," called a familiar female voice.

"Here," she replied, moving toward the open doorway.

"How are you?" questioned Callie Warren, moving inside and hugging Lessie to her. "We were so worried about you."

"I'm fine, Callie, and you? How are you and Viola?" Lessie asked when Viola also entered the hut.

"We're all right now. Mr. Shute and the braves rescued us. You should have seen the uproar in the camp. The ambushers thought they were surrounded, but it was only Mr. Shute, Chulhkan, and Standing Oak," Callie stated, her voice filled with pride.

"I'm so glad. Have you seen Nate? He's here. Able Hand brought him in. I guess that's all of us, except for the poor postmaster and Mr. Albright."

"We saw Nate as soon as we arrived. We've only been here a few minutes. Hart told us where to find you," Viola interjected, feeling left out. She had decided to tolerate Lessie, at least until she was safely back in Natchez. "As for Colonel Sheffield Albright, he's one of the bandits."

"What...what did you say?" Lessie asked, attempting to straighten her hair, which had tumbled around her shoulders.

"I said the colonel is working with the bandits. He told us so before we were rescued," Viola affirmed, exhilarated that her information had so startled Lessie.

"It's true, Lessie. The colonel admitted he was working with the British against the colonials in the territory. They mean to claim the territory for England," Callie added just as Hart stuck his head through the door.

"Come and eat," he instructed. "The food's ready."

Lessie allowed the girls to leave first, waiting to accompany Hart. He took her arm, leading her in the direction of a brightly patterned woolen blanket spread near a campfire. Tchula and Nate sat side by side, staring at bread baking on pieces of bark.

"The girls are eating with Able and Sam. We're eating here. Tchula has made bark bread and coffee," Hart said, assisting Lessie to her place on the blanket.

"Almost done," Tchula stated, shifting the pieces of bark nearer the flames. "Chestnut bark make bread taste good."

"I can't wait," Nate groaned, rubbing his stomach. A night's sleep had left a cavern where his stomach used to be.

Hart settled himself next to Lessie. "Sleep well?" he asked.

"Better, I think," she replied. "And you?"

"Not much. Too much on my mind," he answered. "Lessie, as soon as we can move, we need to get you and Nate to your grandmother's."

"Yes," Lessie agreed.

"I regret having to leave you there," he said, his voice low, meant only for her.

"We'll be fine. The sooner we start earning our way, the sooner Nate can start school," Lessie replied.

"I thought we settled that question. Nate can go to school in Washington, at the military academy," Hart said, then added, "as soon as we've settled this political mess we're in."

"You shouldn't take on the responsibility of educating Nate," Lessie insisted. She had given the matter additional thought. She wanted Nate in school now. She had no idea when, or if, she and Hart would be married.

"I disagree. And I don't consider it a responsibility. I consider it a privilege," Hart began.

"But, you've just said we can't do anything until this political strife is settled. I want Nate to begin now," she persisted.

"Don't worry so. It's all coming to a head soon. Now that we're certain about Albright's part in it, we'll find the others," Hart returned, perplexed by her insistence. It seemed out of character.

"I know you and Tchula are doing all you can. But there's the matter of your brother's death, too. You won't rest until you find the person responsible. It could be years before we can make a proper home for Nate and see to his education together," Lessie concluded, her face serious.

"Not if I have any say in the matter," Hart quipped. "I'm only leaving you at your grandmother's for a few weeks. No longer than that." His voice somber, he added, "Do you think I would part from you for years?"

Lessie searched his eyes, seeking the answer she needed. It was there. She knew that as long as Hart MacAlpin was alive, she and Nate would be important to him. Her happiness and Nate's education would become a certainty. She reached out and took his hand. "Forgive me. It's just that Nate's education is so important to me. My father's greatest wish was for Nate to attend school."

Hart grasped her hand in his, raising it to his lips. "We'll keep your promise to him," he said.

As he released her hand, Lessie asked, "Is the colonel the man you suspected?"

"That's right. The man called Zeke and the one in black have been seen near his home at night. Tchula's braves have been approached by them and offered new rifles if they would help wipe out the colonials. But we need witnesses, proof."

"What will you do?"

"Nothing until we can get you and Nate safely to Nashville," he replied. "After that, we'll try to find them and the colonel and question them."

"Bread ready now," Tchula interrupted, handing the first piece to Nate, who began to nibble voraciously at the smoking pone.

Hart accepted a piece for himself and one for Lessie. They ate in silence, alternating between the hot pone and the dark coffee, which Tchula served in Hart's small tin cups. Lessie's headache eased as she ate the unsalted but nonetheless tasty bread. The chestnut bark on which it was baked did impart a pleasant flavor to the cornmeal.

While they were eating, Able Hand walked over. "Ms. Warren and Ms. Vespar say that Colonel Albright was mighty thick with those Indians. Said he ran when the shooting started?"

"So we've been told," Hart declared.

"Funny thing," Able said. "I wouldn't have thought that of the colonel."

"Oh. Why not?" Hart quizzed.

"I dunno. I guess because he used to visit the governor so often, meet him at his house."

"You saw him there?"

"More than once."

"What were you doing there?"

"Me? I…nothing. I go there to collect pay for playing my fiddle. You know that."

"I see. Then you'd know who the colonel spent his time with. Who was it?" Hart was alert now to the subtle tightening around Able's eyes. He knew more than he was telling.

"Now that you mention it, I don't remember seeing him spend time with any one man," Able said, scratching his head.

"And?" Hart asked.

"Dunno," Able finally replied. He knew who was behind the killing and burning. But he knew better than to talk. That is, it wouldn't be profitable for him to talk. And it might cost him his life. He knew William Smythe, the colonel, and others were moving toward taking the territory. Able wanted to be on the winning side, whichever way it went.

Hart rose, assisted Lessie to her feet, then turned back to Able. "I understand your point of view, Able. I mean, a man needs to look out for himself. You could be on the winning side in this affair, you know. There could be money in it for you," Hart finished, watching greed glimmer in Able's eyes. "Why not bring me any information you can dig up on everyone surrounding the colonel and the governor, I'll pay well."

"I'll do my best," Able answered. This was what he'd hoped to hear. He'd sell information to both sides. When it was all over, he'd be accepted by the winner.

*****

Hart walked with Lessie back toward her hut.

"Are we moving on today?" she asked, wondering if there was a sufficient number of them to pose a threat to possible outlaws.

"No, not today. Tchula is asking around about Black Hat and Zeke. He's found that Zeke does have a wife and son here. Since he was in on the ambush, we're hoping he'll turn up here," Hart explained.

"Will you be here until we leave?"

"I will," he said, noting the uncertainty in her voice.

*****

Nate had finished two of the thick pones of cornbread, relishing every bite. He now stood in the middle of the compound, his eyes taking note of each log building, each hut. Sounds of merriment surprised him. He turned his head in immediate response.

In a cleared area nearby, young men were rushing first one way and then the other waving large sticks with cupped ends in their hands. He walked toward them, his eyes alive with interest. There were at least thirty-five or forty of them. Most of them were swinging the cupped sticks at a large round object that was constantly being flung from one end of the playing field to the other.

"Nate! Be careful. Back away from there," Lessie called when she had at last found him, knowing she wouldn't be heard above the impossible din of voices, but feeling the sisterly need to try. When he didn't respond, she gathered her riding skirt in one hand and rushed toward him.

"Gizzards, Lessie! Why'd you come running up on me like that?" Nate asked when she had caught his shoulder and turned him to face her.

"Don't get in their way, Nate. I don't want you hurt."

"Ah, you fuss too much. I wasn't going to get in their way," he declared, snatching his arm away and turning to watch the game again.

Lessie made no attempt to remove him from what she considered the edge of danger. He liked it there. She stood beside him, wondering when they would be trampled under the feet of the rushing players.

There seemed to be two teams, one guarding each end of the field where there was a wooden goal. As they ran first one way and then the other across each other's fields—and each other's bodies—with laughter ringing their heads, they tried to catch the ball and then sling it toward their opponents' goal.

Shouts of "Falamolichi! Falamolichi!" rang through the air as stampeding feet charged toward the goal at the near end of the field. A long arm, fairer than the others, shot upward from the throng. The swinging ball was thrust from its stick and propelled against the near goal. A lean body dressed in canvas britches was raised into the air. It was Sam Shute. He was carried jubilantly around the field on the shoulders of his teammates. When he passed Nate and Lessie, he cupped his hands to his mouth and let loose with a vociferous noise much like the call of a wild turkey. It delighted Nate, who was dancing up and down in his enthusiasm.

Sam was unceremoniously tumbled onto the ground, and the game started again. Lessie watched, amazed. The ferocity of the play and the sociability of the players was contagious. She found herself cheering. After a few moments, she turned and found that Nate had moved off. He was standing with a young Indian boy clad in breech cloth and leggings. They were conversing and pointing toward the field of players.

Lessie left them alone and went in search of Callie and Viola. She wanted to hear more about their hours of capture and the colonel's part in it.

*****

Ada had been up for several days when she received a caller. She felt better than she had in months. As she dressed to receive him, she regarded her reflection in the mirror. *What are you?* she asked her reflection. She had lost her first child but felt nothing. It had been a little boy. Before she had regained consciousness, he was taken from her. He was now buried behind the house. It was for the best, she had been told. She had not wanted the baby. But for him to die as he entered the world was regrettable. Still.

"Miz Ada, you 'bout ready?" Cleo called from the door. "Your guest is getting fidgety."

"Let him wait."

"Yes'um," Cleo returned, raking Ada with her eyes. *Wonder when that woman's going home*, she thought, closing the door quietly.

Ada finished her toilet, then turned slowly in front of the long mirror to assess her work. The black crape dress hung loosely on her thin form, but it brought out the pale creaminess of her skin. She placed a string of black oval-shaped beads around her neck and started downstairs.

"Good afternoon, Mr. Smythe. What gives us the pleasure of your visit?" she asked, moving into the parlor, where he had been told to wait.

"Ah, Ms. MacAlpin, how very lovely you are, even in mourning," Smythe said as she entered. "Let me assist you to a chair."

"Thank you," she replied, allowing him to usher her toward a striped peacock-blue-and-gold-covered armchair. Once seated, she asked again, "What brings you to visit?"

William Smythe studied the young woman before him. She was beautiful in an earthy sort of way. He watched the way she hid her dark eyes underneath thick lashes until she was ready to reveal their brilliant shine by opening them wide as she lifted her head to look at him. *She's a natural coquette*, he thought before replying to her question.

"I've come both on my own behalf and that of the governor's to offer our condolences for your recent loss." Smythe's face registered empathy as he spoke.

"Thank you both. It's most kind of you to come," Ada returned, her eyes evaluating the magnificent suit of clothes he wore, the way he seemed about to burst from the jacket.

BROADHORN

"May I say also, Ms. MacAlpin, that I've never seen a more beautiful woman," Smythe continued, watching her preen at his remark.

"Thank you again, Mr. Smythe. Won't you have tea?" Ada asked. She enjoyed this flattery. And compared to sitting in her room, this was like being born again.

"I don't want to intrude."

"You are definitely not intruding. And please, you must call me Ada. All my friends do."

"You are gracious indeed, Ada," Smythe agreed, thinking this was much easier than he had believed it would be.

Ada rang for tea. Ash came in response.

"Ash, please tell Cleo to make tea. And tell her to serve some of her wonderful tea cakes," Ada ordered, waving her hand in dismissal when she finished speaking.

Ash turned on his heel and left the room. He'd fetch the tea and the tea cakes, but what he wanted to do, had a burning need to do, was pour the tea on top of that glorious head. Receiving William Smythe so soon after the loss of her child. Shameful, that's what it was. What was Smythe doing here, anyway? Ash wondered.

Trouble was brewing. Everybody was talking about it. The threat posed by the comet was growing less each day now. Reports were that it had turned away from its approach to earth. But the threat of another war with England was growing. Times were turning bad, he figured, as he walked into the kitchen, where he found Cleo hard at work. He'd get a letter off to Mr. Hart after supper. He'd want to know about Smythe's visit.

"Cleo, Miz Ada wants tea and tea cakes. What else do you have?" he asked.

"I can make some cucumber sandwiches," Cleo answered, not moving from the table where she was kneading dough. "I suppose she'll want some jam ones too."

"You know her better'n I do. Better get it ready quick. She's edgy," Ash added, watching Cleo's hands turn the dough, then punch it down, turn it over, and begin kneading once again.

153

"I'll get right to it," she replied, wiping her hands on her apron. "Here, you fetch the water. I'll stir up the fire."

Ash left by the back door to get water from the well, which was situated at the end of the rear porch. He didn't know why Ada always made him angry. No, that wasn't exactly true. She didn't fit with the rest of the family. At least, she didn't fit now that Mr. Bruce was dead. The two of them had been a real pair.

After they'd had their tea, which Smythe had assured her was the best in a long time, Ada walked with him out to his horse, which was tied up at the hitching post in front of the house. He touched his hat as he mounted.

"Thank you for calling, William," Ada said, smiling up at him. "It was a splendid lift for me."

"My pleasure, Ada. May I call again?"

"Yes, please do. Of course, I shouldn't be receiving callers yet, but one's friends aren't really callers, are they?"

"Indeed not. I'll come again," Smythe replied. "By the way, has the family any recent news of your brother-in-law?"

"Adam?"

"Hart. I believe he's called Ishto Impa by the Choctaws," Smythe stated.

"You haven't heard!" Ada began. "Oh, surely you must have. The Natchez caravan was ambushed somewhere up the Trace. The postmaster was killed, but the others all survived. Hart and his Choctaw friend are at the Stand, with the Lord girl and the others," she said but was interrupted by Smythe.

"Did they capture any of the miscreants?"

"I don't know. They don't tell me. What Hart is doing there in the first place is beyond me," Ada continued.

"Thought I'd check for the governor. He's interested in Hart's activities."

"Oh, I didn't know that," Ada replied. "I can't imagine why, can you?"

"I have one or two ideas," Smythe began. "But you shouldn't bother your head with these affairs, Ada. You've suffered such tragedies lately. Tell me, did Hart ever find the man responsible for killing your late husband?"

"No. I mean, I don't," Ada answered, her guard up. Smythe was asking too many questions. He was ruining their brief visit. "You can ask him when he returns. I'm certain he'll have answers for you," she finished.

"You're expecting him soon?" Smythe asked.

"No," Ada answered, anger replacing the pleasure she had found in his company.

"Forgive me, Ada," Smythe said suddenly, smiling down at her. "I don't like puzzles. And I did enjoy our visit." He pressed his right knee into his horse's side, signaling movement. "If I may, I'll come again."

"Please do," Ada answered, smiling in return.

He'd enjoyed himself, Smythe thought, as his horse trotted down the drive. Ada would make a fine wife for a politician. She'd relish the dinners, parties, and such. After the takeover, being married to her would ease his relationship with some of the locals, make it easier for him to govern them. Only, he wasn't so thick as to think he could trust her around men.

Ada stood watching him ride down the drive. She'd enjoyed his company. He was an attorney on the governor's staff. It could be she'd be invited to many events, many dances. That was what she needed—that and Hart. Only, Hart wasn't here.

*****

Not many miles from where Sam Shute had ambushed the raiding party, Colonel Sheffield Albright ran smack into a Chickasaw hunting party. They shot his horse from under him and were about to scalp him when he made them understand red coats, brass buttons, in faulty Choctaw. The leader of the band ordered them to cease and allowed Albright to stand.

"What name you say?"

"Smythe," Albright replied, straightening his clothes and rubbing his hands through his long gray hair. It was still all there.

"You know this Smythe?"

"Yes. We are associates. We fight for British."

The leader looked Albright over carefully, then motioning for his warriors to follow, he led the colonel toward a spare horse. They mounted and headed for Chickasaw Bluffs.

It was two weeks before they made the Bluffs, which sat high above the Mississippi at the northwest corner of the territory. All during that time, the colonel had been afraid for his life. At night, around the cook fire, he watched the eyes of his captors. He knew most of them wanted to kill him. They hated all whites, trusted none. When they finally arrived at the Bluffs, he was gratified to see so many British uniforms. He introduced himself to the one in charge.

"So you're the person working undercover in Natchez. How did you come to be here?" questioned the captain, who had been introduced as Thomas Bean.

"It's a long story," the colonel informed him. "First, I need a bath, some clean clothes, and food, if I may," he added, not wanting to sound too officious.

"Certainly, I'll arrange it," Bean replied. "Then I'll need a report."

"Of course," the colonel agreed.

After he'd eaten and changed, the colonel was escorted to a canvas tent, where he was admitted. Captain Bean had just finished his own meal and rose as the colonel entered.

"Have you eaten?" the captain asked, motioning to the food left on his table.

"Yes, I have, thank you," the colonel said. "I'm here to give my report."

"Fine. Start when ready," the captain instructed, taking out pen and paper.

Colonel Sheffield Albright pulled out a crudely made chair and sat down, wiping at his forehead with his handkerchief. "I left Natchez about six weeks ago in a party of six men, three women and a boy. I was the sixth man. We were ambushed about a day's ride from the Stand by a band of Chickasaws under the direction of our man—"

"Don't say his name out loud, not even here," the captain instructed. "You never know who is willing to sell information of that type."

"Yes, of course, you're right. I didn't…think," the colonel mumbled, disconcerted.

"Get on with your story," the captain ordered, watching the colonel squirm in his chair.

"All went well as far as I know. That is, one man was killed, the postmaster. That should put a crimp in the Americans' information network. Of course, it won't take long for them to appoint another."

"Naturally not. But perhaps this time, he'll be one of ours. We'll be privy to all correspondence between Philadelphia, Nashville, and the Natchez area. We'll be able to set our plans for takeover in motion," Bean advised.

"I see. Well, as I was saying, all went well. I was recognized and spared. Sam Shute was cut down by a club, and the other man, Able Hand, disappeared. The Choctaws put up a good fight but were outnumbered. Two of the women were captured and taken with me to a campsite not far from where your Chickasaws found me. I don't know what happened to the other woman and her brother. I think he was in the woods somewhere." The colonel paused to catch his breath.

"How did you come to be on your own?"

"They ran off and left me," the colonel rasped. "Ran off and left me without a weapon, a horse, anything."

Captain Bean laughed uproariously. You could always count on Zeke to look after himself.

The colonel continued, having warmed to the issue. "Someone attacked our camp that first night just before dawn. They took both the white women, most of the horses, and killed or scattered the majority of the camp."

"Who was it?"

"I'd swear it was Samuel Shute."

"You said he'd been cut down," the captain reminded him, thinking this Shute must have a head of stone.

"I saw him struck down. But I'd swear I saw him making off with the women. He must not have been seriously injured when he fell," the colonel suggested. Shute had earned his reputation for rising from the dead. The man seemed might near indestructible.

"See anyone else? Don't tell me he caused such panic by himself," the captain, his interest aroused, asked.

"No. There were rifle shots from all sides of the camp, then pandemonium, then nothing," the colonel replied.

"Is that all of it?"

"That's all of it," the colonel stated tersely. He was tired of being cross-examined by an inferior. "You know," he said, his voice that of his old self, "I outrank you."

"You used to outrank me, Colonel," Bean stated, rising and pulling back the flap to his tent, dismissing the colonel. "Your rank is useless here."

The colonel moved to exit, but not before he recognized smug satisfaction on the younger man's face. *I was enlisted because of my war-time experience and my British sympathies*, he said to himself. *But I've not been allowed any authority. I'm near bankruptcy. And I've never been given the sum of money I was promised.*

His face sagged as he walked to the dirty-smelling hut where he would spend the night. What was he going to do? How could he even go back to Natchez now? What about Mildred and Ada and her child?

*****

Chulhkan watched the white woman carry her laundry to the stream near the camp. Hart MacAlpin had suggested Tchula and the braves stand watch in case her man returned. She held a heavily loaded basket on her shoulders Indian style. Repeated desertion by her man had forced her to work for the women of the Stand in order to provide a hut and food for herself and her small boy. The factor had long since cut off her charge at the store. She owed much, had little, and worked extremely hard.

Her small son sat cross-legged near the stream, watching a brave practice with his seven-foot-long reed blowpipe. He was hitting his mark across the stream at a distance of thirty or more yards. Chulhkan smiled. *I could do better.*

The woman had finished her wash and sat down on a large rock to watch the child at play when a man of short stature walked out of the bushes and moved toward her. His movements furtive, he circled around behind a corn crib before suddenly jumping forward. The woman backed away as though frightened, then turned, seeking her child, as the man grabbed for her arm.

"It's me, Annie. Don't back away like that. I might get the idee you're skeered o'me," the man said.

"No, no, Zeke, I ain't skeered o'ye. I just didn't know ye, that's all," the woman's voice pleaded.

"That's it, is it?" Zeke prodded. He had her by the arm and was pulling her toward the bushes when the boy, not more than six years old, ran out of the water and attempted to pull his mother away from Zeke. Zeke raised his fist and swung downward in a hard blow, sending the boy tumbling. "Git outer my way, brat."

Hart happened by and saw Zeke at the same instant that Chulhkan broke cover. They both rushed forward.

"Hold it, Zeke!" Hart shouted, running toward Zeke and the woman, letting the singing bola fly to its mark. "Don't fight it!" he shouted, as Zeke fell to the ground, gagging, attempting to pull the wrapped leather throngs from around his throat. "Chulhkan, get him on his feet," Hart directed, pulling the bola from around Zeke's neck.

Hart glanced around for the woman and child. They had scurried for cover in one of the nearby huts.

Zeke surrendered readily. He knew when he was outnumbered. And one of them had weapons he'd never seen. He knew who the tall blond man was, though. He had been described to Zeke. He was Hart MacAlpin. He knew the governor had set this MacAlpin and a chief called Tchula against them.

"Whatcha gonna do?" Zeke cried as Tchula and the braves led him toward their campsite.

"That depends on you," Hart answered, walking along beside him. "You should be thinking about what's going to happen to you if we don't get the right answers to our questions."

"Whatcha mean?" Zeke wheezed, rubbing at his throat. Great red swellings were growing where the bola had left its mark.

They arrived at their camp and tied Zeke to the nearest tree. Hart consulted Tchula before approaching Zeke. "You question him, Ishto Impa. We help if needed," Tchula declared.

"Zeke, we know who you are. We know you're practicing treason against the United States. You know what the penalty for that is, don't you?" Hart spoke carefully, watching Zeke's eyes widen in fear, then narrow cunningly. "We want to know who pays you."

Like a trapped animal, Zeke waited, his eyes seeking escape. "I don't know whatcha mean," Zeke replied, his voice not much more than a whisper. "You nearly killed me with that thing. What is it?"

"It's called a bola. It's good for catching game," Hart answered, a sardonic smile lengthening the scar above his lips. "Four-legged or two-legged."

"You hatten oughter do that to a man," Zeke whispered.

"I usually don't, Zeke, not to a man."

Zeke's eyes flared. He got the point.

"No use fighting your ropes, Zeke. That's another trick I know. I learned it aboard ship. It's called a square knot," Hart explained, watching Zeke twisting his hands in an attempt to slip loose.

An idea began to form in Hart's mind. Zeke wasn't likely to give in to force. He was trail-tough and torture-wise. But he might be bought. Money and the freedom to leave the territory might purchase the name of the agent behind the takeover attempt. He discussed the possibilities with Tchula and the others. They agreed it was worth trying. He walked back to the tree where Zeke was tied.

"We can see you're not a man to be bullied, Zeke," Hart began, watching Zeke's head come up.

"So I'm a man now, is it?" Zeke laughed, then spat near Hart's feet.

Hart ignored him. "You've two choices, Zeke. One, you can remain silent, go to jail, take your chances with the courts. Two, you can tell us what we want and go free—with traveling money."

"Say again. About money, I mean," Zeke said, his attention fully captured.

"Just what I said. We're willing to pay you to tell us what we want. Who is the man that wears the black hat? Is he the man in charge?" Hart asked, pulling gold coins from inside his bonnet, rubbing them between his fingers.

Zeke's eyes fastened on the coins. "I'd be as dead iffen you shoot me or he does," he said. "They's got spies everywhere. I'd not git far, I think."

Hart decided to change tactics, give Zeke a moment to consider his future. "We'll talk more later about that, Zeke. But there's something you could help us with. It would be in your favor if you go to jail."

"What's that?"

"My brother Bruce was killed a few months back. Shot. He was found near Brightway Plantation. Do you know anything about that?"

"No. No, I don't," Zeke replied, fear gripping his mind as he looked into the eyes of the man questioning him. He'd seen bad men many times. Men who'd kill for fun. Their eyes were cold, empty. But he'd never seen eyes like the ones staring at him now. They blazed with white hot heat, like branding irons. Zeke shuddered, then looked away. This man was not like the others. But he had killed.

"You're certain you don't know anything?" Hart prodded, his eyes fastened on Zeke's.

For answer, Zeke turned his head, shaking it from side to side, fear consuming him. He had to think. He wanted the money. But it wouldn't do him any good iffen he was dead.

For the next few minutes, Hart attempted to persuade Zeke to talk. But he steadfastly clamped his lips and refused to answer. Finally, Tchula and Chulhkan began to work on him, applying pressure in ways they knew best. Zeke didn't talk. As Hart had suspected, he was tough. When twilight fell and he had not said anything useful, the group left him tied for the night and went to look after the horses, feed themselves, and arrange for supplies for the second leg of their trip up the Trace.

"I give him bread and water," Tchula said when he'd finished his own meal. "Need strength to talk."

Sam, Hart, and Tchula took turns watching him throughout the night, each sleeping for three hours at a time. Around dawn, just as the brilliant moonlight paled to the shadowed sun of day, Hart rose from his blanket and went to take his second turn on guard.

He'd begun to think Zeke might not know Black Hat's true identity; either that or he was one fine actor. When Hart took his first watch and asked him a second time what he knew about Bruce's death, his small eyes had narrowed suspiciously.

"What's the reward for that bit o'knowledge?" Zeke had asked, sitting at attention, his animal-like antenna tuned. "I don't believe you said."

"That depends, Zeke, on whether or not I believe you and whether or not we capture the murderer," Hart had said.

Zeke laughed, a short, bitter snarl of a laugh. "Fat chance o'that."

"Do you know who killed him?" Hart had demanded.

"Maybe. Maybe not," Zeke snarled.

"I'll pay one thousand dollars for his capture," Hart amended, thinking Zeke incapable of turning down that sum.

"And what would happen to him?"

"That's for the judge to decide. But if found guilty of murder, he'd hang," Hart had finished.

He'd watched as Zeke's mind assimilated that last bit of information. As he'd watched, Zeke's eyes lost their greedy glint. Hart knew then that he wouldn't talk. He was more afraid of his friends than of anything that might happen to him in their hands. It was a shame that such a man held the fate of the Mississippi Territory in his hands.

The territory was diabolically enormous. No one could be expected to find those who wished to hide in its forests—forests filled with deadenings, cane fields so thick no life pervaded them, woods that dwarfed the human mind with their heinous proportions until the sojourner resigned himself to occupancy. The man in the black hat could be anywhere. If he chose not to expose himself at one of the settlements, he and his bloodthirsty crew might never be captured.

Zeke was watching him approach, his small mouth almost smiling. Fog was drifting about three feet off the ground, moving thickly between Hart and the captured man. Suddenly, Zeke moved.

Hart pulled his pistol and fired toward the tree just as something sharp hit his shoulder, knocking him backward. Zeke started to run, a gleeful chuckle following him. He seemed to jump as the boom of a rifle assaulted Hart's ears. Zeke jumped, then collapsed in midstride.

"Help me," Lessie screamed. "Help me. He's bleeding so," she said as Sam and Tchula reached her side. She stood with her arm around Hart, supporting him. A smoking rifle lay on the ground near her.

Sam examined the wound in Hart's shoulder, then signaled for Tchula and Chulhkan to help Hart to their blanket by the fire.

"Is it bad?" Hart asked, his voice raspy. "Who fired that shot?" he continued, his breath coming in short bursts.

"I did," Lessie replied, attempting to stop the flow of blood, which was soaking the sleeve of her blouse.

"Lie down, Hart," Sam ordered, accepting some hog-gut thread and a bone needle from his wife, Sophie. "I've got to sew this up as soon as we pour some liquor on it," he continued, taking the bottle of spirits from Chulhkan, who had retrieved it from Sam's bags near the fire.

When the ordeal of suturing the three-inch wound was over, Hart was on the point of collapse. He had lost a lot of blood. "Is Zeke dead?" he asked on a long sigh. "Ms. Lessie, you stay with him for a while. Watch that bandage. If it turns red, fetch me. I don't think it's going to fester, but you never can tell," Sam said, pulling a brightly colored blanket under Hart's chin.

As he walked away to check into Zeke's condition, he saluted Lessie. "Mighty fine shot, miss. Didn't know you could handle a weapon like that."

"All kinds of guns, Mr. Shute," Lessie returned, her eyes resting on the bandage on Hart's shoulder. "Our father owned a gun shop in Mobile. Nate and I can both shoot fair."

"Looks like the young Mr. MacAlpin owes his life to you—or possibly to your Daddy's foresight," Sam declared, winking at her.

Hart slept most of the day. Each time he woke, Sam poured whiskey down his throat. "Nothing better to make a man sleep," Sam would say when Hart resisted. Lessie sat beside him through the long hours, wondering if he would mend. He had lost so much blood.

The Factor came to check on him, asking questions about his wound and congratulating Lessie on placing a good shot. She turned sick every time she thought about the way Zeke looked when the shot struck him. She and Nate had hunted small game. It was never a pleasant experience for her. Her father had insisted that both his children know how to use a weapon to defend themselves or feed themselves. What he hadn't explained was what to do if you didn't have a weapon. She had been lucky in finding Hart's rifle laying where he had slept, a few yards from his approach to Zeke. She had seen Zeke prepare to throw the knife. The fog had dissipated briefly as she aimed the rifle and fired. But she hadn't been quick enough to save Hart from injury.

"Zeke's dead," Sam stated, bending to check Hart's wound again.

"I must explain to his wife," Lessie whispered, not wanting to wake Hart.

"Don't bother, miss. She weren't his legal wife, just his consort. The Factor told me Zeke used to show up every few months, beat her something awful, then leave again. She's better off without him. Her and the boy can leave here now, find her family, if there is any," Sam explained.

The next day, Hart was up. He insisted on continuing their trek to Nashville. His wound was healing under Lessie's and Sam's watchful eyes, and except for his shoulder being stiff and sore, he could manage.

*****

Abel Hand saluted as he rode away south, back to Natchez. He had finished his business at the Stand. He and the Factor had come to terms. Abel would bring luxury items from Natchez four times a year. He'd buy low and exact a higher price from the Factor. Travel expenses had to be covered and profit made. He'd make certain he cleared a good profit and the Stand would have a few luxuries.

Able rode one horse and led another. He had bought a fine gelding from Sam Shute. He'd been surprised to find that Sam had been raising horses and selling them to stranded travelers for several years. *Wish I'd thought of that*, Able mused.

Hart watched Hand ride out of camp. He'd wondered about Able's profitable lifestyle. Now he knew where his greater profits were acquired. Able Hand was a dealer. He dealt in anything he could buy cheap and sell high. When asked how he came to know about the Factor's desire for supplies from Natchez, he had grinned and said he overheard old Angus and a guest discussing it at the MacAlpin soiree.

Hart now regarded Able with distaste. While he walked around the rooms playing his fiddle for other folk's pleasure, he was eavesdropping on private conversations. Music, the way he played it, did pay well.

"I see Able's off," Sam said.

"Yes, he's off and with his pockets heavily lined. He'll do all right," Hart pronounced, "if he doesn't run into bandits or get caught in the middle."

"Did you send your letter to the governor by him?" Sam asked, watching Able's back disappear into the far trees.

"No," Hart replied. "I decided against it. He spends too much time at Government House. Anyway, I posted a letter to the governor the evening we arrived by Choctaw runner."

"Then we're ready to travel?" Sam asked again.

"Yes. We'll leave now," Hart answered, turning toward the assembled group of travelers.

The two of them walked toward Chulhkan, Standing Oak, and Tchula, who were waiting by the assembled horses. Hart checked Blister, tightened his cinch, then moved to check Lessie's and Nate's horses. Sam had loaned them two of his older horses, both mares in their twenties. Safe horses for unseasoned travelers, he had said. The horses were saddled well.

"We're ready now," Lessie advised, turning to mount her horse. "Nate has chosen the dappled gray, Hart. He said it looked something like yours."

Hart winked at Nate who had clamored into his saddle, anxious to be off. "She does look something like Blister. Has a nice gait too," Hart remarked, mounting Blister and taking the lead.

Tchula moved up front with Hart. This time, the braves would be riding with the party. There were now five men who could shoot and one woman. Odds were a little better, Hart decided. He'd hoped others would join the party, then he and Tchula could go about their hunt for Black Hat. Since no others asked to accompany them, he decided he must see the women and Nate all the way to Nashville.

Callie and Viola had never learned to use a gun. Viola cringed when she learned of Lessie's heroics in saving Hart's life by causing Zeke to miss his mark. She didn't see how any well-brought-up young woman could kill a person. She had begun regarding Lessie with a mixture of respect and loathing.

Nate had been given a small blowpipe and taught how to use it by his young friend at the Stand. He carried it proudly and had become adept at hitting his targets.

Viola had fussed too about having to ride one of the spotted mares. "What will everyone think when we ride into Nashville astride these spotted ponies?" she argued.

"Hush, Vi. We owe our lives to Indians and Sam, here. You should be more grateful," Callie challenged.

Sam punched his Bible down inside his saddle bags, winked at Callie, and clucked to his horse. This promised to be a very interesting ride—baring bandits.

*****

Hart had asked Nate to ride up front with him. The boy seemed to grow before his eyes; he was that proud. After a few hours of answering endless questions about his rifle, his bola, his hat, and almost everything that grew along the Trace, Hart began to question his generosity. At one point, he had turned in his saddle to glance back at the girls. Lessie was riding in the center, slightly in front of Vi and Callie. She had been watching the exchange between Hart and Nate. When she saw Hart turn and look in her direction, she lifted both hands in a gesture of surrender. Hart chuckled. He knew exactly what she meant.

"What's funny, Hart?" Nate asked.

"Eh, just something I thought." Hart straightened himself, pushed his boots down in the stirrups, and turned his attention back to the road.

"Nate, ride back and check on Sam, will you? He's probably in need of some company about now."

"Sure, I will," Nate beamed, turning his horse and trotting to the rear of the column.

Hart glanced at Lessie as he watched Nate's passage. She was smiling. He winked at her.

In the middle of the afternoon on the third day, they came to the Tennessee River. At a narrow gorge where the river ran shallow, they stopped to rest before crossing. Tchula was there ahead of them.

"Anyone near?" Hart asked, dismounting and letting Blister drink his fill from the river's edge.

"Sign two days back," Tchula said.

"None today?"

"No. You not cross at Colberts?"

"Don't trust him. Too many Chickasaws there," Hart explained. "Too many people have disappeared passing through there."

Tchula concurred, nodding his assent.

"Good. We'll let the ladies rest awhile. The horses can feed," Hart directed, moving to assist Lessie from her saddle. Nate was there ahead of him.

"Why, thank you, Nate," Lessie was saying as he took her arm, helping her off her horse. When he had her safely on the ground, he ran over to assist Callie.

"Looks like Nathaniel is growing before my eyes," Lessie said to Hart as they walked toward a group of large rocks to rest. "I think he's taller, too."

Hart laughed. "I doubt that. But he's taking his responsibility as a man seriously. He informed me that he'd do the heavy work until my shoulder heals. I suppose he thinks helping ladies off horses heavy work. But now that he has the idea, he'll remember it."

"Is that how it happens?" Lessie quizzed, amazed at Nate's seeming metamorphosis.

"Most times, I think," Hart answered, sitting down beside her and offering her a drink of clear cold water from the spill off the rocks.

"I see. It seems both the Lords are learning on this trip," Lessie continued, accepting the drink.

Hart called to Chulhkan to bring Ms. Warren and Ms. Vespar over for a drink of the cold water. Sam walked over with them.

"This is a good place to eat. We oughter move across soon. This crossing is well known. We'd be better off far up the Trace when dark falls," Sam suggested, stooping to drink from the cascading stream.

"Couldn't we fish first?" asked Nate, who had rushed over after Sam.

"Not here, son. Maybe at a place I know," Sam answered.

Lessie heard something strange. She turned to Hart, a question in her eyes. Hart stood up and motioned for Sam to listen. The two of them turned, looking toward the west. The beating sound grew in intensity, its volume swelling.

"There they are!" Sam pointed to the west, off to the left of where the girls were sitting. Everyone turned to see what they were, fear in their hearts.

A unified gasp escaped the lookers. Countless numbers of birds were circling toward them. As they watched, the flight began to settle slowly to the ground a short way down the river on a sandbar.

"How beautiful! What are they?" gasped Callie, shading her eyes to see better.

"Passenger pigeons. See how rosy pink their bellies look? That's how you can tell them from regular pigeons. That and their size," Sam said, gazing in wonderment at the countless numbers of them. "They'd make a find supper, Hart."

"No, no! Please don't shoot them," Callie begged. "They're so beautiful."

"We've plenty of provisions. I bartered for some bear steak back at the stand. We'll grill it over an open fire," Hart said. "We let these go untouched," he added, glancing at Lessie's enraptured face.

"Thank you, Cousin Hart," Callie said. "I wouldn't be able to eat a bite of them, anyway."

The assemblage watched the pigeons while the horses fed on the thick moist grass that grew near the riverbank. Nate stretched out on a flat-topped rock and fell instantly asleep.

The women went to the river to wash their faces and hands and refill their water bags. Chulhkan had moved off in one direction, Standing Oak in another. Tchula had climbed to the top of a tall projecting rock and was smoking his pipe.

"I should check the horses. We don't want one to come up lame," Hart said to Lessie when she had returned from washing up at the river.

"Fine. If you don't need me, I'll rest here until you're ready to move on," she answered.

He moved off deliberately, pushing to the back of his mind the way her freshly washed skin glowed, the graceful way she moved to check Nate as he lay sleeping, and the wonderment he saw in her eyes when she looked up and caught him watching her.

"You ready to cross, now?" Sam asked. He had noted Hart's studied observation of Lessie and the look that passed between them when she caught him watching her.

"We'd better move," Hart said, pulling his attention away from Lessie.

"I'd say so," Sam agreed, grinning.

CHAPTER 10

S mythe watched the governor sign the arrest order for Colonel Sheffield Albright. The governor's face was solemn, his hand steady, as he affixed his seal to the letter.

"Deliver this to Major Scott. He and his militia are to seek out and capture Albright as soon as possible. I have written the militia in Nashville informing them of this man's treason. Between our forces, we should have him in hand soon." The governor handed the folded document to him.

"Certainly, sir," Smythe returned. "However, if I may, sir?"

"Yes, what is it?"

"I wonder if it wouldn't be prudent for us to gather more facts, find some witnesses who can point to the colonel's culpability in this affair before we issue an arrest order. We don't want to garner hostility from the local inhabitants unless we're certain of his guilt." Smythe's voice was civil, his eyes carefully watching for signs of indecision on the governor's part.

"We've got our witnesses, and we've got the word of Ms. Warren and Ms. Vespar, who heard the colonel admit his guilt. Chief Tchula and Hart MacAlpin are certain of Albright's part in the arming of the Indians against us. I don't see any need for hesitancy," the governor replied. "Issue the order as I directed."

"Certainly, sir," Smythe answered, turning and moving from the office. He'd hoped to delay action of any kind. Now due to Albright's stupidity, action was being taken before he and Bean were ready to move.

*****

By the fifteenth of November, the Natchez party had reached Duck River on the final leg of their journey to Nashville. There, they rested for two days before going on toward the small farm that belonged to Grandma Lord on the southwestern edge of Nashville.

Hart's shoulder had healed rapidly under the care of Sam and Lessie. There were no further attacks on the party. Except for Viola's constant irritability, the group had few problems.

Viola found fault in everything and everyone. Nate's constant chatter grated on her nerves, the endless days of slow riding bruised her dignity, and the wilderness fare they ate in the evenings around their camp fires made her quite ill, or so she declared.

"Now, Vi, don't fuss so," Callie insisted, offering her cousin one of the syrup cookies Lessie had made for them.

Their provisions were dwindling. Hart and Sam, and sometimes Tchula, would hunt each day, occasionally bringing in fresh venison or turkey. But for the most part, they lived on small pones of cornbread, some coffee, and the ever-available rabbit stew.

"Oh, hush yourself, Callie. You've been bossing me ever since we left Natchez. Don't you ever get tired?" Vi queried.

"I do, Vi. I get very tired of hearing all your endless complaints. We can all do without them," Callie asserted, rising and moving off to sit alone to finish her meal.

"Now don't fight, girls," Hart instructed. "We need to support each other. Viola, you do complain too much, and, in truth, Callie, you correct Vi too often."

Callie walked back over to Viola and sat down beside her. "Let's call a truce, Vi. I won't correct if you won't complain. How's that?"

"All right. I'll do my best to see something worthwhile in this awful wilderness. I'll do my best, but I'll make no promises."

The assembled diners all laughed. Viola was a trial. But she had a way of making them laugh.

"We should all get a good night's sleep. We'll cross the river by ferry in the morning," Hart advised. "This ferry is operated by the Nashville postmaster."

"Will the horses have to swim it?" Nate asked, his voice expectant.

"No, Nate. There will be room for everyone and the livestock," Sam informed, moving to rinse his plate in the pan of water by the fire. "Everybody, wash your plates and cups here," he instructed before moving off to check into sleeping arrangements for the men.

"The women will sleep in the cabin near the river." Hart pointed toward the large log structure that sat imposingly on a small knoll near the ferry. "The postmaster has generously allowed the ladies to stay with him and his wife."

*****

A well-trod road lay before them. It wouldn't be long now before they reached the Lord farm. Lessie hardly knew how she felt.

"What are you thinking about?"

The question caught her off guard. She had not noticed Hart ride back to join her.

"Just about my grandmother—and the fact that you will be leaving us here," she answered honestly.

"I'll be leaving you. But if your grandmother will allow, I'll leave Standing Oak and Chulhkan with you. They'll help you get through the winter, cut fire wood, hunt to provide their own provisions and some for you. You'll be fine," Hart insisted.

"I'm certain we'll be more than fine, Hart. You've already done so much for us. We can't thank you enough," Lessie replied.

"I don't want to leave you. You and Nate are very important to me. Remember that," he directed as he turned his horse and moved back to the head of the line.

The Lord farm, seen from the curving plateau of land over which the road ran, sat on level ground within a grove of maple trees. Wooden buckets hung from each tree, where they had been used to collect sap for making sugar. A shed where the sap was reduced by boiling stood near a small stream behind the cabin. Smoke curled from the rock chimney. The smell of cooking pervaded the air.

Hart walked to the cabin door and knocked.

A voice from inside immediately answered. "Who is it? What do you want?"

"I'm Hart MacAlpin from Natchez. I've brought Ms. Lessie Lord and her brother Nathaniel. Is this the Lord farm?"

The door slowly opened. Blue eyes stared into Hart's. The point of a rifle, which was aimed at his chest, poked through the door. After a moment, a young woman stepped out. She still held the rifle raised in shooting position, but it was now aimed upward and away from Hart's chest.

"I'm Sarah Lord. Grandma Lord was my grandmother. Who did you say you had brought with you?" she asked, looking directly at Lessie and Nate, who had moved their horses forward, expecting to dismount.

"Us," Lessie said, dismounting and moving toward the armed girl. "This is my brother, Nate. I'm Lessie Lord."

"I've heard of you," the girl said. "Gramma read me a letter she got from your father about a year back. I knew you were coming. But it's too late. She's dead."

Lessie was stunned. Too late. They had come all this way, and it was too late.

"Ms. Lord, perhaps we could all go inside," Hart suggested. "We can talk there. The rest of our party can take a few minutes' rest." He took Lessie's arm, giving her hand a light squeeze as he led her inside.

Once inside the cabin, the girl turned to Lessie. "You sit there. I'll fetch you a cup of tea. Would you others care for some?" she asked, moving toward the enormous rock fireplace that occupied one side of the room. "I was making some soup. You're welcome to eat."

"I would," Nate said, finding a bench near the stove and straddling it with his legs. "I'm that hungry."

"Nate!" Lessie corrected. "We'll accept a cup of tea with gratitude. We haven't had any for a while. But we need to talk. Nate and I will have to decide what to do," she continued.

Hart watched Sarah as she placed cups on saucers and filled them with steaming tea, then offered one to each of them. She was a pretty thing, with enormous blue eyes the color of cornflower blue, long, straight black hair, and a heart-shaped face. He could see some resemblance to Nate, but none to Lessie. The girls did not share the same coloring.

"Do you live here alone?" Hart asked.

"Yes, I have been since Gramma died," Sarah answered.

"Don't you mind? I mean staying here alone at night?" Lessie asked. She felt an immediate response to her cousin.

"Not much. You see, neighbors down the road a piece look in on me almost every day. We have a signal for trouble. If I fire my rifle, they can hear it well. They'll come quickly and well armed," Sarah told them as she moved to refill their cups. "They have four sons. All of them are good shots."

"Sounds as though you're well looked after," Hart responded. "Have you any plans for leaving here before the first of the year?"

"No, no, I haven't any plans for leaving at all," Sarah said, a question in her eyes as she watched her visitors.

"How far is it to Nashville?" Hart asked.

"Ten miles," Sarah answered.

"Then may I propose an alliance?" Hart asked.

"An alliance?" Sarah repeated. "What's that?" This man was interested in her cousin Lessie. Sarah was young, but she could see the signals pass between them. And the boy, Nate, hung on his every word. *Cousins*, she thought to herself. She had cousins.

"It's like this. I've some work to do in Nashville. Lessie and Nathaniel need somewhere to stay for a while. They had intended living here with their grandmother Lord." He paused, glancing at Lessie. "I have two cousins outside who need somewhere to stay until we start back to Natchez. Could we impose on your hospitality? Could you take in three young women and one boy for a few months?"

Sarah's face lit with pleasure. "Oh please, yes! I've been so lonely since Gramma died. And to have my own cousins here with me would mean so much. They would stay through Christmas?"

"Yes, we would," Lessie broke in. "And thank you, Sarah. We'll be able to bring each other up to date on our families."

"I'm that pleased," Sarah said, moving to retrieve their empty cups.

As she offered to refill them once again, Hart rose. "I'll tell Viola and Callie they'll be staying here. When they're ready to take care of their business in Nashville, I'll come for them," he finished. Then as he moved toward the door, he paused. "I want to leave two Choctaw friends here. They'll protect you, hunt to provide part of your food. Is that permitted?"

"I'd be pleased to have any friends of yours here. They'll have to sleep in the sugar mill, though. I don't have enough room here in the cabin," Sarah returned.

"They would prefer that," Hart reflected.

After introductions had been made and the women had retired to the cabin for the evening, Sarah told Lessie, Vi, and Callie something about her life. She had been raised in North Carolina. Her mother had passed away two years ago, and since Gramma Lord was the only relative she could find, she had found transportation here to the farm, where her grandmother had taken her in. The two of them had made plans for the three women and the boy to sell the farm, which brought in revenues from sugar each spring, and take a small house in Nashville, where Nate could go to school. But as often happens, fate had other plans. Gramma Lord had taken ill and died.

"I have some money," Sarah said. "My mother ran a tavern after my father died in an Indian uprising. When she died, I sold the building and brought the money with me. Gramma made me put it in the bank in Nashville where it would be safe. She said it would draw interest, and with the money from this farm, we could live off the interest and Nate could go to school. Gramma said you were serious about that, Lessie. Your father told her you'd only come if Nate could go to school."

"That's right. It's very important to me," Lessie said.

"But I don't want to," Nate informed them, looking up from the wooden puzzle he was attempting to work.

He was ignored.

"Sarah, it's good of you to allow us to stay here. We don't have any money, except a small amount I borrowed from our cousin John for traveling expenses. This is your home, not ours. Although we're first cousins, we don't make any claim on the farm or anything else

175

Gramma Lord may have left," Lessie stated. "We'd intended working the sugar mill with Grandmother Lord for our income," she continued. "Things have changed. We'll need to decide whether to move to Nashville or stay on here. But I'm delighted to find you here, to get to know you. We had thought all of you dead in the uprising."

"Most everyone was killed. My mother and me were in the woods, picking sassafras at the time. We didn't know anything about it until we got home. It was a shock. My mother never got over it," Sarah said, memories of horror mirrored in her eyes.

"I'm sorry," Lessie said, placing one arm around Sarah's shoulders. "We're together now. We're family. We'll be fine."

Hart spent a restless night. His mind labored between plans for hunting down Black Hat and the need to stay near Lessie and Nate. He had nearly lost them before he was truly aware of how much they meant to him. He was determined to guard them well.

He had told Lessie good-bye before they turned in for the night, as he, Sam, and Tchula, planned to leave for Nashville before daylight.

"Promise me that you won't leave the cabin unless Chulhkan and Standing Oak are with you. Promise me," he demanded.

"I promise," Lessie replied.

When he could tear himself away from her, he left her at the door of the cabin and went to his bedroll near Blister, the old feeling of desertion plaguing him.

*****

The captain of the militia listened raptly to Hart's tale of the burning and destroying of farms around the Natchez area, of the gunrunning, the attack on their caravan, the murder of the postmaster, and Zeke's consequent death. His interest peaked when told of retired Colonel Sheffield Albright's part in the scheme to take over the territory.

"We've only recently become aware of the strength of these rumors of takeover, Mr. MacAlpin. There is, we believe, a well-formed plot to drive us colonials out of the territory from a line near Canada to the Gulf. Major General Jackson believes another war with England is eminent. However, the Tennessee Militia cannot march against the British unless war is formally declared."

"I understand that, Captain. But what are we Natchezians to do if they attack Natchez?" Hart asked.

"Defend it with all force necessary. We cannot attack the British as a nation without a directive, but we can defend ourselves from attack," the captain explained.

"So what do we do about Sheffield Albright?" Hart continued. He disliked this hesitancy, this passive attitude in the face of proven treason.

"We've received an arrest warrant from the militia in Natchez, issued by the governor of the territory. I believe a Choctaw runner brought it in only this morning. Albright will be arrested and returned to Natchez."

"Thank you, Captain. Now all we have to do is find this Black Hat. Perhaps then we'll be able to stop the murdering and pillaging. It seems a large order, doesn't it?" Hart commented as he moved to leave the office.

"A large order, indeed, Mr. MacAlpin. But we have them between us now. Our militia on the north and yours on the south. Secrecy was their main ally. Now that we know what they're up to, we'll run their brass buttons all the way back to Canada."

"Thanks again," Hart said. "I'd like to see that."

"You may, Sir. You may," the captain said, rising and shaking Hart's hand.

*****

"How long is it till Thanksgiving, Lessie?" Nate sat on the floor of the cabin, shelling walnuts. He smacked each nut lightly with the bottom of the iron that Sarah had just finished using to iron his shirt and trousers. The warm scent of roasting nuts filled the room.

"It's tomorrow, Nate," Lessie answered. "Be sure to pick out all the shell bits. Don't put any in the bowl with the nut meat," she directed. She was churning butter in her grandmother's ancient hickory churn. The butter was coming nicely.

Sarah's two cows were cooperating with her efforts to have a plentiful Thanksgiving feast. Her few chickens were doing the same, laying better than Sarah could remember. They had eggs, butter, buttermilk, cream, and sweet milk for drinking.

Gramma Lord had not kept hogs. Sarah had said she thought them dangerous. But she did enjoy bacon or ham when she could get it. She often traded maple sugar or syrup for meat and provisions that she could not provide for herself.

The Lords and their guests, Viola and Callie, Chulhkan and Standing Oak, along with young Nathaniel fared well. A mill near Nashville provided flour and cornmeal. Sarah's garden provided mustard and turnips.

Lessie was content, except for worrying about Hart, which she did most of the time. He and Tchula had backtracked along their path to the farm and found where Albright had been captured by the band of Chickasaws. They had attempted to follow this new trail in the hope of capturing him and extracting Black Hat's identity. But the autumn rains had set in. The trail became a sodden mass of unreadable sign, leading nowhere.

Lessie's contentment and the unusually exultant attitudes of the braves and the girls was due, in part, to the seeming disappearance of the threatening comet. Its cloud of light had grown dimmer each evening since the middle of October. On one of Hart's visits to the farm, he had commented that Nashville newspapers stated that the comet had turned outward in its orbit and was moving steadily away from the earth. Everywhere he went, he had said, people seemed to be awakening from a state of shock. Those who had packed up and attempted to run were returning to their homesteads, bringing their children, livestock, and goods with them. Even the forest animals and birds were returning to their native haunts.

The autumn sun seemed brighter, the nights darker, as the great comet slipped away into the black expanse of the universe.

*****

The sun had not yet crawled above the forest roof when Nate rose. He rubbed the sleep from his eyes and pulled on his trousers, shirt, and jacket. Lessie had knitted him a woolen cap and mittens. He pulled them on as he quickly and silently closed the cabin door behind him. It was Thanksgiving. Hart was coming. He wanted to wait for him near the road to Nashville.

Walking along the path from the cabin to the edge of the road, Nate whistled happily. He was rewarded by Hart's prompt arrival just as he finished his tune. Blister was trotting, his tail up and his mane flying. He enjoyed early-morning runs when the weather was cool. It was hard to keep him in a trot.

"Hello, Hart! Hello," Nate shouted above the sounds of Blister's hooves.

"Hello, yourself," Hart replied.

At the sight of Nathaniel waiting to greet him in the early morning chill, the fatigue that plagued Hart seemed to dissipate. He and Tchula had been riding for days, seeking information concerning any known gun dealers. They were both exhausted.

"I'll take your horse," Nate said, grasping the reins as Hart dismounted.

The cabin door opened, and Lessie emerged, dressed in a Carmelite-brown dress. Square points of cream-colored lace met just beneath her chin. Her fair hair shone in the morning sun. She smiled when she saw him. "You're here at last," she said when he had dismounted and gathered her into his arms.

"I've missed you," he said finally, placing his arm around her shoulders and moving toward the cabin. "It's cold out here. We'd better get inside."

"Nathaniel. Come inside as soon as you put Blister in the stall. We'll have breakfast," Lessie called, a lilt to her usually soft voice.

"Okay," Nate yelled, trotting along beside Blister toward the stall at the rear of the cabin. "Good boy, Blister," he crooned. "Good boy."

*****

Chulhkan and Standing Oak had brought in a deer. Venison roast was on the menu. There would be greens with ham, dry beans, and buttermilk biscuits. Lessie was making a large pan of egg custard, which she would sprinkle with maple sugar. Gramma Lord had a large dutch oven with two shelves that sat to one side of the huge fireplace. Lessie would place the custard there until the top was browned and the sugar melted. It would be delicious. When it was time, biscuits would be baked on the bottom shelf.

"Lessie, can I have some of that custard now?" Nate begged. "I don't think I can wait."

"No, Nate. We must wait for the others," Lessie instructed. She knew how he felt. Her own stomach seemed to shrink by the minute as the preparations for their small feast grew.

A knock at the door brought Hart to his feet. When he asked who was there, Tchula answered.

"Come inside," Hart invited. "Nate, how about taking Tchula's horse around back?"

"Okay." Nate jumped to take care of the horse. At the open doorway, he turned and exclaimed, "He's brought a turkey!"

"I brought bird to include for meal," Tchula informed them, a pleased expression in his eyes. "It's cleaned and ready for roasting."

"Now that's the way to bring a bird to a party," Hart replied. "Here's Sarah with a cup of coffee for you. Where'd you get the turkey?"

"It flew in tree near where I passed. I got it with one shot," Tchula explained, pleased with himself.

"Hart, let's set a table up outside for our meal," suggested Callie. "It's such a lovely day. It'll be warm by early afternoon."

"Sounds good to me," Hart returned, glancing at Lessie, who was picking greens and placing them in a bucket of water.

"I'm for it," Sarah replied. "We'll eat as the early settlers did, out in the open."

Nate had returned from stabling Tchula's horse in time to hear the discussion about eating out of doors. Happiness shone from his eyes as he spoke. "We'll be just like the pilgrims, Lessie. Just like Mama read us in the book."

"Yes, Nate. Just like the pilgrims," Lessie agreed.

Sam arrived just before the meal was served in the warm autumn sunshine. He had been back down the Trace to visit Sophie and his children. She had told him to leave because a fever had broken out at the Stand. She was afraid he would catch it. He had reluctantly agreed, after providing her with venison, a twenty-five-pound bag of flour, which he had purchased in Nashville, and sugar, which Sarah had sold him. He worried at leaving them, especially at such a time. But Sophie had insisted that she and the Indian women would know how to deal with the fever. She was better off not having to worry about him.

Thanksgiving turned out to be the nicest ever for the assembly. Standing Oak and Chulhkan ate ravenously, having provided substantially to the feast. Sam finally sat back on the wooden bench, placed his hands on his abdomen and groaned.

After rapturous discussions all around concerning the food, the fantastic weather, the growing absence of the comet, the congeniality of those gathered, and a good deal of teasing of Hart and Lessie, whose love for each other was evident to all, Thanksgiving at Lord farm came to a close.

*****

The weeks following the gathering for Thanksgiving were filled with preparations for the coming winter. Standing Oak and Chulhkan were earning reputations as the world's greatest hunters. They brought in bear, from which both meat and lard was derived; deer, which was quartered and smoked in the hut they had built for the job; honey from a giant oak near the stream behind the cabin; and fish from various lakes they crossed while hunting.

Hart, Tchula, and Sam were gone most of the time. Hart and Tchula were visiting area farms, talking with the squatters, explaining the threat posed by the British. At one outpost not far from Nashville, they found a farmer who had seen the man called Black Hat riding with Chickasaws.

The farmer had been hunting along the edge of the Chickasaw nation that covered the western half of Tennessee. He could not identify the man in the black suit but remembered the way he had been dressed.

"All that black amidst those bare chests and leggings stood out, I can tell you," the farmer said. "I wondered if he was a parson."

"When was this?" Hart asked.

"Oh, 'bout a year back now, I guess," the farmer explained. "Didn't see him but that one time."

The next few weeks were spent similarly. It seemed to Hart that he now knew every back trail, every road, and every stream between Nashville and the Stand. But only the one squatter had ever seen Black Hat. Hart was beginning to wonder if the man was a mirage. Occasionally, Sam would find him, bring news of the Stand, the farm, and his own efforts at finding Black Hat. With Zeke's exodus from the scene, Black Hat's connection to the Stand was terminated. No one there had ever seen him.

Except for a brief note from Ash, which arrived by the usual method of runner, Hart had no news of his family. The note had stated that they all knew about Albright's part in the treason, that the governor had issued an arrest order for the colonel. Ash also mentioned that William Smythe had been visiting Ada, adding that he didn't trust the man. Hart understood. He had distrusted the man on first sight.

On December 16, the great San Madrid earthquake struck. It shook the earth from around the base of centuries-old trees, heaving them onto the ground. Those fleeing from its center at New Madrid, Missouri, told tales of horror and death. The ground sank all around its center. Great mile-long trenches were opened along the Mississippi River, allowing the water to flow backward, filling them, then forward along new erosions, changing the course of her path to the Gulf of Mexico.

When the tremors were felt at the Lord farm, Nathaniel was fishing in the stream behind the cabin. The flowing water began to slosh, to run backward, then forward, spreading into new areas. Nate was stunned, his cane pole still hanging out over the trembling water, his line weighted. Even as the earth trembled and shook beneath his moccasin-clad feet, he started to run, dropping the pole and his bucket of freshly caught fish.

His path toward the cabin was irregular, his forward movement shifted by the sideways movement of the earth. He didn't realize he was yelling at the top of his voice until he reached the yard just in front of the cabin. It began to shake, the windows breaking even as he watched, hypnotized.

"Lessie! Lessie!" he could hear himself screaming. "Come out!"

The door was pushed back, sagging awkwardly, as the four women pushed through.

"Nate! Here," Lessie called, reaching for him.

They clung together, standing in the middle of the path leading to the front door. Viola, Callie, and Sarah did likewise. Two frail groups of humanity united in fear as the trembling and shaking suddenly stopped.

No one moved. There was not a sound. The entire world was silent in the face of nature's onslaught. Afterward, they could never remember how long they had clung together in silence, fear holding them captive.

"I think it's safe now," Nathaniel suggested, releasing his grip on Lessie. "Let's see about the animals and the cabin."

Lessie moved toward the cabin, pausing at the door. She pushed with all her might to see if it would collapse. It stood firm, the doorway permanently angled, glass gone from the two front windows.

"Is it safe?" questioned Sarah. "Can we go inside?"

"I think so," Lessie answered. "Everything's a mess. We'll have to clean up."

Nate returned from the sugar mill just as the women were entering the cabin. "The animals got loose. They're all fine, except for one of the chickens. It was trapped under the henhouse. It's dead."

"Providence be thanked," replied Viola, her face white.

"Where's Standing Oak?" asked Callie. "He was standing guard today. He was down by the mill."

Nate looked at Lessie, his face solemn. "I'm afraid he's dead too."

"Oh no! Take us to him," Lessie directed, running out the door and around the cabin.

When they found him, he was lying facedown, a huge maple tree across his back. After climbing through the limbs, they examined him. Callie looked at his eyes. They were unblinking and staring. His back had been crushed.

Nathaniel went for a saw. The five of them began to work at sawing away the limbs and cutting up the huge trunk to free Standing Oak's body. Everything else was forgotten. They had removed enough of the tree to roll the last remaining section of trunk from his body when Blister appeared behind them, sweat rolling off his hide, great puffs of hot breath escaping his flared nostrils.

Hart dismounted and ran forward. "Are you all right?"

"All of us here are," Lessie replied, moving to his side. "But Standing Oak is dead. He was on guard. The tree fell on him."

Hart looked at his friend, his face reflecting both anxiety and grief, the long scar colored with his efforts to reach them. "I tried to get here as soon as I could. I was only a few miles back when it started."

"Was it an earthquake?" Nate asked.

"Yes," Hart answered. "A great one."

The following day, Chulhkan returned from his hunting trip, safe but suffering from the same kind of shock as the rest of them. When told of Standing Oaks death, he remained stoic. Not until late evening did he visit the grave where his cousin lay buried according to colonial custom. He said nothing, simply turned and walked away, heading south toward his family. Hart and the women understood. He needed to know if his family had survived.

Christmas came and went. Hart and Tchula were at the farm for the holiday. Sam had returned to the Stand to be with his family. He would join them in the spring in Nashville.

*****

The Cumberland River dock was a bustle of activity on the spring morning of March third. Various boats were being built, loaded, or dismantled all along the pier. The MacAlpin broadhorn was the object of scrutiny since it was the largest raft being built on the river.

Two other quakes had occurred, one in January and one in February, both doing minor damage over a wide area. Runners from the Chickasaw village at Chickasaw Bluffs had told the story of pandemonium and death in the wake of the December quake, which was centered near them in the Mississippi River valley area. They bragged that the great Shawnee, Tecumseh, had forewarned of this event, that he was indeed a great and knowledgeable man. The colonials were still too stunned to argue the point.

Sam Shute blew smoke rings into the air. He was perched on top of a stack of eighty-foot logs that were being used to build the broadhorn. Much as an owl would sit and scan the ground seeking prey, Sam watched over the construction. He'd had experience in building broadhorns and knew how to handle the work crew. Hart had hired a Nashville carpenter and his apprentices to build the craft. Sam had been put in charge of overseeing the job. And overseeing it, he intended to do. Nothing escaped his owl-like gaze.

The boat would be eighty feet by forty feet in length and width on the bottom level. A second level of forty feet by twenty feet would stand in the exact center. The lower level would be partitioned off to hold hogs, cows, and hardware for the commissary in Natchez and the horses that the group owned. The upper level would be used for sleeping and eating, with a kitchen boasting an iron stove that would be dismantled and sold in Natchez.

The front end of the broadhorn was raised higher than the sides, with a wide-pointed prow, which greatly improved navigation. Long oars attached four to the side maintained its stability. If they were lucky, they would make it to Natchez in one piece with the craft intact where it would be cut up and sold as lumber.

The work crew already had the lower level floored. The huge wooden structure floated just offshore, an extension of the pier.

Hart approached Sam's stack of logs, his eyes taking in every detail of the rapidly growing broadhorn. He'd been in town making arrangements for the cattle and swine his father had wanted brought to Natchez.

"How's it going?" he asked.

"Fairly well, I reckon. Those gents seem to know what they're about," Sam returned, knocking the ashes from the pipe he had been smoking.

"When do you think it will be ready?"

"If the weather holds, I'd say by the end of the week."

"Good. You know what to do, Sam. I'll leave it with you. I'll pay the men off when I return with the women. I'm going for them today. They can stay in the boarding house until we're ready to leave. Callie has business to take care of," Hart explained.

"That's fine by me," Sam said. "I'll be stocking up on needfuls while you're gone. I didn't want to buy any until I could put them in storage on the boat and stay aboard at night. We don't want them liberated before we set off."

"Good thinking, Sam. By the way, I've been concerned about handling the craft. Do you think the three of us can handle it? There will be four women aboard. Sarah Lord is coming with us. They may have to help row," Hart declared.

"Seems to me women are more useful than otherwise. Having four of them aboard might be an advantage," Sam stated, as Hart prepared to remount Blister and return to Lord Farm. "Probably don't need to hire extra men."

Hart saluted as he turned away, a grin stretching the facial scar wide. Sam had his own ideas about women—ideas which he didn't mind articulating. He preferred them to men in most instances. Said you could always count on a woman to run true to form. It wasn't so easy figuring a man.

Thinking of the women caused Hart's thoughts to turn to Lessie. He was amazed at the change in his own attitude toward women since he'd met her. His previous determination to enjoy their fellowship without entangling himself with any particular one had evaporated since that first evening. Ada's betrayal had made him distrust all of them, causing him to look only at the surface, the transitory aspects of each. Lessie had taught him a valuable lesson. He would now evaluate women more fairly, each independently of any other, as he did men.

*****

Sarah and Lessie took one last look at Gramma Lord's farm—at the sturdy log cabin, which had withstood three earthquakes; at the sugar house, which had been partially destroyed; at the grove of giant maple trees, some down as a result of the quakes but most still stand-

186

ing, each festooned with a wooden bucket; at the small garden plot, already green with sprouting turnips; and at the iron pot beside the stream used for washing clothes, making soap and hominy.

"I'll miss this place," Sarah cried softly, a single tear escaping down her cheek. "I was happy here with Gramma."

"I have a good feeling about this place, Sarah. We'll be coming back here sometime," Lessie said. "Gramma left it to us. We've leased it to your friends down the road, and we'll receive money from it yearly. And with Hart as our business manager, we'll do well."

"Com'on Lessie, Sarah. Don't be so poky!" Nate called from aboard his horse.

"All right," Sarah said at last. "We're coming."

When Hart had assisted them into their saddles, the Lord family, Hart, Tchula, Viola, and Callie set off for Nashville and the trip down the Mississippi aboard their broadhorn. The ten-mile trip didn't take long, and they arrived at the boarding house downtown by noon. The women removed only what they would need for the night from their baggage. The broadhorn was ready. They would be leaving early in the morning.

"I'll return here for dinner this evening," Hart told Lessie. "The O'Donald's serve a good meal."

"We're going to walk around town, do some shopping after lunch," she replied. "Viola wants some special lace, which she thinks she can find here."

"Just stay on the walks and out of the alleys," Hart advised. "Muggings have taken place in secluded areas."

"We will," she agreed as he turned Blister toward the street. He and Tchula rode off toward the dock area.

"Boat looks like house on water," Tchula said, when they rode into sight of it. "Big."

"It needs to be. We need ample room. The stock will be more content if they're not so crowded while aboard," Hart replied.

Sam saw them coming and walked to the edge of the gangplank, his open Bible still in his hand. He'd been doing his daily reading while awaiting their arrival.

"Good day, Sam," Hart said, dismounting and tying Blister to one of the iron hitching posts along the wharf.

"Good day, yourself," he replied, nodding to Tchula, who was coming aboard right behind Hart.

"It looks fit," Hart said, standing on the upper deck, surveying every corner.

He entered the raw-timbered kitchen and checked the iron stove, which sat in one corner with its chimney poking through the board roof. Then he opened the two sleeping compartments, taking note of the four bunk beds in each. Everything had been done according to his directions.

"You've done well, Sam. You deserve a bonus."

"Thanks, but I'll just take what's due me," Sam returned, his Bible tucked under his arm. "Nothing more, nothing less."

The three of them had descended the wooden stairs to the water level to inspect the holding pens and storehouses when a shot brought them up short.

Hart reached the gangplank first. Tchula stood to his side. Sam aimed his loaded rifle from behind the high walls of the prow.

"I don't see anything," Hart said.

"There! Running this way," Sam shouted, pointing down the dock area to the east. "Looks like a runaway slave."

The tall black man ran straight for them. When he came abreast of the broadhorn, he hesitated. Looking at Hart, he pleaded wordlessly for help. Hart stepped out, putting the slave between himself and Tchula who had his rifle ready.

"Stand off there!" commanded a burly-faced man as he raced his horse toward them. "Stand off. That slave is a runaway. I intend taking him back."

"No! No! He's trying to steal me," the slave said, his body partially hidden by Hart's.

"Wait just a minute!" Hart was adamant. "This man says you're trying to steal him. What about it?"

The burly face turned beet red. "That's none of your business. Now get outer the way, or I'll go through you."

The pistol was in Hart's hands and cocked before the man had finished speaking. Angry eyes stared at it, not blinking. Indecision held him fixed where he sat. His horse whinnied, sweat foaming around its neck and shoulders. It was a standoff. Hart stood poised, ready to shoot. The stranger sat his horse, his rifle leveled at Hart. For a moment nothing moved.

Then a brusque voice from the broadhorn rasped out, "You're outnumbered, friend. Think it over."

At that moment, the bulbous eyes moved. Tchula leaped from behind Hart. He pulled the man off his horse, pinning his arms behind him.

"What's your name?" Hart asked the slave. "Do you have papers?"

"My name's John. I had papers. This man took me out of a field near Coily. I belong to the Benne family. He stole my papers," the black man's words sizzled with hate. "I got family back there."

Hart considered the situation. A sizable crowd had gathered. He saw two militiamen walking their way. He motioned to Sam to keep his weapon aimed, then turned to John. "If what you say is true, you'll be returned there. If not, you're on your own."

When the militiamen arrived, Hart told them what had happened. The bulbous eyed man insisted he'd been accosted by Hart. It was decided that the man and the slave would be held until their stories could be checked.

"Thanks, mistuh. Thanks," the slave said over his shoulder as he was led away. "I got a family back there."

"You reckon he's telling the truth?" Sam mused.

"Probably so. I'm told it goes on all the time. If the slave has papers or can prove his ownership, he'll be returned. The other one will go to jail. It's a crime to steal slaves and resell them. Some of these types steal them a second and third time, reselling them, moving them around the country until someone gets wise."

"Seems unnatural to me, one man owning another," Sam said.

The three men stood watching the slave being led away. Each man's thoughts were his own.

CHAPTER 11

Rain soaked the broadhorn that first morning. The four women huddled together in front of the stove. The air was damp and cold. Nate wouldn't be kept inside. He wanted to be in the prow, watching the river as they floated rapidly, awkwardly along.

Sam was at the tiller, guiding the heavily loaded vessel, striving to keep it square with the shore. Hart was on deck, watching for floating logs, which might send them into a spin. Tchula was attempting to quiet the animals. They were nervous, unsettled, on this first day of their journey down the Cumberland to the Mississippi.

Lessie ventured on deck, a warm shawl over her head, her pelisse fastened tightly against the March wind. She relished the taste of spring, which the rain and wind tossed abroad, carrying the scent of sweet blossoms, the pungency of wet pines and cedars. The attack on their caravan, the comet's threat to earth, even the earthquakes, seemed distant now, almost as though they had happened to someone else.

Hart saw her standing with her back against the wall of the cabin, her head lifted. "Enjoying the fresh air?" he asked, walking along the deck toward her.

"Yes, it's heavenly, but cold. The weather is so changeable this time of year," she stated as he joined her.

"It's warm in the cabin," he said, taking her hands, feeling their chill.

"I know. But I want to stay here for a while longer. I don't know, it's cold, but there's freedom here with the damp and the wind in my face," she stated, smiling at him.

He smiled in return. He knew what she meant. He'd felt something similar many times as he stood on the vast pampas in solitary contentment. But as he studied the way her damp hair curled around her face, he knew he'd never again be content alone.

"I have work to do. You distract me," he added, grinning at her. "Call me at noon. I'll want something to eat."

"Yessir!" she answered, laughing softly.

It was because Hart was here. It was because of their complete faith in each other that she felt this bonding with the earth, with the rain and wind. Nothing that happened would ever overshadow that.

*****

"I don't believe it!" Mildred Albright stated vehemently. "This is all some grotesque mistake."

"I'm sorry, Mildred. But I felt you should know that an arrest warrant is out for Sheff. The governor says he has sufficient evidence to try him on charges of treason."

Angus was weary. He'd been with the governor all morning. There was nothing he could do. The fact that Hart had sent the letter incriminating Sheff, with Viola and Callie's corroboration, had convinced even Angus that Sheff must be guilty.

"If you're all so certain that my husband is guilty of treason, where is he?" Mildred demanded. "He left here with the Lord girl and her brother. He must be where they are. Unless they all died in one of the quakes," she finished, her voice quivering.

"No, Mildred," Angus continued, his face tightening, "the letter stated that the colonel had joined a group of Chickasaws after the attack on the caravan, that he held some authority with them. My own nieces, Viola and Callie, were captured by these same Chickasaws. They too witnessed Sheff's treasonable behavior."

"I...I...just...won't believe it," she cried, her eyes dry, her voice pained. "And yet, I did see—"

"Now, Mama, don't get upset. You know how Papa does things. It's probably just some silly mistake," Ada enjoined, patting her mother's hand. "It'll be straightened out in time. I'm sure it will."

"This Black Hat you mentioned, Angus, he must be the culprit, not Sheff. Sheff must have been taken in somehow."

"Black Hat's at the head of it. We know that much. But we don't have a clue about his identity. That's what Hart and the others are trying to uncover," Adam interjected. "I wonder if he's the caped figure who was following Bruce that night."

"Caped figure? What caped figure?" Mildred gasped, her attention now on Adam.

Adam glanced at his father. He'd let the cat out of the bag, he supposed. His father's nod permitted him to continue. "We've evidence—Hart has evidence of someone else at the scene of Bruce's death. Someone wearing a dark cape, riding a pony." Adam stated these facts candidly, watching the appalled expression grow on Mildred Albright's face.

"Is that all you know...about this caped figure?" she asked, glancing around the room.

"That's about it, Mildred," Angus answered. "We know that Bruce died of a blow to the head, not from being shot."

"I suppose you're blaming that on Sheff as well," she argued.

"We're not blaming him with anything, Mildred. We're simply apprising you of the facts involved in the warrant for Sheff's arrest and what we know about Bruce's death," Angus stipulated.

"I suggest you find the person responsible for it all, then, instead of accusing my husband when...when he isn't present to defend himself," Mildred continued. She looked faint. The news of the arrest order had greatly shocked her. "And I suggest you issue an arrest warrant for that Lessie Lord. She's guilty of murder. I believe it's still unlawful to shoot a man. You said yourself that she had fired on a man at the Stand and killed him."

"Shush, Mama. We'll go home. I'll stay with you for a while," Ada suggested, glancing at Adam as she spoke.

Adam rose and offered his arm to Mildred as Angus apologized for the second time for bringing her such bad news.

Mildred glanced at him, her head high. She'd never liked Angus MacAlpin very much. As children, they'd never been able to get along. As adults, they were the same. "Your apology is not accepted,

Angus MacAlpin. You should have championed Sheffield. After all, he is the father of your daughter-in-law. He is a part of your family. But you seem to prefer waifs to genteel folk." She turned, brushed Adam's arm aside, and spoke to Ada. "Come. We're going home. The treason, if there is such, lies in this house."

When they had gone in a flurry of carriage wheels and flying dirt clods, the MacAlpins retired for the evening.

Flora couldn't sleep. Worry creased her brow. She wondered what was happening to Hart and his party. The letter he'd sent to the governor had told them little. She feared the worst. She had heard such stories of horror. The Trace claimed so many of those who attempted to travel over it. And the earthquakes. There had been three, one each month for three months, as well as numerous small shocks. Did they survive? Where were they now? Were they all right?

Before she had climbed the stairs to bed, Adam had tried to reassure her. "Don't worry so, Mam. Hart can take care of himself, and he has Sam and Tchula with him. The women will be fine too. He'll look after them," Adam stated.

There had been a look of fear in his mother's eyes ever since word had come of the attack on the caravan. It was December 16, about two in the morning, when the letter arrived. Adam had answered the heavy knocking. A Choctaw runner stood on the porch. He offered a leather pouch to Adam just as the ground began to shake. It had vibrated slowly at first, then stronger motion was felt. Adam gripped the door frame for support. The Indian braced himself against one of the pillars as the shock waves moved under their feet.

All of Natchez now knew that it had been an earthquake, that its origin had been somewhere north along the Mississippi River, that it had wrought destruction in its path. Even in Natchez, boats had broken their moorings, glass had shattered, people had fallen to the ground, unable to stand against the trembling. Another had occurred just after Christmas, on January 23, and a third on February 7, yesterday. He could understand his mother's worry. He was worried himself.

"I do worry, Son," his mother had said. "Even the strongest, the smartest, the wisest are sometimes deceived.

"What do you suppose Ms. Albright saw?" Adam asked, changing the subject.

"How do you mean?"

"She said she did see something the night Bruce died. I think she knows more than she's telling," Adam suggested.

*****

The broadhorn was docked for the night. Hart had pointed out an inlet on the north side of the river, where it formed a large lake. Sam had guided the broadhorn there. They would enter the Ohio tomorrow. From there, they would float southwest into the mighty Mississippi, the mother of waters.

"Hart, can I pull some of that fresh grass for Blister and the other horses?" Nate asked when the boat had been securely tied ashore.

"Some. Not much. They'll have to get used to it a little at a time," Hart responded, glad the boy wanted to help. "Then ask your sister if she needs the ashes removed from the stove, will you?"

Nate nodded his head, already scampering off after grass for the horses.

When they had attended to the animals, the evening meal was served. Everyone ate aboard the boat, on deck. The weather had turned warm. Stars shone brightly in the clear evening sky. If anyone remembered the horror of the past several months, it wasn't evident, as they chatted conversationally with each other.

"How much longer will it take?" Viola asked Hart from her position on a bench by the railing.

"About ten days. Once we enter the Mississippi, we'll float faster. The currents are very strong," Hart answered. "I pray the river is navigable after those quakes. Stories have it that it changed its course."

"What will we do if it has?"

"Find some other means of getting to Natchez," Hart returned quickly. He didn't want panic aboard. They'd do what they had to.

"Thank goodness. I'll never leave home again," she declared. "I don't see how we've made it this far."

"I will," Nate responded, holding out his hand for more bread. "I'm going to be a wilderness man."

"You'll be no such thing, Nathaniel. You're going to school. Our grandmother left us land for just that purpose," Lessie corrected.

"I don't want to go to school. I'd be a sissy," Nate returned, not in the least threatened.

"Whoa," Sam said, knocking the ashes from his pipe overboard. "Hart there went to school. In fact, some of us had decided he always would," he continued, casting a sly glance in Hart's direction. "I wouldn't call him a sissy, would you?"

"Hart went to school! I didn't know that," Nate answered, his determination slipping. "Did you Hart?"

"Yes."

"What for?"

"To learn about the world, the stars, many things," Hart replied.

Nate searched Hart's face intently. Maybe there was something to this school thing after all. He'd have to think on it. "I'll think on it, then," he stated affirmatively, sinking onto the floor and finishing off his plate of food.

The next day, late in the afternoon, they sighted the Mississippi, its muddy waters a mile wide or more where the Ohio joined it.

"Sam, hang tight to the tiller," Hart warned. "Tchula! Get to the other side and man the fore oar. Sarah, you and Callie take the two behind him. Lessie, you and Vi follow me. There are whirlpools here."

Everyone did as they were instructed.

"Nate, go up on deck. Watch for any floating debris that's large enough to turn us, even if most of it is underwater," Hart ordered.

With a speed previously unknown to most of them, the broadhorn slid into the Mississippi, slipping sideways for a while as Sam struggled to correct its position.

"We'll be moving much faster now. Watch carefully, Nate," Hart called again.

Managing the broadhorn in such swift water took all the strength they possessed. Everyone aboard had to work diligently, either handling the oars, the tiller, or watching for the ever-present, ever-threatening debris, which had been left in great abundance by the quakes and moved first above water, then below, as the various currents took it.

Every night, the recumbent craft rested beside land, securely tied to a standing tree, its passengers exhausted. On the evening of the third day on the Mississippi, the horses went for a swim. Everyone was in their usual place, attempting to maintain the boat's direction southward without the hidden currents taking it ashore, or turning it into a spin, which would finally end in capsizing it.

"Watch horses!" yelled Tchula, who had seen them pushing toward a weak section of their railing. "Horses go over!" he yelled again, just as they did, in fact, break through the log railing and begin to slide, one by one into the water.

Hart and Sam were frozen, one to the tiller and the other to his oar.

Suddenly, Lessie was beside Hart. "Go. I'll handle the tiller."

Hart ran toward the left side of the prow, where the horses had been penned. Most of them were in the water. Blister had skidded against the side, attempting to keep a foothold on the deck. Hart grabbed him, hanging on as the broadhorn rammed into a small island.

"What do we do now?" asked Callie, her usually gentle expression one of consternation, her hands glued to the oar.

"Watch the horses! They're swimming ashore just behind us. We'll go ashore and collect them," Sam yelled.

For answer, Hart and Tchula grabbed ropes, while Lessie and Callie tied the broadhorn to a tree, their skirts dragging in the muddy water.

The island wasn't large, but the horses wouldn't be caught. Hours went by while the three men chased them. Finally, just after sundown, the last of them gave up grazing and returned to the edge of the river. Tchula went ashore and caught it, leading it back onto the broadhorn.

Sleep came quickly. Snores could be heard from several directions as the evening grew late. Finally, even Tchula was fast asleep, his rifle beside him.

The wooden boards of the broadhorn creaked. Tchula opened his eyes, adjusting them to the dark. He lay still, his heart pounding.

Something was wrong, he thought, just as a knife blade thudded into the deck beside his head. Feet, bodies, and hands were all around him. He cried out. Instantly the others came awake. A rifle was fired from the gangplank, another from shore. A body dropped beside him as he grappled with another.

Sounds of battle grew as the three men attempted to stave off a boarding party of Chickasaws. All at once, gunfire from the upper deck was heard. The women were shooting, dropping two of the Indians at once. The others decided they were outnumbered and either jumped overboard or dashed back across the gangplank to the island, where they were immediately swallowed up in the dark.

"Get a lantern, some light," Hart ordered, groping for his rifle. He'd been fighting with his dirk, the only weapon he could find in the dark.

The door to the dining hall opened, light shone through. A gun fired again, just off to the right of the broadhorn, as a figure ran forward, crossed the gangplank, and collapsed beneath the railing, cowering low.

Hart held up the lantern that Lessie had handed to him. The figure was Sheffield Albright! He seemed a wasted man. His clothes were muddy, covered with dirt, his face white, devoid of expression.

"We can't leave him, Hart," Lessie pleaded as Sam dragged him to his feet and prepared to run him back down the gangplank to the waiting Chickasaws.

"Hold on, Sam. We need him. He can tell us who Black Hat is," Hart insisted.

"Looks as though his friends have turned on him," Sam said, pulling Albright back aboard and shoving him down near Hart.

Hart reached down and helped the man to his feet. "Can you stand, Colonel?"

"Yes, I think so," the colonel replied, his voice weak. "They were going to kill me."

"Why?" questioned Hart.

"I began to realize what a fool I'd been to get involved with them. They didn't want me free, afraid I'd talk, I suppose," the colonel replied.

"You're not off the hook. You've a lot of talking to do if you want to live. Where'd you come from?"

"There," the colonel said, pointing eastward toward high bluffs along the far edge of the river. "It's a Chickasaw village. There're British soldiers there too."

"How did you happen to get away?"

"I hid a canoe, expecting to take it after dark and float down river to New Orleans. From there, I had no plans." The colonel's voice shook with cold and terror.

"Tell me, who is the leader in this plot to take over the territory?" Hart demanded, his hands in the colonel's lapels.

"I don't—wait! I'll tell you when you land at Silver Street Wharf in Natchez—not before. I will pay for my safe passage with his name," the colonel stated, color beginning to creep into his face. "But I take the broadhorn on downriver to New Orleans. Its lumber will buy my passage to Bermuda. I'll be safe there."

"You've a lot of gall," bellowed Sam, still wanting to throw him back to the Chickasaws.

"That's my deal. Take it or leave it," the colonel replied, stubbornly. "Don't you see? I can send for Mildred in a year or so if I find work. It's our only chance. I'll be hung if the militia find me," he pleaded, his eyes on Hart's.

"I'll take it," Hart said, his eyes watching the colonel's, seeing the fear that lay there, "if you answer one question. Did you have anything to do with Bruce's death?"

The colonel's faced blanched again. His body began to tremble. He staggered as he attempted to sit down on a bench by the rail. Hart assisted him, ordering brandy and a blanket. The colonel dropped his head into his hands.

"I'll get him the brandy, Hart," Lessie said, moving toward the stairs. "You'd better cover him. He's wet all through."

Nate brought a blanket, and Hart pulled it around the colonel's shoulders. When Lessie returned with the brandy, he straightened himself and drank some before looking directly at Hart.

"I regret to say that I caused your brother's death. It was the blackest day of my life. You know I wouldn't have killed him deliberately," he added, as Hart moved toward him, his right hand gripping the dirk.

"Caused it? How?" Hart demanded, his voice low, cold.

"He followed us one night to the south of Brightway. You know, just where you found him. He wanted us to pay him for his silence. He attempted to blackmail me," the colonel stated. "I became angry and accused him of mistreating Ada, of cheating on her. He grew angry too. The next thing I knew, I had started to swing my fist into his face when I accidentally hit Zeke's gun hand. His gun went off, killing Bruce. That's all there was to it. One minute he was standing there, attempting to blackmail me, the next he was on the ground," he finished, pushing himself as far away from Hart as he could get.

"Don't look at me like that! I didn't pull the trigger. I told you it was an accident. Anyway, I was told by Captain Bean that the man called Zeke was dead," Sheffield added, attempting to distract Hart from the all-too-obvious idea forming in his mind.

Hart slowly replaced his dirk in its sheath, turned, and walked off by himself. No one moved to follow. Tchula and Sam got the colonel on his feet. After they searched him for hidden weapons, they left him on his own. There was nowhere for him to go.

"I'm sorry about your brother," Lessie said. She was standing beside Hart. "At least you know how it happened."

"That's just it. The doctor said he was struck on the head, that the blow actually killed him, not the gunshot wound. The colonel didn't mention a blow to his head. It must have been done after he left Bruce for dead. But who?"

"The person wearing the cape?" Lessie questioned.

"Must have been," Hart replied.

The two of them stood together, watching the dark water move beneath the broadhorn, giving Hart time to adjust to his feelings of rage and pity.

*****

"Nate! Nate! Where are you?" Lessie called, her voice growing with each unanswered call. She began to run, holding her skirts in her hand as she searched along the railings, in the cargo area, in the storeroom, in the sleeping quarters and on deck. He was nowhere to be found.

"Nate!" she screamed.

Tchula was the first person to reach her. He caught her and shook her until she stopped screaming. Then as Hart reached them, Tchula handed her to him and began to search for the boy himself. Sam took one look at Hart's face and did the same. The girls stood nearby, stunned.

"Sam, head for shore on this side. We'll walk back and search for him," Hart directed.

"When was the last time you saw him?" he asked Lessie.

"Last night after the colonel came aboard. He was in his bunk. Hart, where is the colonel?" she asked.

"Tchula, where's the colonel. Have you seen him this morning?"

For reply, Tchula lifted his rifle, jumped off the broadhorn just as it bumped into the grass-covered bank, and began to run back the way they had come, searching the shoreline.

When Sam had knotted the anchoring rope around a stump, he and Hart jumped ashore and began to search for the two missing passengers. But search as they did, they could not find them. Hart's voice grew husky as he called the boy's name again and again. Finally, when it grew dark, they returned to the broadhorn to rest. The next morning, they would row the craft over to the opposite shore and search back along that side to a point across from where they had been docked.

Lessie stood near the deck railing, watching the churning water. When Hart attempted to console her, she turned away in silence. Her silence hurt. He held himself at fault for not watching the boy more carefully. He'd known from the beginning that Nate possessed an adventuresome spirit, that he needed close supervision. It was his fault that Nate was lost, that Lessie was suffering from grief and shock.

When dawn burned its way over the eastern horizon, the three men rowed the broadhorn across the expanse of the river and tied up on the eastern shore. There they separated and began to search along that side, calling Nate's name loudly. They didn't bother calling the colonel's name. They figured he could look after himself. Once again, they returned to the broadhorn without either of the missing passengers. It was concluded that Nate must have caught the colonel attempting to get away and been carried off with him. The colonel could hide forever if he knew how to feed and clothe himself. But what about Nate? Would the colonel allow him to live? Callie asked the question.

"No, no, the colonel would not hurt Nate," Hart insisted, seeing the horror build in Lessie's eyes. "He might bring about the death of a man, accidentally, but he'd never harm a boy."

Hart had gone straight to Lessie when they returned from searching along the eastern shore.

"Let it go, Lessie. Don't hold it inside. It'll make you ill. I know," he added, shaking her slightly. "I know."

She raised her head and looked at him. Gone was the glow of vitality, the sparkle that had recently been found in her every glance, her every movement. Her eyes were now pools of misery in which he was drowning. He released her and walked away.

And that's the way it stayed between them. Nothing Hart could do or say reached her. She moved about the boat, handling the oars when necessary, cooking, eating, and pretending to sleep. But she said nothing.

They gave up the search after three days and resumed their journey down river.

"How much longer, Ishto Impa?" Tchula asked. He watched Lessie as she walked up and down the deck above them.

"Two days, I think," Hart responded.

He too had been watching her solitary walk. She seemed determined to suffer alone, to blame herself for Nate's death. He'd tried to talk to her time and time again, but it did no good. He'd lost her. He'd lost her just as surely as they'd lost Nate.

"I agree," Tchula said. "I know this place." He pointed toward the eastern bank of the river. "Good hunting in winter."

"Will she be all right?" Hart asked, his eyes still following Lessie's pacing form.

"Maybe," Tchula said. "She need time. You wait."

"I don't know if I can," Hart answered. "I hate seeing her like this."

"You strong. You wait," Tchula insisted, casting Hart a positive look. "She worth it."

Hart knew Tchula was right. She was worth any amount of time left to him on this earth. But he didn't know if he was strong enough to watch her suffer. It was the hardest thing he had ever been forced to do.

The broadhorn floated steadily down the river, rounding bends, avoiding rapids, secured by a heavy rope at night. Its human inhabitants talked little, stood apart from each other, spoke only when necessary. Nate's loss and Lessie's suffering had divided them.

At noon, on April first, 1812, they sighted the Silver Street wharf.

Viola sang out, "We're home. We've made it."

Hart looked at Lessie, who was standing in her usual place, watching the river, her expression unchanged. His heart broke at the sight.

*****

Sam agreed to see to the unloading of the animals and other cargo while Hart went to help the women ashore. He found them gathering their bags, talking amiably. The sight of home had restored their spontaneity—all except Lessie. She was standing quietly by her packed bag. A smaller one sat beside it.

"I've sent Tchula up to the store to borrow the buggy. He'll drive Viola and Callie out to their farm. I'd like you and Sarah to come home with me," he began.

"No, thank you, Hart," Lessie answered, her voice lifeless. "I want to go home—to Wellsley Farm. Sarah is coming with me."

"Fine," he replied curtly. "Tchula can drop you off first." Her continued withdrawal tore at his insides until he wanted to shake her, wake her up to his own pain, his own suffering. But instead he said, "Sam, I'll see you at the tavern, later. Thanks for all your help."

"We're not finished," Sam said. "We'll get the leader yet."

"I have to admit it looks hopeless at this point," Hart returned. "I've an idea he's right here in Natchez. In fact, there's something about one of the governor's aides that teases my memory. But we have no proof."

*****

"Hart! Oh, Hart, you're back!" Ada cried, rushing forward.

Hart was standing in the open doorway of Crapewood. He'd arrived in time to witness an embrace between Ada and the man whose stance teased his memory.

"I'm so glad to see you, so glad you're all right. We've been so worried. Welcome home," she said, standing on her toes to kiss him lightly on the cheek.

"Where's Papa and Mam?" he asked, pushing her gently away from him.

"They're in the parlor," she replied, her voice chilling slightly. "We thought you were dead."

"I never gave up hope," Flora said, rushing across the hall. "We've been awaiting your return."

Hart kissed her on the cheek, then turned to shake his father's hand, just as Adam entered from the back hall.

"You see, I told you he'd show up in one piece. Welcome, Brother," Adam interjected, adding his welcome to the others.

"It's good to be home," Hart replied, glancing at Smythe, who was attempting to edge his way around the family toward the door.

"I don't want to intrude, Ada. I'll leave. I'll come back later," Smythe explained when she went to his side, claiming his arm and attempting to stay his departure.

"No. Please don't go, Bill. I want you to meet my brother-in-law, Hart MacAlpin."

Ada returned to Hart's side, took his arm, and attempted to draw him toward Smythe. "As my two favorite men, you two should get to know one another," she said, preening before them.

"We've already met," Hart stated. Turning to his father, he spoke privately. "The colonel has escaped. We had him on board the broadhorn. He disappeared during the night. We don't know whether he's alive or dead. Young Nate Lord disappeared with him."

"That is bad news about the boy," Angus began, "but as for the colonel..."

A carriage rolled rapidly up to the hitching post. The assembled group turned to see who had arrived. Tchula appeared at the door, opening it for Lessie, Sarah—and Nate.

Hart could hardly believe his eyes. He stared into Lessie's. What he saw there started him forward. "He's alive! But how? Where?" he began, just as Nathaniel pointed to William Smythe and spoke in a clear voice.

"That man is Black Hat. He's the one with Zeke the night they caught me in the woods."

Hart froze in midstride, his eyes now on Smythe. As he searched the man's face for signs of confirmation, Smythe pulled a small pistol from inside his jacket.

"Stop right there, MacAlpin!" Smythe ordered.

"Don't be foolish, Smythe," Hart stated, his own hand near the dirk which hung from his right hip.

"What are you doing?" Ada cried, moving to intercede. "That boy is not telling the truth. Bill couldn't be this...this Black Hat character."

"Stay out of the way," Hart warned as she grabbed for his arm.

A movement caused Smythe to look over his shoulder just as Tchula prepared to rush him. He fired, the gun pointed at Hart. The bullet struck Ada instead.

Hart caught Ada just as Lessie rushed forward. "Here, let me see," she said, attempting to check Ada's wound.

"You get away from me," Ada hissed, her breath short, her hands clutching at Hart.

"Why? Why did you leave me...to Bruce?" Ada whispered, her voice weakening. "It hurts, Hart, it hurt..." Her body went limp. Hart picked her up and carried her upstairs to her bed, leaving Smythe to Tchula and Adam.

"No move," Tchula commanded. He was holding Smythe, his arms clamped behind him.

In the confusion surrounding Ada's death, Tchula reached to retrieve Smythe's gun from the floor. Smythe twisted free of his hold and lunged through the open door. Adam raced after them, shouting for Hart, who ran out onto the upstairs veranda, saw what was happening, and swung himself over the edge, dropping onto the drive below. Ash was there beside him.

"Get Blister. Bring Tchula a horse, mount yourself. Adam, get Jubal. We've got to catch him," he directed.

"Nathaniel, you stay here, in the house until I return. Do you understand?" Hart directed his strained voice to the boy who was watching the events wide-eyed. "I will speak to you later."

"Yessir. I'll stay right here," Nate said, backing up a foot or two. His friend Hart had become threatening, his face as cold as his own father's death mask. "I'll stay," he repeated.

The four of them caught up to the buggy, which was careening dangerously, just as Smythe drove the weakened horses to a stop in front of his house on Broadway. Smythe jumped out, pushed his way through the front door, slamming it behind him.

Hart held up his hand, halting Ash and Tchula. "Let's split up. Adam, you take the side entrance. Tchula, you watch the front door. Ash and I will go around back. He's probably got a horse there."

"Smythe! You may as well give up. You can't get away," Adam called.

Hart edged his way around the house, dismounted, and moved along the rear porch. Ash moved to the other side. Silence prevailed from within. Hart stood against the rear wall, his pistol ready, listening for sounds of movement.

Ash signaled to Hart. He was going in through a side window. Hart watched. Suddenly a shot was heard from within. Hart raced up the back stairs and entered the house.

"In here! In the library," Ash said, pointing the way.

Hart stared at the gaping hole behind the linen press. He'd heard of these hidden entrances, but had never seen one. "Who fired?" Hart asked.

"I did. I thought I saw him going in," Ash answered.

"Bring a candle from that bureau and follow me," Hart said, entering the hole. The tunnel walls were earthen; the roof was covered with board planks. The two of them walked carefully downward.

"It must lead to the river," Ash suggested, just behind Hart.

"Probably," Hart agreed.

Just ahead they saw light. They were near its end. Hart motioned for Ash to stay back, not to get too near the entrance until they made certain of Smythe's location.

Nothing moved outside. The afternoon sun glinted off the muddy waters of the river. A small breeze set leaves turning around the entrance. Hart walked out, stopped, and looked at the gangplank attached to a post near the tunnel opening. There was no sign of red dust or mud. Smythe had not been here.

The Natchez militia had arrived, found the inside opening, and followed Adam and Tchula through. They were all scanning the river, searching for a boat.

"Where'd he go?" Adam asked, puzzled.

"I've an idea," Hart said, returning through the tunnel. "He's probably right here in the house."

Ash had followed Hart back and moved off toward the center hall. Smythe was standing near the back entrance, a valise in his hand. Ash dove for him, catching him as he attempted to leave through the back door.

"Get out of my way," Smythe snarled, thrusting himself away from Ash.

"Hold it," Hart yelled. "I'll shoot if you so much as move."

"You'd be shooting an innocent man," Smythe said, attempting to straighten his clothes, which had been twisted as Ash grabbed him.

"Explain that," Hart instructed, leveling his gun at Smythe's chest.

"The boy saw me, it's true. But I'm not the same person as this Black Hat."

"You were with Zeke in the woods. Now that I think about it. I recognize you too. Your stance gives you away," Hart rebutted.

"You'll never prove it. I have friends in this town—powerful friends," Smythe said, regaining some of his accustomed composure.

"That may be, but they'll hang you high if they find you guilty of treason. This country has already fought one war against the British. We may have to do it again," Hart returned. "The colonel was a guest of mine a few days back. He told me about the shooting of my brother, Bruce," Hart said, laying a trap. "He said you were there. That would make you a British agent."

"Hardly. I know nothing of your brother's death, except what I was told by the governor, that he was shot in the left shoulder," Smythe said, attempting a bluff. MacAlpin was a fair man. He could handle him, he thought. He was totally unprepared for MacAlpin's next statement.

"You've just convicted yourself with your own words," Hart replied, the scar stretched under a wide grin. "No one knew he was shot in the left side of his chest, except those who were present at the time. The governor didn't know. Only the doctor, Adam, and I," Hart finished.

After speaking with the captain of the militia, Hart instructed Ash to turn Smythe over to them. He was marched off to jail, where he would await trial on charges of treason. When they had a chance to check his books, records, and bank account, they'd probably have all they needed to convict him.

"Thanks, Ash. That was some tackle. He'd have gotten away without you," Hart said, offering his hand to Ash.

Ash took it, accepting Hart's thanks.

Tchula mounted his horse and led the way down Broadway, through crowds of spectators. Hart recognized a number of friends and acquaintances as they passed. Questions were hurled at him. He didn't answer.

"Smythe turned out to be the spy arming the Indians against us," Adam called as he rode past.

"Who caught him?" someone yelled.

"Ash here," Hart said, pointing to Ash, who was riding beside him.

The crowd applauded. Ash beamed, bowing low in the saddle.

*****

Once again, the MacAlpin household was in mourning. Ada was buried beside Bruce and their child, her mother weeping softly by her grave. Angus and Flora stood by through it all. Afterward, they escorted Mildred back to Brightway. It was raining during the funeral. Mildred took a pelisse from the hall tree at Crapewood, placing it around her shoulders as she left for home.

Hart, Tchula, and Sam gave a full report of everything that had happened since the night Hart had gone in search of Nathaniel Lord and found him in the clutches of gunrunners.

The governor was satisfied that the plot to overthrow the territorial government by force had been successfully terminated. However, the threat of another war with England grew more likely each day. He appealed to Tchula, Sam, and Hart, offering each of them commissions in the militia. They refused, each of them preferring to live a quieter, more private life. Ash was commended for his gallant capture of Smythe, received a reward and a grant of land next to that the MacAlpins had given him.

After explanations had been made at Crapewood and Ash had been sent to notify the Wellsleys that their cousins would be returned much later, Hart went in search of Lessie. He found her in the library with Nate. They were seated side by side. Nate's face was solemn, Lessie's expectant. She rose when he walked into the room.

He crossed it and gathered her to him, holding her close. "I've missed you," he said, his voice a caress.

"Forgive me," she begged, her eyes seeking his. "I couldn't think of anything except Nate. How I'd cost him his life," she began.

"Hush," he insisted. "It's over." He released her from his embrace and turned to Nate. "Now, young man, you and I have some talking to do," he stated. "What happened to you?"

"I've already told Lessie and Cousin John and almost everybody. Do I have to tell it all again? I'd rather go down to the barn and see Blister."

Hart laughed. "Go on," he decreed. "I'll worm it out of your sister."

"Right," Nate sang, disappearing through the door. "She'll tell you all about it."

"It is the most amazing story," she began when Hart led her back to the sofa and they were seated. "Nate was sleeping near the colonel the night they disappeared. Something woke him. He went out on deck, leaned over the rail to see what was making the noise, slipped and fell in.

The colonel must have heard him get up because he was there as Nate fell, grabbed for him, and fell with him into the river. The current was too strong for them. Nate said he called out once before the current took him so far downriver that we couldn't hear him yelling. He never saw the colonel again.

"And?" Hart pressed.

"He caught hold of a log and held on. Before morning, he had drifted up on the eastern shore, right into a Choctaw hunting party. He used Tchula's name to identify himself, and they brought him straight home to Wellsley Farm."

"He certainly has the luck of the Irish," Hart teased, playing with a strand of her hair that insisted on escaping from underneath her cap. "He's trouble, I admit," he added, "but he's bright. He'll turn out fine."

"And I'm forgiven?" she asked again, her large eyes serious.

"Without asking," Hart answered. "Always without asking."

*****

Later the same day, Hart rode over to see Mildred Albright. He went alone. When she had received him, she offered him tea. He refused.

"Well, sit down then," she said, seating herself across from him. "What brings you here, now?"

"A caped figure seen following my brother on several occasions before his death," Hart said, speaking slowly, seeking his way.

"Oh that. I remember that being mentioned before," Mildred said. But a small finger of fear began to creep along her spine.

"It was you, wasn't it?" Hart asked bluntly.

Her reaction startled him. She began to weep hysterically, uncontrollably. He waited until she could control herself. "I'm not sorry. I'm not…you understand that, Hart MacAlpin," she cried, wiping at her eyes with her handkerchief.

"You admit hitting Bruce on the head, killing him?" Hart continued.

"Yes, yes. He deserved it. Ada was going mad married to him. She knew where he was going every evening. I started following him. I only wanted to help my poor daughter. She never got over you, you know."

"Get to the point, if you don't mind," Hart insisted.

"As I said, I had been following him for some weeks. He visited that bordello several times a week. Then on the night of his death, I had intended confronting him on his way home, offering him anything if he would spend more time with Ada. But he didn't go home. He rode off toward Brightway. I followed at a discreet distance. My pony moves quietly. He never knew I was there."

"That's when you killed him?" Hart suddenly felt a need to get out of her home, away from her.

"No, no, I didn't intend to kill him, you understand. But after that little man shot him, I waited for him to die. He deserved it, you know," she repeated. "When he regained consciousness, made an effort to get up, something came over me. I picked up a piece of wood and hit him," she admitted as simply as if she had been talking about the weather.

Hart didn't move, just sat there watching her. If she wasn't deranged before Bruce's death, she was now. She was probably telling the truth about not planning to kill him. She had lost her husband, her daughter, and her grandchild. The shame of the colonel's betrayal would follow her always. Asking for her life in exchange for Bruce's would serve no good purpose. He rose.

"Thank you for telling me the truth. I'll not repeat what I've heard here as long as you live quietly, causing no trouble for anyone," he said, moving to leave.

"How did you know?" Mildred asked as he walked toward the hall.

"Your pelisse. It was raining during the funeral. You put it on before you left for Brightway. Then I remembered you owned a pony.

I'd found pony tracks near Bruce's body. I put two and two together," Hart said, walking through the door into early evening, leaving the Albrights behind him forever.

*****

Two months later, Hart Fowler MacAlpin, aged thirty, recently of the Argentine and the Natchez Trace, married Ms. Lessie Renard Lord, aged twenty-four, spinster. The wedding was held at Wellsley Farm. Guests came from as far away as Nashville, Mobile, New Orleans, and the Stand, for Sam Shute and his family attended. Tchula was Hart's best man.

Flora Fowler MacAlpin had helped the bride to sew her wedding dress. The bodice was made of Valenciennes lace, cut square in the neck, with long sleeves pointed at the tip. A hood of the same lace was attached to the neck of the bodice. The bride wore it pulled over her curls, which had been arranged in an upsweep. The skirt draped softly and wide, flowing out into a six-foot train behind. She had satin slippers and gloves to complete her fashionable attire.

The wedding was the high point of the summer in Natchez. The couple honeymooned in New Orleans. The city buzzed with rumors of war. The young MacAlpins took no notice. One morning, just after a leisurely breakfast, Hart presented Lessie with a single rose, golden in color.

"This being our first anniversary, Cousin," he teased, "name your gift, and it's yours."

"I can't possibly imagine wanting anything other than what I have," Lessie replied, sniffing the rose's heady perfume.

They were seated on the second floor veranda of a downtown hotel. Hart moved his chair next to hers and took her hand.

"Contented woman, are you?" he questioned, the long scar widening with his smile.

"Very," she replied, tracing the scar's outline with her finger. "However, I do have some news."

"What's that?" Hart asked, perplexed.

"Did you notice the way Sarah and Adam behaved during the wedding?"

"Can't say that I did, why?" The look of astonishment on Hart's face was genuine.

"I think they're in love," Lessie replied, sniffing the rose's fragrance again.

Hart rose, took her hand, and led her into their suite. "Adam will have to worry about himself," he said when they were inside and he had closed the door.

*****

"Didn't you just love the wedding, Vi? It was so glorious," Callie exuded. She, Sarah, and Viola had been bridesmaids.

They had worn celestial-blue silk gowns. A wide row of turquoise silk had circled their waists, creating a bow in back and trailing to the floor. They had worn blue gloves and blue bonnets to match the color of their gowns.

"It wasn't bad. Actually, I enjoyed myself until I started to take a sip of punch and saw a toad looking up from my punch cup. That brother of Lessie's needs handling."

Callie laughed her honest, light laugh. "You were the hit of the reception, Vi. I mean, when the toad jumped from your cup and you started jumping up and down, I nearly died, I laughed so hard."

"Laugh as you will, Callie Warren," Viola exclaimed. But she was growing used to it. Everywhere she went, she was the brunt of frog jokes. "I couldn't very well step on the creature, could I? I mean, at a wedding reception."

"Well, you came out of it fine, Viola. Everyone cheered when you finally picked up the creature, carried it to the open window, and tossed it outside," Callie continued.

"That may be, but if I ever get my hands on Nathaniel Lord, I'll wring his scrawny neck," Viola stated, her voice vibrating with sincerity.

*****

Hart and Lessie returned to Crapewood from their honeymoon. They had decided to remain in the Natchez area. Hart rushed in at lunch, demanding that Lessie put on her pelisse and come with him.

He had something he wanted to show her. She left the kitchen and joined him.

They took the light buggy and rode north across St. Catherine's creek. Hart stopped the buggy a few miles east of Springfield Plantation.

"What do you see?" he asked, standing in the buggy, waving his left arm toward the wide expanse of land before them.

Lessie stood up. "I see acres of good farm land, ending in a promontory on the Mississippi," she replied.

"It's ours," Hart exclaimed. "I bought it at auction this morning. There's 3,300 acres here, more or less, ending in that piece of land jutting out toward the river."

They left the buggy and walked to the promontory, looking northward along the Mississippi. It was spring again. Daffodils carpeted the thick thatch of last year's grasses, great oaks spread their burgeoning boughs outward and upward, reaching for the sky. Birds sang giddily as they flew from tree to tree.

"What shall we call it?" Hart asked, his arm around her waist.

"I know," she answered immediately. "We'll call it Broadhorn."

CPSIA information can be obtained
at www.ICGtesting.com
Printed in the USA
LVHW051136110521
687090LV00003B/251

9 781641 146913